The Turnaround:
A Rancher's Story

David Pratt

This book is intended to provide insights and principles for building and running sustainable ranch businesses. Its purpose is to educate and entertain. It is designed to provide accurate, authoritative information in regard to the subject matter covered. It is sold with the understanding that the publisher and author are not engaged by the reader to render legal, accounting, financial, investment , management or other professional services. If legal, accounting or other professional assistance is required by the readier, the services of a competent professional person should be sought. The author and publisher shall have neither liability not responsibility to any person or entity with respect to loss or damaged caused, or alleged to have been caused, directly or indirectly, by information contained in this book. *Adapted from a declaration of principles jointly adopted by a committee of the American Bar Association and a committee of Publishers.*

The Turnaround: A Rancher's Story
Copyright© 2020 David W. Pratt

All rights reserved. No part of this book may be used, reproduced, distributed or transmitted in any form or by any means, including photocopying, recording or other electronic or mechanical methods, without written permission from the publisher except in the case of brief, appropriately cited quotations. For permission requests contact:

Ranch Management Consultants, Inc.
www.ranchingforprofit.com
ISBN
978-0-9910634-4-4

Published by Dave Pratt
Art: Dan Lorenz
Printed in the USA

**To my teacher,
Stan Parsons.**

Table of Contents

PART III: SUGGESTED TASKS, APPENDICES & GLOSSARY

Suggested Tasks

Appendices

Glossary

Acknowledgments

I don't know about every book, but while this one has one author, it would never get published without the support of a team, and I've had a great one.

First (and last) mate on my team is my wife, Kathy. She's makes everything I write better. Having critically read my drafts too many times to count her suggestions have made the story tighter and concepts clearer. A bad sign for an author, I haven't found words that adequately convey my appreciation for her support throughout this project.

My respected colleague, RFP alumnus and best friend, Roger Ingram reviewed a draft of the manuscript and helped me finalize the tasks that are included in this work. I am grateful for his enthusiastic support

I asked John Marble, a rancher in Oregon to review the manuscript, because in addition to being a friend, and an RFP grad, he is a gifted author and storyteller. John offered suggestions that improved the flow and clarity of the story. I particularly appreciated the inside jokes John wrote in the margins.

Dallas Mount, owner and CEO of Ranch Management Consultants has the mind and heart to lead RMC into the future. Dallas was instrumental in determining the scope and design of this book. He offered suggestions that helped make complex concepts more understandable. I appreciate his help on this project and am confident RMC has a bright future under his leadership.

RFP grad and former Executive Link member Dan Lorenz of Corner Post Meats in Colorado drew several terrific sketches for this work. I am grateful for his talent and his contributions.

I am also grateful to Sara Henneberger and Jill Keith for editing and formatting. No one knows more about where and where not to put a comma than Sara and Jill is the best there is at formatting pages. Jill has helped me on several projects for nearly 20 years and has never let me down.

People who've attended the schools I've taught think of me as their teacher. What they probably don't realize, is that they are my teachers too. I explain concepts and share their stories in the classroom. But by applying RFP concepts to their ranches they've made concepts more than an academic theory. They have taught me more than I've taught them.

Forward

If you're reading this book as prework for the Ranching For Profit School, welcome to RFP. If you came to this book outside of RFP, I invite you to explore our website and social media pages and consider attending a Ranching For Profit school.

A skilled teacher can take complex and difficult concepts and make them simple and understandable. Dave Pratt is the best teacher I've ever met. He is a master in the classroom and a gifted storyteller. I think you will find, in the pages that follow, that Dave has embedded a lifetime of knowledge into an engaging story.

Dave taught the first Ranching For Profit School I attended. When I walked in the classroom I was assigned to a team of smart and engaged ranchers. Though I felt a little self-conscious, thinking I didn't belong with this group of established ranchers, Dave soon had us working together, looking inside our businesses and our lives and empowering us to create change within ourselves and our businesses. I'm still in contact with some of those people on my team. In fact, one of them now provides facilitation work for Ranch Management Consultants with our Executive Link program.

I was an Extension Educator working with livestock producers in Wyoming when I took that first RFP school. When I returned to Wyoming I tried to recreate the same magic I experienced at the RFP class through my extension work, but I never felt like I had the same impact. A few years later, Dave invited me to consider attending another RFP with the goal of seeing if I might want to train to be an instructor. It was exciting and intimidating. I felt like a high school quarterback getting a call from Payton Manning to see if I wanted to learn how to throw. Over the next 7 years Dave and RMC provided me opportunities to work with the most progressive, kind, humble, and knowledge-seeking ranchers that exist. In 2019 my wife Dixie and I purchased RMC from Dave and Kathy Pratt and we strive everyday to carry on the tradition of excellence started by Stan Parsons and continued by Dave and Kathy.

The Ranching For Profit School was the most impactful education program I had ever experienced. The experience began before the class with a prework book, *Putting Profit Into Ranching*, by Stan Parsons. The book was written at a simple level but included powerful concepts and tasks that readers were encouraged to complete to prepare for the school. Written in 1986, the principles were still solid, but we had added new things to the school and the story it told felt dated. I was thrilled when Dave offered to re-write the book as his first 'retirement' project.

This book introduces you to many key Ranching for Profit principles and processes. By reading it and completing the tasks provided, it will help you hit the ground running when you attend the school.

As you read the story of discovery that follows, I encourage you to take the time to be self-reflective. Look for ways to apply the principles to your situation. It is easy to think, "It won't work here" or, "That's not the way it's done." It is more effective to ask deeper questions like, "What is the result we are looking for?" or, "What would it take to make this work?" The principles we teach at RFP have been tested all over the world in just about every climate. The way the principles are applied will look different in the Red Desert of Wyoming than they do on the Gulf Coast of Texas. Take the time to work through the exercises at the end of the chapters so that the knowledge gained will result in positive actions.

I'm deeply grateful to Dave for writing this book. I am confident it will help you become familiar with and deepen your understanding of the RFP principles, and I look forward to seeing you in class!

Dallas Mount
CEO Ranch Management Consultants, Inc.

Introduction

The characters in this story are real. At least they are to me. Kate and Lori are Jennifer and Kinsey and Melody and Sarah and Wendy and dozens of other amazing women. Chris and Wayne are Robert and Derek and Dillon and Kyle and John and dozens of other terrific men … men and women I met in over 3 decades teaching the Ranching For Profit School and two decades leading the Executive Link Program. My hope is that you will also see yourself and the people you love in these and the other characters in this book. At the very least I think you'll recognize their frustrations and challenges. They are the challenges that all family ranches must overcome if they are going to stay family ranches.

The story is told in two parts. In the first part the main characters work together to learn and apply the Ranching For Profit economic planning process. The second part describes how RFP graduates apply grazing and husbandry strategies taught at the school. Of course, nothing matters if people can't work together effectively, so there's a healthy dose of principles for building effective personal and working relationships in both sections.

The third part of this book includes suggested tasks that will help you apply Ranching For Profit principles and processes to your ranch. Tasks 1.1 to 8.1 are recommended prework for the Ranching For Profit School.

A recurring theme in this story is that knowing how to raise livestock and knowing how to run a business that raises livestock are two very different things. In my opinion, most ranches aren't businesses. They are a collection of expensive assets and a lot of low-paying, physically demanding jobs. The lifestyle associated with these ranches has some definite perks, but when people rely on off-farm income, can't pay themselves a competitive wage and are eating into their equity to keep things going, that lifestyle also involves a lot of stress.

A lot of people assume that transforming a ranch into a real business will detract from the ranching lifestyle. They've got it backwards. This transformation is the key to turning things around. Ranching For Profit School graduates know that the result is healthier land, happier families and more profitable businesses.

But turnarounds are hard. They don't happen overnight and not everyone is up to the challenge. This is a story of people who have the courage and optimism to turn around their ranches and their lives.

Part I

The Three Secrets for Increasing Profit

Chapter 1

The Ride Home

Wayne stared out the window as they drove west on Highway 41. He was used to being behind the wheel and didn't particularly like being a passenger. He and his wife, Lori, had reluctantly gone to a workshop on ranch profitability with their friends, Chris and Kate. Now, heading home, everyone was lost in their thoughts. Kate and Lori were in the back of the crew cab. Wayne rode shotgun as Chris drove. Breaking the silence, Wayne grumbled, "That guy was nuts."

"What guy?" Chris asked.

"The guy at the meeting today."

"The teacher?" asked Chris.

"Yes, the teacher," Wayne barked. "He said he doesn't own one acre and doesn't have any cattle, but he's supposed to be some kind of expert? What does he know about ranching out here?"

"You didn't think what he said made sense?" Chris asked.

"Well, maybe in a classroom," Wayne conceded. "But let me quote Yogi Bear on this one: 'In theory there is no difference in theory and practice, but in practice there is.' What does he know about ranching?"

"It's Yogi Berra," Lori corrected. "And it sounded like he's been on more ranches in the last year than we'll probably see in our lifetime."

"You're against me too!" Wayne complained.

"Nobody is against anybody," Lori chided. "What's eating you?"

"Nothing's eating me." He sat stewing as he told himself to drop it. A few moments later, unable to follow his own advice, he erupted, "Three secrets? Three secrets my foot!"

"What?" Kate asked. Chris's wife, Kate, had been lost in her own thoughts, and Wayne's comment startled her.

"'Three secrets for increasing profit.' Who does he think he's kidding? I can come up with 10 things that affect profit: Genetics. Cattle prices. Marketing. Reproduction. Weather. Competition. Cattle prices. Government regulation. Management," he rattled off with satisfaction.

"Family dysfunction," Lori said quietly.

"Ranching For Profit," Wayne continued with contempt. "Now there's an oxymoron."

Lori was fed up with Wayne's attitude. She wasn't going to put up with it for the two-plus hours they still had to go.

"If you really think ranching can't be profitable, and you're still ranching, who's the moron?"

"Play nice," Chris said.

"Okay, okay. I know ranching can be profitable. We made a good profit these last two years," Wayne said.

Lori's frustration boiled over. "Then how come I still have to work at the bank? How come we still can't remodel the kitchen? How come you have to work so hard all the time?"

Chris began to regret having invited Wayne and Lori to the workshop. He and Kate had attended the Ranching For Profit School 10 months earlier. They thought the workshop would be a good refresher for themselves and a good introduction for Wayne and Lori.

"Was there anything he said that you agreed with?" Chris asked.

"Not really," Wayne answered sourly. "I mean, he said ranching isn't a business. Where does he come off saying something like that to me ... to us? Our ranch is not a hobby." Wayne was defiant. "I'm busting my ass trying to make sure it passes to a fourth generation. I'm not working this hard to support a stinkin' hobby! Where does he get off telling us that ranching isn't a business?"

"That's not exactly what he said," Chris corrected.

"Close enough," Wayne said.

"No, it's not," Lori argued. "He didn't say ranching isn't a business. He said that, in his *opinion*, most ranches aren't businesses. That really struck a nerve. I don't think our ranch is a business."

"What do you mean? Of course, it's a business!" Wayne insisted.

"I don't think so," Lori said with less annoyance in her voice. "You said it yourself yesterday, 'We need to run our place more *like* a business.' *Like* a business? I never really thought about it before, but when you put it that way, you're admitting that it isn't really a business."

"Geez. Remind me not to talk to anyone anymore about anything," Wayne said.

Kate spoke up. "Our ranch wasn't a business," she said. "If we sold it, we wouldn't be selling a business. We'd be selling an asset … a big, expensive collection of assets. A business is more than just a bunch of assets."

"You spend a week at a school and now you're an expert?" Wayne asked sarcastically.

"What's wrong with you? That's no way to talk," Lori scolded.

"It's okay," Kate said. "It doesn't take an expert to know that what we were doing wasn't working, and what we're doing now is better. We've finally started turning things around."

"What wasn't working?" Lori asked. "You've always seemed to have your act together."

"Appearances can be deceiving," Kate said. "We didn't tell anybody, but you know the cabin we had just south of Jackson?"

"The place your folks left you?" Lori asked.

"Uh-huh," Kate confirmed. "We had to sell it."

"But you loved that cabin!" Lori protested.

"It was either sell that or lose the ranch," Kate said. "We were so far in a hole we didn't see any other way out."

"I had no idea," Lori said, placing her hand on Kate's.

"How could you? We didn't tell anyone." She sighed. "Who really knows how anyone else is doing? It's not like anyone talks about that sort of thing. When's the last time you showed anyone but the banker your balance sheet or your cash flow?"

"Heck, he usually shows it to me!" Wayne said. The sale of the cabin surprised him, and he was at a loss as to what to say to Chris and Kate. He was even more surprised that they revealed what must have been a very difficult, personal decision. There weren't that many people in Wayne's life who shared that kind of thing with him.

"Knowing what we know now, I don't think we would have sold it," Kate said. "We've been able to do some other things that have put us in a much better financial position. But live and learn."

"The thing that hit me the hardest when I first learned about Ranching For Profit is the thing that's eating you right now," Chris said, glancing at Wayne.

"What's that?" asked Wayne.

"The idea that we didn't own a business. All we owned was a collection of expensive assets and a job. That was a slap in the face," Chris said. "And it was a punch in the gut when the teacher asked, 'Or does the job own you?'"

A few seconds passed before Chris said, "I'd thought about going to that school before, but I didn't think we could afford it, and I sure didn't see how we could both be away for a whole week. Kate and I hadn't been away from the ranch that long since we got married — that's 11 years! Anyway, at that point I realized that we didn't own a business. Heck, we didn't even own a job. The job really did own us!"

"Twelve," Kate corrected. "We've been married 12 years. It just seems like 11 because you're so happy being married to me!" Turning to Lori, she asked, "When's the last time you two got away?"

Just as Wayne started to respond, Chris interjected, "Bull sales don't count."

"For a week?" Wayne asked incredulously.

Lori just shook her head, rolled her eyes and mouthed, "I wish," to Kate.

"We just decided we had to do it," Chris explained. "It's ridiculous. When you add up the land, the cattle, and the rest of it, we've got almost $3 million in assets. And yet we were living like church mice. Of course, it's almost all in the land."

"Land rich and cash poor," Wayne mumbled.

"We got Chris's mom to watch Sally and Robyn," Kate explained, "and we got Tim to check on things while we were gone, and we just went. It's the best investment we ever made. I think Chris was surprised, and maybe a little disappointed, that everything was just fine when we got back."

"So now everything is hunky-dory, I suppose?" Wayne didn't mean for his tone to sound so sarcastic.

"We didn't say that," Chris said. "We've still got challenges, but things are better. In six months, Kate's going to half time at the hospital and by this time next year she'll be on the ranch full time. We aren't where we want to be yet, and we know we have a long way to go, but we have a plan. And if we stay with it … well, it's been a long time since I've been excited about our future. I felt like I was working harder and harder and getting nowhere. In fact, sometimes it felt like we were going one step forward, two steps back. But now I'm excited about what's ahead."

"And, we're having a lot more fun," Kate added.

"I know what you mean about one step forward and two steps back," Wayne said quietly.

"The problem was that because we knew how to work livestock, we thought we had a pretty good handle on how to run a ranch," Kate explained.

"Y'all know what you're doing," Wayne said. "Your place looks great. You've got a good set of cows."

"If we were doing such a good job and had such good cows, then why were we going broke?" Chris asked.

"Because we didn't know how to run a business!" Kate answered. "Like the teacher said, 'There's a difference between knowing how to grow crops and raise livestock and knowing how to run a *business* that grows crops and raises livestock.'"

"We realized that unless we learned how to run a business, our success would be dependent on weather, markets, and other things beyond our control," Chris added. "We wanted to — no, we *needed* to — learn how to run a business."

"There was one thing in that workshop that did hit home," Wayne said. His tone was more positive now.

"Just *one* thing?" asked Lori sarcastically.

"Hey, cut me some slack. I've had a hard day," Wayne joked. He was starting to feel a little better. "The thing the teacher said about the difference between efficiency and effectiveness. He said efficiency was hitting the bull's-eye and effectiveness was aiming at the right target."

"It doesn't do much good to hit the bull's-eye if you're shooting at the wrong target," Chris said. "There are a lot of things ranchers do that are efficient but ineffective."

"I liked the example he gave of the guy near Montgomery," Wayne said. "He said he'd been so busy trying to do things right, he never thought to question whether he was doing the right things. That got me thinking about the seeding and brush clearing project we're planning. We're getting cost-share money to do it, but we'll still have to put a lot of money into the project ourselves. I know the seeding mix is right, but after what he said, I'm wondering if we ought to be seeding anything at all."

"Good Lord! You're thinking that *now*?" Lori gasped. "You're supposed to sign that contract next week!"

"No one has a gun to our heads. If it isn't the right thing to do, I don't have to sign it," Wayne said defensively. "I was just wondering if there's a more *effective* way to spend our money."

"Better to figure that out now than later." Chris thought Wayne was smart to question the cost.

"The people on my team at the school had lots of examples of things they were doing that were exactly that — very efficient but completely ineffective," Kate said.

"Like what?" Wayne asked.

"Ron was a guy on my team who was repeating the school. He said he used to brag that his cows had a 95% breed up and weaned 600-pound calves. When he crunched his numbers at the school, he realized he was losing over $100,000 a year. He got by because he'd inherited the land, didn't pay himself a wage, and his wife worked a full-time town job," Kate said, as she gave Chris a gentle poke in the back.

"Ow!" Chris said. "Just finish the story."

"So anyway," Kate continued, "the economic loss was over $100,000. After making changes, he said they're now making an economic profit of over $100,000. He showed us his numbers."

"What changes?" Wayne asked.

"Changes that made him less productive but more profitable," Chris said.

"Ron changed everything," Kate explained. "He didn't make the changes to be less productive. He made the changes to cut costs. He said that now his conception rate is closer to 90% and he weans lighter calves. The weight weaned per cow is probably down something like 20%, but he cut his costs by way more than that."

"And he's running more cows now," Chris said.

"Less productive, more profitable," Wayne said. "He was hitting the bull's-eye but shooting at the wrong target."

"There were several people in our class who were repeating the school, and that's something they all had in common," Chris observed. "I think they all had an example of something they stopped doing that made them more profitable." Looking at Kate in the rearview mirror, he added, "Remember Walt? He told us that he left the school with 'to do' *and* 'to don't do' lists and said that the 'to don't do' list may have been even more important."

"Work less, make more?" Lori asked skeptically.

"I know, it sounds like snake oil," Kate said. "But everyone repeating the school had an example."

"When you start to look critically at what people do, you see lots of examples of things that are efficient but not effective," Chris concluded.

A few moments later, Wayne turned to Chris and said, "There was something else the teacher said that rang true. Those examples of things that are efficient but not effective ... they're a lot easier to see on your neighbor's place than your own."

"Take me now Lord, I've heard it all!" Lori said. "Wayne was listening!"

SUMMARY OF CHAPTER 1
CONCEPTS

- Knowing how to raise livestock and knowing how to run a business that raises livestock are two completely different things.
- Most ranches consist of a collection of expensive assets and a lot of low-paying, physically demanding jobs. A business is more than that.
- It is possible to be very efficient (hit the bull's-eye) but completely ineffective (aim at the wrong target).
- The most productive ranch is unlikely to be the most profitable.

Chapter 2
Should I Do It vs. Can I Do It

Miles passed. The only sounds were the wind whistling past and the occasional rattle of the racks on the truck as they rolled home.

Wayne wrestled with reconciling things the teacher said with his own experience. He and Lori had the same enterprises as everyone else in their area. They calved when everyone else calved. They retained replacements and backgrounded calves and put up hay and fed it out for three to four months every winter, just like everyone else. And he and Lori relied on off-farm income the way most everyone else did. Even so, things were tight financially, and he and Lori had been feeling the stress.

Lori was thinking about how much she didn't want to go to work on Monday. She liked her colleagues and the customers at the bank, but she wanted to be home. Their plan had been that she would work in town for three or four years while Wayne grew the business. Then she would be full time on the ranch. That was nine years ago, or was it 10? She was tired. Tired of the drive every day. Tired of scraping by. She feared that she was growing tired of Wayne. Mostly, she was tired of being tired. She looked over at Kate and envied her. She couldn't remember what it felt like to be excited about the future.

Kate's mind was on the cozy cabin that they'd sold near Jackson. She'd never mentioned it to Chris, but she'd imagined that she and Chris might live there one day when the kids were older and running the ranch. No chance of that now. It had been her idea to sell it, but if it hadn't been for the debt on the ranch, the sale wouldn't have been necessary. She realized she held some resentment toward the ranch for that. While it was on the market, she'd been able to suppress her feelings. She rationalized that they hadn't even visited the cabin in nearly two years. They had been too busy. Losing that link to her past and to her family's legacy had been an abstract concept. But once she signed the papers, the loss was real and she grieved all over again for her mother and father, who had died a few years earlier.

They were coming into Sweet Creek, with its one church, two bars and a gas station with a small café, when Chris asked, "Anybody hungry?"

"I'm starving," Wayne said. It was a relief to turn his attention to something else.

They pulled into the Gas n' Go to fill up and grab a bite. Kate and Lori went in to the diner while Chris and Wayne gassed up.

"I'm not so sure the B to C ratio here is very healthy," Wayne quipped.

"The B to C ratio?" Chris asked.

"The bar to church ratio. Two bars to one church? I'm not so sure that's healthy!" Then, with the pump clicking away, $2, $3, $4, he added, "Is it right what the teacher said about the cost of gas going up faster than cattle prices?"

"Pretty much all inputs have gone up faster," Chris said over the hum of the pump. "Land prices are most out of whack. In a lot of places land's gone up more than 10 times faster, and in some places it's been closer to 20." $7, $8, $9 ...

"What did the teacher say about technology?" Wayne asked. "That if technology were the solution to our problems, we'd have fewer problems, and that we've substituted technology for management. What'd he mean by that?" $11, $12, $13 ...

"He's got a broad definition of technology," Chris explained. "He's talking about inputs like implants, vaccines, supplements, embryo transfer, AI, insecticidal ear tags, DNA testing, stuff like that."

"He's saying we shouldn't use vaccines and supplements?" Wayne asked.

"No, not at all," Chris said. "His point was that people tend to jump to quick fixes using inputs, as opposed to thinking through strategies that might eliminate the need for the inputs. Technology involves the use of this," Chris said, holding up his wallet. "Management uses this," he said, pointing to his head. The pump clicked on. $16, $17, $18 ...

"What did you think of the benchmarks he talked about?" Chris asked.

"At the workshop?" Wayne asked.

"No, on your spaceship to Mars. Yes, at the workshop." Chris shook his head with mock despair.

"I don't know. He went through that part pretty fast. I liked the analogy he used of taking a shotgun blast and turning it into a rifle shot, showing that you could use those benchmarks to pinpoint problems."

"Holy cow, you were listening!" Chris said.

"Hey, I'm not just a pretty face." $20, $21, $22 …

Chris was encouraged that Wayne had connected with at least one thing he'd heard. "You know, I never really had a handle on our numbers until I attended that class. That stuff always intimidated me. Now it's actually fun."

"Fun? You think doing the numbers is fun?"

"Maybe fun isn't the right word," Chris admitted. "I used to hate putting the numbers together. But the fact is, I never really knew *how* to do it. No one ever showed me how to make a projection, at least one that meant something. No one ever showed me how to calculate a gross margin. Heck, I didn't even know what a gross margin was. Now that I know how to do it, I actually enjoy it.

"If someone had asked me what a gross margin was, I probably would have thought they were talking about something to do with the futures market, or something," Chris added. "I didn't even know there was a difference between economics and finance." $28, $29, $30 …

"There's a difference between economics and finance?" Wayne asked.

"Yeah. I hadn't thought about it before the class, but there is a big difference. It's simple, but it's important. Economics is all about profit. Finance is about money."

Wayne looked confused. "You lost me. Economics isn't about money?"

"It's more than that," Chris said. "You usually keep about 80 or 90 heifer calves as replacements, right?" $34, $35, $36 …

"Not last year. It was so dry I only kept 50." Wayne said.

"Okay, so you sold more heifers last year than the year before, right? So, you made more money, right?" Chris asked.

"No ... well, I had more income, but ..." Wayne paused. He sensed that Chris was using some sort of Jedi mind trick. "I sold them because of drought."

"Doesn't matter why you sold them. The fact is you sold them. Is that all you sold?" Chris asked.

"No, I culled pretty deep into the cow herd and I sold another 40 pairs late in the season. I didn't have the grass and didn't want to buy more hay. Took a beating on the culls, but I did okay on the pairs."

"So, you made more money than normal, right?" Chris wiped his forehead and said, "Thank goodness we have a drought so we can finally make some real money! Gosh, let's hope it never rains again."

"That's crazy, but you're right, income does go up in a drought. But that's not profit, is it?" Wayne looked at Chris for confirmation.

"Income usually goes up in the first year of drought — at least it goes up if you destock. But no, just because income goes up, it doesn't mean that you made a profit. You also have to look at the value of the inventory you sold.

"If you buy a cow that's worth $1,000 and wind up selling her for $100, you didn't make $100. You lost $900, right?" Chris asked.

"Sure. That's just common sense," Wayne agreed.

"It is. It's also economics," Chris said. $45, $46, $47 ...

The pump stopped. Chris put the nozzle back in the pump and screwed on the gas cap.

Wayne leaned on the tailgate, one boot on the bumper. Chris leaned on the side of the truck next to the pump.

"Let's say I buy a cow," Chris said. "I used to think that the cost of the cow was whatever the price I paid was. It's not."

"How do you figure?" Wayne asked.

"It's like a trade. I had money and I traded it for a cow. My business is out the money, but now I've got a cow worth, hopefully, whatever I paid for her."

"Until she dies," Wayne said glumly.

"Okay, until she dies. When she dies, I have a big cost. My business lost value. But did money leave my business on the day she died?" Chris asked.

"No, of course not," Wayne said. "You won't be out money until you replace her."

"Right," Chris agreed. "In economics you follow the movement of value, not just money. The purchase of the cow is a capital investment. Same as this truck. The purchase of the pickup is a capital expense. The costs of having the pickup are the interest I pay on the loan, depreciation, fuel, repairs, and insurance."

"And it's the same for cows?" Wayne asked.

"Exactly. The purchase of the cow is a capital investment. The costs are interest on the cattle loan, feed, health costs, and depreciation."

"Depreciation?" Wayne asked.

"Sure, she's eventually going to lose value. You said it yourself. The cow that died? She's completely depreciated! She lost all of her value." Chris smiled.

"Look," Chris continued, "those drought sales you had? Income went up, but your business probably lost value because prices were down. Or turn it around. Let's say you raise a bunch of heifers and get them bred, but you don't sell them until next year. They are in your inventory at the end of the year and they've increased in value. You didn't sell anything or make any money, but your business produced a lot of value."

"So, in economics you need to consider more than money. You need to consider the change in inventory value, right?" Wayne asked.

"Exactly."

"Okay, well, if that's economics, what's finance?" Wayne asked.

"It boils down to this," Chris said. "In economics you ask, 'Should I buy this cow? Will she be profitable?' In finance you ask, 'Can I buy this cow?' Something could be profitable to do, but what if you can't pull together the capital to get started? Or what if all the income happens at the end of the year? How do you pay your bills in the meantime?"

"You seen my credit line? That's how," Wayne said with a frown. "But I think I get it. Finance is two questions: Where do you get the money to start the ball rolling, and how do you keep the ball rolling? Right?"

"Right," Chris confirmed. "But there's a third question that's just as important: Where are you going to put the money?"

"Where you put it? I'm not following," Wayne said.

"There are three places where we can put money in our businesses," Chris explained. "We can build reserves. That's money, or things we can turn into money quickly, that we can use to pay unexpected expenses or invest in opportunities and grow the operation.

"The other two places we can put our money are fixed assets and working capital. The way I learned it, fixed assets are things you intend to keep, and working capital includes all the things you intend to sell. So, working capital would be the calf crop and the inputs into those calves. Fixed assets would be things like land, machinery, and cows."

Wayne frowned. "A cow is a fixed asset?" he asked.

"I was confused about that too," Chris admitted, "but think about it. Do you hope every cow is open and dry so you can cull her this year? Or do you hope they are all wet and pregnant so you can keep them? Isn't your intention to keep them?"

Wayne nodded. "I guess so. I never thought of it like that."

"Where you have your money is important. Most of our money is tied up in fixed assets and that's a problem."

"What's so bad about that?" Wayne asked. "I like owning land and I like owning cows and I like machinery — especially new machinery."

"I like it too, but it's why we are all broke. Wealthy on the balance sheet, broke at the bank," Chris summarized. "Look, when all of your money is tied up in things you intend to keep, there's hardly anything to sell. So, we have a ranch worth millions that doesn't produce very much income, and then what little income we have gets spent maintaining those fixed assets. They aren't cheap."

"No, they're not," Wayne agreed. "Between insurance and interest ..."

"... and repairs and depreciation," Chris added, "they were sucking up just about every dollar we produced."

Wayne nodded. "Us too." He thought for a moment. "You know, that's funny. Not 'ha ha' funny, but strange funny. Take Chuck Davis to the south of us."

"He's the hedge fund guy that bought the McBride ranch, isn't he?"

"Uh-huh," Wayne said, nodding. "He's got green paint disease. He just bought a brand new dually and a gooseneck trailer. Last year he bought a new tractor, a baler, and a rake. He built a new set of pens and put fresh paint on all the buildings. I think there are only 400 cows there and he's got two employees."

"I'm sure they're busy too," Chris said. "Someone has to keep paint on those buildings."

"He bought some fancy bulls for ... I don't know how much, but I'll bet he paid three or four times what we pay for ours," Wayne said.

"It must be good to work on Wall Street. He must have had a lot of money to spend," Chris concluded.

"Had is right," Wayne laughed. "He's not buying things that will make him money, is he? He's buying things that cost him money."

"And they will cost him year after year after year," Chris added. "We've been looking at options for reducing our investment in fixed assets and reallocating that money into working capital — things that actually produce income."

"Options like what?" Wayne asked.

"Lots of things," Chris explained. "Leasing stuff instead of owning stuff. Having someone else come in to cut our hay so we don't have to own equipment. Expanding our stocker program. Things like that."

"It doesn't seem like that'd make that big a difference," Wayne said.

"It adds up. At least it does for us," Chris said. "I'd never challenged it before. I just assumed that ranchers had to own this stuff. Just about everyone we know does. But maybe that's one reason why just about everyone we know has off-farm income too.

"They say it takes money to make money, but what if you don't have much money?" Chris asked.

"I guess you'd better put what money you have into things that make money," Wayne said.

"Right, and that means putting it in working capital, not fixed assets," Chris said.

"Kate's going to think we've been kidnapped," Chris joked. "We'd better go in."

"Kidnappers would probably have to pay Lori for her to take me back!" Wayne said as he followed Chris.

As they walked, Wayne asked, "What was that thing the teacher said about accountants?"

"He said that accountants help you minimize taxes and his job was the opposite. The teacher said that he wants us all to have tax problems," Chris said.

"That's nuts," Wayne said dismissively.

"Not when you think about it," Chris countered. "Of course an accountant's job is a lot more than helping you avoid taxes, but the teacher questioned some of their advice, like buying fixed assets at the end of the year to minimize your profit and avoid paying taxes. He calls the things we buy to avoid paying taxes 'monuments to tax avoidance.' Sure, they can help reduce this year's tax liability, but next year they just add to our costs without adding to our income.

"His point was that we do lots of things to ourselves that make it even tougher to make a profit. I'd rather make a big profit and have big tax problems than never make a profit. Most people put tax avoidance ahead of finance and finance ahead of economics. They've got it backwards ¬— profit ought to come first, finance second, and tax avoidance third."

"I don't like paying taxes," Wayne complained.

"Well then don't make a profit and you won't have to worry about it," Chris quipped as he held the door for Wayne.

Lori and Kate looked up from their menus. "What took you so long?" Kate asked. "We were about to send a search party."

"We were talking about the difference between economics and finance," Chris said.

"Did you tell Wayne about the engine and the gas?" Kate asked.

"No, but that would have been a good way to explain it. Why don't you tell him?" Chris suggested.

"At the school you work in teams. Each morning there's a review. Each team member picks something from the previous day's class. You summarize the key points and explain how they apply to your own situation," Kate said.

"Oh, I could never do that. I hate talking in front of people," Lori said.

"I thought it'd be uncomfortable too, and I was a little nervous the first time," Kate continued, "but you're in a small group and everybody is learning. The reviews turned out to be one of my favorite things about the class."

"So, what was it about the engine and the gas?" Wayne asked.

"In my review I said that economics is the business's engine. If you had a big place or leased a lot of grass, you had a big engine. If you had a small place, you had a small engine. If your enterprises weren't very efficient, your engine needed a tune-up."

"So where does finance fit in?" Lori asked.

"Finance is what you use to buy the engine and pay for the gas that makes it go, right?" Wayne guessed.

"That's right," Kate said. "So, which comes first, economics or finance?" she asked.

"Well, you don't want to buy an engine that won't run!" Lori said.

"Or put gas in it," Chris added.

"That makes sense. Economics has to come first," Wayne said.

"Our banker uses ratios he calculates from our balance sheet to tell us why he won't loan us more money. Those are *financial* ratios, aren't they?" Wayne asked. "But the ratios and benchmarks that the teacher talked about in the workshop were *economic* ratios, right? They measure the power of the economic engine. They show if it's running efficiently and what's holding us back, right?"

"That's a good way to think about it, since the things that make you profitable are called *profit drivers*," Chris said.

Lori passed Chris and Wayne menus. "Did we come here to talk or eat?" she asked.

Chris and Wayne looked at each other and in unison said, "Yes."

SUMMARY OF CHAPTER 2
CONCEPTS

- Key economic questions:
  - Is this profitable?
  - Should I do this?

- Key financial questions:
  - Can I afford to do this?
  - Can I get the start-up capital?
  - How will the cash flow?
  - How will I allocate capital (e.g., fixed assets, working capital, and/or reserves)?

- Fixed assets are things you intend to keep.

- Working capital are things (and the inputs that go into the things) you intend to sell.

- Investment in fixed assets are capital expenses. Economic costs of ownership include interest, insurance, depreciation, repairs, and maintenance.

- The biggest financial problem in agriculture is the misallocation of capital.

- If most of your money is tied up in fixed assets, you will have a very expensive business that produces very little income. (Wealthy on the balance sheet and broke at the bank.)

- Economics is the business's engine.

- Finance is the money used to buy the engine and pay for the gas.

- Economics comes first! Finance comes second. Tax consequences should be the last consideration.

- Avoid investing in "monuments to tax avoidance."

Chapter 3
Napkin Math: Creating a Profit Target

"Too early for a beer?" Kate looked at her watch. 2:30.

"I'd better not. I don't think I could stop with one," Lori lamented.

They ordered cheeseburgers and sodas all around.

While they were waiting, Kate asked, "Lori, was there anything that really stood out in the session for you this morning?"

"Well, like I said, I've been stewing on the question of owning a business or just a bunch of jobs ... or do the jobs own us? I feel like we work harder for the ranch than it does for us."

Chris saw Wayne shift in his seat. It was obvious he wasn't comfortable with where this was going.

"Everyone talks about the ranching lifestyle, but for me that lifestyle involves a 40-minute commute twice a day to a job that ..." Lori's voice trailed off. "To tell you the truth, sometimes I just get mad at myself!"

"Mad at yourself? Whatever for?" Kate asked.

"I get mad because I get jealous. I get jealous of Wayne. I know he works his rear end off, but he gets to work it off at home. He doesn't have to commute five days a week." Lori wiped a tear away. She continued, "I get home and the house is a mess, someone's got to get dinner going." Her fist came down on the table harder than she had expected, making the silverware rattle. After a moment she looked up at Kate and said, "I'm just worn out. I'm impatient with the kids. I'm impatient with Wayne.

"Funny thing is I don't dislike what I do. I like the people I work with, but I want to be on the ranch. I want to be able to homeschool Matthew and Justin. I don't want to *have* to work in town. I know we need the money and the insurance. God knows, with this drought, it'll be the only thing bringing in any money.

"The thing that really eats me up is that I take my frustration out on Wayne and the kids. It's not fair to them and ..." With tears rolling down her cheeks, she concluded, "Sometimes I just don't like who I've become."

Kate hadn't expected the conversation to take this turn. No one knew what to say, especially Wayne, who sat there feeling guilty, but for what he wasn't sure.

Chris finally said, "You are dealing with some tough issues." He was reluctant to pry and thought it best to avoid the temptation to offer advice. He knew that sometimes it was important to just let people know you heard what they had to say. After a few seconds of silence, he asked, "What would it take to quit or at least scale back your job at the bank?"

Lori was embarrassed about her minor meltdown and pretended not to hear the question. She wanted to let the subject drop and shift the focus away from herself.

Chris rephrased the question, "How much more would the ranch have to make for you to be able to quit your job at the bank?"

"More than we make now," Wayne answered.

"Our place isn't big enough to support us and Buddy," Lori said.

Wayne's dad, Buddy, had ruled the ranch with an iron fist until 13 years ago when he'd had a stroke. The stroke affected his vision and left him with limited use of his left arm. Wayne, who had always wanted to come back to the ranch, dropped out of college to help out.

Chris wondered how far he should push the conversation. "Look, it's clear we are on sensitive ground here, but it's also clear that you aren't happy with the way things are. I wonder if there could be some way to make the ranch more profitable. Do you want to explore some possibilities?"

"There isn't much point," Lori sighed.

Kate spoke quietly to Lori, "A year ago, I thought it'd be impossible to ever be full time on the ranch, but I'll be half time in six months and if things go the way we expect, I'll be able to be full time on the ranch by this time next year." Looking Lori in the eye, she added, "You know how frustrated I was."

Chris shot Kate a questioning look. He suddenly realized that she may have been more frustrated than she had let on. Kate saw his look and responded with a slight shrug. Then, talking directly to Lori, she said, "One of the questions they asked us at the school was, 'What is something that seems impossible to do, but if you could do it, it would change everything for the better?'"

"That's easy," Lori said. "For the ranch to make enough money to support us full time."

"That's it," Wayne agreed. "Word for word what I was going to say."

Jumping right to the point, Chris asked, "How much? How much would the ranch need to clear for you to be able to quit?"

"I don't know." Shaking her head slowly, Lori repeated, "Chris, I really don't know."

"Wayne, what do you think?" Chris asked.

"I don't know, $100,000?"

"Why $100,000?"

"I don't know," Wayne said. He was growing irritated at his friend for pushing him into a sensitive, uncomfortable subject. "It's a big number. It ought to be enough."

"Enough to do what?" Chris was pushing his luck and he knew it.

"Enough for Lori to quit," Wayne said slowly and loudly as though trying to communicate with someone who did not understand English.

"I know I'm being pushy, but go with me on this a little," Chris pleaded. He glanced at Wayne, then Lori. Lori frowned but nodded her agreement to go ahead. "Look, quitting is describing what you don't want," he explained. "You don't want to have to work at the bank or need to rely on an off-farm job. You don't want to have to commute every day. But what *do* you want?"

"What do you mean, 'What do I want?'" Lori asked. If she had ever thought about what she wanted, it had been a long time ago. She and Wayne were so busy trying to get by and keep *bad* things from happening, it didn't feel like there was much point to think about *good* things that they wanted to make happen.

Lori sat there staring across the booth at nothing and slowly shaking her head. "I want to quit …" She caught herself, "No that's what I don't want." She asked herself again, "What do I want? I want … Wayne to be happy. I want," she paused as though once she said the first two words the rest would come automatically. "I want my boys to be safe and enjoy their childhood." She thought for a moment about the doctor appointment she had for Justin next week. Justin had broken his collar bone last month when he was helping work cattle in the corrals. He didn't do anything wrong. It was just a crazy cow that decided she wanted to be someplace else and Justin was in her way. He climbed the corral fence, but she came climbing after him. Lori had never been so scared as when she saw him lying unconscious in the pen. She thought about the frequency with which close calls happened. "It's a miracle we aren't all crippled or dead," she muttered. Trying to refocus, she mumbled, "Okay, I want …" She was obviously struggling to come up with things.

Kate suggested, "It sounded like you wanted to homeschool the boys."

Lori appreciated the suggestion. "Yes, I think so. I mean, really, I just want to have more constructive time with them. I don't want to feel like I'm always nagging. There I go with what I don't want again. It's so much easier to describe what you don't want, isn't it?"

"Yeah, it is," Chris agreed. "But the absence of something bad doesn't mean you've got something good." He continued, "Do you want to retire?"

"From the ranch? Every day!" Wayne joked. Then he said seriously, "Well, I'd like the kids to have it someday. I guess I don't want to be a burden on them." Wayne realized that he was answering a question posed to Lori again. He had a bad habit of doing that. "Sorry," he said.

"Don't be sorry." Chris said. "It might be a good idea if you each made your own list. Kate and I did, then we discussed each thing on our lists. That was a big deal for us. I assumed I knew what Kate wanted, and I had a lot of it right, but I missed the mark on some things."

"And we got into more than just what each of us wanted," Kate explained. "We got into *why* the things we wanted were important to us. Identifying the *why* behind the *what* was the most valuable part."

Looking at Wayne, Chris continued, "A minute ago you said you wanted to be able to retire someday. What kind of income would you need to not be a burden on the kids?"

"I don't know, $50,000?" Wayne guessed.

"To get a solid number you'll need to really think through what you want your life to look like then. You'll probably want to travel a little?" Chris suggested.

"More likely the kids will want us to travel," Lori joked.

"It's probably going to wind up being more, but let's leave it at $50,000 for now," Kate suggested. She saw Lori's frown. She knew that Lori, who liked detail, would be uncomfortable with "ballparking" figures. Kate tried to reassure her. "Look, every number we put down will be wrong. We just want to get close." She added, "You can get more precise later."

Chris continued, "So, $50,000?" He looked at Wayne for confirmation. When Wayne nodded, Chris asked, "So what are you now, 50?" He knew Wayne was 36.

"Hey, play nice," Wayne grumbled.

Chris shrugged and said, "Let's say you want to retire 30 years from now. If you had a million dollars invested and got a 5% return, that'd be $50,000."

Chris realized that he was oversimplifying things. For one thing, he wasn't accounting for inflation or interest, but it was a place to start.

"How much do you have squirrelled away right now?" It occurred to Chris that Wayne and Lori might think it was none of his business. "Have you guys got anything saved for retirement?"

"The ranch is our retirement," Wayne said. He had figured that they would be secure when they got older by putting all their money in the ranch. Suddenly he wasn't so sure.

"How's that working for your dad?" Chris asked. He was pretty sure that Wayne's dad, Buddy, had put every nickel he ever made back into the ranch. Even though Buddy was unable to do much work anymore, he probably still depended on income from the ranch. It might have supported one family before, but now it needed to support two. "Do you guys have any retirement savings? Kate and I didn't until recently, and what we have isn't nearly enough."

Wayne wasn't sure how much he and Lori had in savings, and he was even less certain he wanted to discuss his personal finances with Chris and Kate. He felt defensive, but he was too tired to argue so he lied, "About $120,000."

Lori gave him a questioning glance. She knew they didn't have anything close to that in their savings and nothing specifically for retirement, but she didn't say anything.

Chris continued, "Fine. Like Kate said, every number will be wrong, but we'll see if we can get in the ballpark. Let's say you need to put away another $900,000 over 30 years." Chris did the math out loud while Kate used the calculator on her cell phone. "$900,000 divided by 30 years …" Chris's eyes darted up to the ceiling as though he expected the answer to be written on a ceiling tile.

"That's $30,000 per year," Kate said.

"Good Lord, we won't be able to afford to eat," Lori said.

Kate added, "You'll probably have some Social Security income. That will reduce the amount you need to save. We haven't accounted for interest on what you save and invest. That will contribute a lot. We haven't accounted for inflation either. Regardless, it's still going to be a wad of money."

"Let's just say that after you adjust for inflation and figure in the interest you'd earn, you need to put away $20,000 every year for retirement," Chris said. He wrote "Retirement $20,000" on a napkin. "I'm thinking that might be a little high, but it's safer to guess too high than too low. I bet it's in the ballpark."

"What else do you need money for?" Chris asked.

Lori started listing, "Groceries, clothes … "

"No, that's not what I mean," Chris said. "Those are personal expenses. You pay those out of your salary. What I want to know is what you need profit for. If you made a profit, what else would you do with it?"

"What else?" Wayne asked.

"Well, we just figured you need at least $20,000 in profit every year to invest for retirement savings," Chris explained. "What else would you use your profit for?"

"I might actually pay myself a salary," Wayne said.

"That's good, but that's not coming out of profit. Your salary is a cost to the business. Profit is what is left over *after* your salary and other costs. What else would you do with it if you made a profit?" Chris prodded.

"I suppose we'd pay down our debt," Wayne said. He knew there must be other uses for profit, but he was drawing a blank.

"It would be a load off my mind if we had some reserves, some savings," Lori added.

"We got that didn't we?" Wayne asked. "$20,000 for retirement."

"No," Kate said emphatically. "Your retirement savings are off limits. I think Lori is talking about an emergency fund — two or three months of operating expenses in reserves. Is that what you meant?"

"Exactly," Lori confirmed.

"Look, we'll have our food in a minute, and I want to push this through," Chris said impatiently. "How much for paying off the debt and how much for reserves?" When no one responded, he asked, "What if you could add $10,000 to your reserves for the next five years and pay your long-term debt down by $50,000 each year?"

"Sure." Wayne was anxious to be done with this. The cook must have had gone out to slaughter a cow. It was taking forever to get their meal.

Pretending to be oblivious to Wayne's impatience, Chris wrote "Pay Down Debt $50,000, Reserves $10,000" on the napkin. Then he asked, "Would there ever be a dividend to shareholders?"

"A dividend?" Wayne thought Chris had lost his mind. "You've got to be kidding."

The discussion went back and forth, but eventually Chris's napkin had a list showing things that Lori and Wayne could do with their profit, if they ever made one, and how much profit they'd need to do all of those things. Some things were filled in, others just had a question mark. At the bottom of the list, Chris wrote "Profit Target ≥ $100,000."

Profit Target	
Retirement	$20,000
Pay Down Debt	$50,000
Build Reserves	$10,000
Expansion	$20,000
On-Farm Improvements	?
Off-Farm Investment	?
Dividends to Owners	?
Donations	?
Profit Target	≥$100,000

"Good Lord," muttered Lori. That seemed like an impossible target. She had started feeling a little hopeful, but as soon as she saw the target, her hope vanished. If Wayne's salary had to come out before profit, she wasn't even sure it was possible to break even. It felt like this had been a cruel waste of time. Even so, she didn't have the energy to tell Chris to stop

"It's pathetic isn't it?" Lori asked. "We've never talked about the ranch in terms of it being a business. We've never ever talked about making a profit. We've always just focused on all the work we have to do just to get by. We've certainly never ever talked about what profit is for."

"You aren't alone," Kate spoke softly. "We hadn't either before that class. I don't think anyone else in the class had ever thought about what profit was for or had ever set a profit target. But it's pretty hard to hit a target that doesn't exist."

Lori shook her head slowly as though she was looking at a mess the kids had made that she would have to clean up. But she couldn't point her finger at anyone who was responsible for this mess.

"It's funny," Chris said. "I don't think anyone is motivated by money. At least no one I know. I'm not. Kate's not. I don't think either of you are. It's not the money. It's what you can do with the money that's important. Having a secure future. Supporting the kids. Taking a trip to Australia ..."

"Oh, that's something Wayne has always talked about," Lori said.

"Us too," said Kate. "And we want to do it with the kids, before they are off to college. We know we need to be responsible and prepare for the future, but we want to experience life *now* too."

"Have your cake and eat it too?" Wayne asked.

"You could put it that way. But why not? I'll bet on our balance sheets we're both worth a couple of million, but I know we both live like we're flat broke. That's crazy," Chris said.

"No, that's agriculture," Wayne said.

"It is for some. It may be for most, but it isn't for everyone, and it isn't going to be for us," Chris insisted. "I really don't want to keep talking about the school, I know you're tired of hearing about it, but there was this guy and his wife who were repeating the class who told us that they'd struggled to get to the school the first time they took it. He said that they'd never been away from the ranch for a week. A couple of years later they took their family on a vacation. How long was it, Katie?"

"Chuck and Bonnie?" Kate asked as she searched her memory. "Bonnie was on my team. I think she said they were gone for three months. They went to Australia. They visited a half dozen properties and stayed with families that had taken the course over there. One family had a tame kangaroo ... Bonnie showed me pictures of their kids with this kangaroo. They are so weird looking."

Chris continued, "One night after class we were in the hotel bar with other people from the class talking about our families. We were talking about how busy we are all the time. It was like each of us was trying to prove we were busier than the next guy." Chris puffed out his chest and boasted, "I work 20 hours a day." Then, in a lower voice, said, "That ain't nothin', I work 28 hours a day!

"Anyway, Carl, this guy about our age, said something about wanting to go to Australia and Chuck and Bonnie are sitting there. Chuck says, 'You'd love it. You should go.' Carl looks at Chuck like he came from another planet then starts going into all the reasons it would be impossible to go. Then Chuck cut him off and asked, 'I know why you can't go, but what would have to happen for you to be able to go?' I'm listening to Carl's answer and, as he's talking, I started to realize that if we really want to do this, we can find a way. If we don't, we can keep making excuses. Anyway, three years from now, in March, we are going. Me, Katie, Robyn, and Sally. We are going," Chris said with determination.

"To Australia?" Lori asked.

"Yep, Australia. That's what our profit is for — at least part of it. It's not about the money. It's about our life."

Kate nodded. "We are doing it," she said resolutely. After a moment she added, "So, you don't have to figure it all out right now, but it's something you might want to think about. What is your profit for?"

SUMMARY OF CHAPTER 3
CONCEPTS

- Your salary and your business's profit are two different things. Salary must be deducted as a cost when calculating profit.

- Investing all of the profit the ranch earns back into the ranch may create big challenges for retirement and generational succession.

- It's impossible to make an intelligent plan without a goal.

- One important goal is your profit target.

- To establish a profit target, you must first determine why you want to make a profit. What is your profit for?

Chapter 4
The Other Side of the Napkin: Gross Margin Target

Seeing Kate's resolve brightened Lori's outlook. She asked Kate, "Once you have a profit target, how do you use it? I mean, just identifying how much you need, doesn't mean you are going to be able to get it."

"That's right, but it is impossible to hit a bull's-eye if you don't have a target to shoot at," Kate said. "Most of us just do what we do, get what we get, and hope that there's something left over at the end of the year. In Ranching For Profit, you start by identifying what you want to have at the end of the year and then work backward to determine what you will need to do to create it. It starts with determining your profit target, but that's just the start."

"Do you want me to show you the next step?" Chris asked.

Lori said, "I'd rather eat." She looked over her shoulder to the kitchen. "But we might as well keep going until our food's here. Lay it on us, Chris."

"Okay. I'll make it short and sweet," Chris said. We need to estimate your overhead costs. Those are the costs that don't change much, whether you have 300 cows or 400. Pretty much all of your land and labor costs are overheads. Let's start with labor costs."

Turning to Wayne, Chris asked, "How much would it cost to replace the work you and Lori do if you had to hire someone else to do it?"

Wayne remembered this from the workshop earlier that day. "$20,000?" he guessed. He thought that keeping the number low would make the numbers Chris was writing on the napkin look better than they might otherwise.

"You can sell that load to someone else," Chris argued. "Are you telling me that I could hire you for $20,000?"

"I'd make more money than I do now," Wayne joked. He wondered if that was true. "No, $20,000 is fair. I'll make up the balance in sweat equity."

"Don't go there," Chris warned with a laugh. "If you want to get the teacher on his soapbox, just bring up sweat equity. He says if you are the one doing the sweating, you'll inflate its value, and if you are another family member, you'll dismiss or at least discount its value." Chris shook his head, "No, you need to put down a fair wage for the work you do. If the business can't afford to pay it, you can write it on the books as deferred wages."

"Is this the economics versus finance thing again?" Wayne asked. "Deferred wages would be an economic cost but not a cash expense — at least not until the day it got paid."

"Exactly," Chris confirmed.

Lori's eyes grew wide listening to Wayne talk about economics versus finance. She was surprised and more than a little impressed.

"So, what should your wage be? There's no way to get someone to do all you do for $20,000," Chris insisted. "You can try to lowball this if you want to scrape by and keep working for the ranch for the rest of your life, but let's see what it's going to take to make your place really work for you. I'm writing in $50,000, and that's probably low. You can change it later if you want."

"What about Buddy?" Chris asked. "What's a fair wage for Buddy?"

"Gee, I don't know." Wayne looked at Lori and shrugged.

"Maybe $50,000 too," she suggested.

Wayne nodded and Chris continued, "Any other labor? How about John? John's just seasonal now, isn't he? So, what's he get? $15,000, $20,000?"

"Once you add in payroll taxes and workers' comp, I'll bet it's closer to 25 or 30," Kate offered.

"Let's write in $25,000." Chris added it to the list. "Remember, every number is wrong. Now, how much for insurance?"

"That's one of the reasons Lori's job has been so important, we can't afford …"

Chris cut Wayne off. "Never mind that for now. How much do you think it might cost? We pay about $10,000."

"It's closer to $12,000," Kate corrected.

"Okay, let's go with that," Chris said. "Now, you've got your truck and your car — that's about $15,000 each."

As he wrote "Vehicles $30,000" on the napkin, Wayne asked, "How do you figure that? One of them isn't worth more than the tires."

"Doesn't matter. If it's new you probably don't have much in the way of repairs, but the insurance, interest, and depreciation are higher," Chris explained. "If it's old, you've got more repairs, and you always have fuel. If it's as bad as all that, you'll be replacing it soon."

Lori laughed, "As long as he's got chewing gum and baling twine, he'll keep that piece of junk running."

"Okay, then, how much for the gum?" Seeing that no one thought he was funny, Chris let it drop.

Wayne thought back to something from the workshop. The teacher said that the cost of hiring an employee with a $40,000 per year salary was closer to $90,000! That was hard to swallow. But now, adding in the truck, housing, equipment, payroll taxes, health insurance, and workers' comp, he could see how that might be true.

"You know we have 2 ATVs, one for John and one for me or the boys," Wayne offered. "I suppose we need to account for those costs too."

"Right." Chris was pleased Wayne was contributing. "So, let's put a lump sum in for the ATVs, equipment, horses, dogs, and all the other labor costs."

"Dogs and horses go with equipment?" Lori questioned.

"Sure," Kate said. "They all do work or support the work you do."

"I guess so. So, things like dog food and feed for the horses, those are labor costs?" Lori asked.

"And the vet bill when they took that foxtail out of Bandit's ear, that's a labor cost too?" Wayne asked.

"Absolutely," confirmed Chris. "What do you think for all that? $20,000? $50,000?"

"Let's go with $40,000," Wayne suggested. "We had a lot of repairs on our hay equipment."

"Okay now, land costs," Chris said. "If you were to rent your ranch out to someone, how much could you get?" He suspected that would spark a reaction.

"Over Buddy's dead body!" Wayne roared.

"Over yours too!" Lori added. "Actually, mine too. None of us wants to rent the place out and Buddy would never go for it."

"I'm not suggesting that you rent it," Chris clarified. "I just want to know, if you did, what could you get? Let's say that this ranch didn't belong to your family. How much would you have to pay to rent it?"

"I suppose it would rent for $50,000," Wayne said without conviction.

"I suspect it would be more than that, but let's go with $50,000 for now." He added it to the list, then said, "You know, that could be one way to gain some independence." He knew there had been tension between Wayne and Lori and Wayne's dad. According to Wayne, Buddy second-guessed even the smallest decisions Wayne made. Maybe most frustrating was Buddy's spontaneous spending. According to Wayne, Buddy would spend money without telling anyone, often for things they had discussed and agreed *not* to buy. "You could rent the ranch from Buddy."

"Rent the ranch from Buddy?" Wayne asked.

"Yeah, rent the ranch from Buddy," Chris repeated. "That would give him some income and it'd give you some independence — and the same when your boys are ready to step up. They could lease it from you. That could be retirement income for you, and your boys could ..." Chris suddenly regretted making this suggestion. He knew they already had enough on their minds today without adding that.

Lori stared at Wayne for a moment. She wondered if it was possible to be free to operate the place without Buddy's criticism and meddling. It sounded too good to be true.

"Anyway, let's add that in," Chris said.

"Add what in?" Lori asked, as if coming out of a dream.

"The rent," Chris said. "I'll put in $50,000 for rent. Would there be any other property maintenance fees? Your fences are in good shape, aren't they? Not a lot of repair and maintenance there. And if you are renting, those would probably be landowner costs."

"But we're not renting," Wayne reminded him.

"Yes, you are," Chris corrected. "Your operating business is renting from the landowner. Y'all just happen to be the landowners. Okay, let's add this up."

Overhead Costs:	
Wayne's Salary	$50,000
Buddy's Salary	$50,000
John	$25,000
Health Insurance	$12,000
Vehicles	$20,000
Other Labor	$40,000
Rent	$50,000
Total Overheads	$247,000
Profit Target	+ $100,000
Gross Margin Target	≥$347,000

Kate had already entered the numbers on her cell phone. "$247,000 in overheads," she said, flipping the napkin over to check the profit target. She turned the napkin back over and wrote "Profit Target $100,000." She added that to the overheads and wrote "Gross Margin Target ≥$347,000." Kate turned to Lori and said, "You need a total gross margin of at least $347,000."

"Good Lord!" exclaimed Lori.

Chris saw the waitress coming and suggested, "Let's put this aside for a while and eat."

The burgers were good, and it was clear they were going to need more napkins.

SUMMARY OF CHAPTER 4
CONCEPTS

- Rather than doing what you do and accepting whatever is left over, determine what you want to have left over and create a plan to achieve it.

- With the exception of shearing, all land and labor costs in a livestock business are overhead costs.

- Labor-related overheads include salaries, benefits, housing, vehicle and equipment expenses, and expenses for working animals.

- Set your salary at what you would have to pay to replace the work you do. If you can't afford to pay yourself, record the unpaid balance as "deferred wages" and determine the interest to charge on the amount owed. The business must repay you someday.

- There is no such thing as sweat equity!

- Land-related overheads include, rent, infrastructure maintenance, and repair.

- If you own your land, separate your operating business from your land investment, at least on paper.

- Your livestock business must rent ALL of the land it uses, including the land you own. Charge a fair market rate rent to your livestock business.

- Overhead costs tend not to change much as the units of production (the number of animals) change.

- 60%-80% of the costs in most traditional livestock businesses are overhead costs.

- Overheads are not fixed. They can be changed.

Chapter 5
The Three Secrets for Increasing Profit

It was a relief to everyone when the discussion shifted to kids, school, and gossip about the neighbors. As they got up to go, Lori folded the napkin with the profit target calculation and the list of overhead costs. As she put it in her purse, she saw Wayne give her a subtle nod of approval.

By the time they were back on the road it was almost 3:30. After a full meal, the warmth of the sun through the windshield made them all a little sleepy. By the time they had gone three miles, Wayne was dozing with his head resting against the window.

With her voice low, so as not to wake Wayne, Lori leaned to Kate and said, "You know, I was chiding Wayne when he said Ranching For Profit is an oxymoron, but maybe I should be pointing the finger more at myself than at him."

"What do you mean?"

"Well, when Chris was asking how much profit we wanted, I thought, right, like our place can really pay us wages and make a profit. But your place isn't any bigger than ours, and it sounds like you had more debt than us. We've got a lot of operating debt and owe some on the cattle, and we have some land payments too."

Kate looked up in surprise. "Mortgage payments? I thought ..."

"I know, I know," Lori said. "But Buddy put a second on the home place to buy a feedlot near Spring Valley. That's another issue." She rolled her eyes. "Even if we agree to a plan, nobody pays any attention to it. Everybody just does what they want. It drives me nuts. It's no way to run a business. Anyway, what I wanted to say ... well, you seem to have figured out how to turn things around."

Kate felt confident but was not one to boast. "We have a lot to learn and a long way to go."

"No," said Lori, "you have found something and, from where I sit, it looks like it has changed your outlook, your confidence, even your relationship with Chris."

"Things have changed for us," Kate agreed. "Creating a vision of the life and of the business we want and establishing a profit target made us hopeful about the future. But the biggest change comes from having a plan. That gives us confidence about the future. Chris and I don't feel like we're at the mercy of the weather or the markets. We realized that we aren't helpless."

"Are you telling me that weather and markets don't have any effect?" Lori asked skeptically.

"No, of course not. Those things have a big impact. But we've worked through how drought and cattle prices and other things beyond our control could play out. We've incorporated those what-ifs into our plan." Kate paused before adding, "And we've tested the plan."

"You've tested the plan? What's does that mean? How did you test it?"

"We made a projection for what we think is likely to happen if we make the changes we're thinking of making," Kate explained. "It shows that the changes should make us a lot more profitable. But you never know how much it'll rain or what prices will be, so we ran other scenarios. In one we assumed that production would be 10% less and prices would tank. We cut calf prices by 30 cents and our initial projections were conservative to start with."

"And?"

"Oh, and then we increased all of our input costs by 10%," Kate remembered. "It was kind of a worst-case scenario."

"And?"

"The projection for what we thought would happen looked really good and the projection for the worst-case scenario was survivable," Kate said with a smile. "In fact, the worst-case scenario came out to be a little better than what we actually did last year — and last year was a better than average year for us! Having a plan and knowing it will work sure helps you sleep at night."

Lori was about to respond when Kate added, "Oh, and remember, we included renting our land and paying fair wages to Chris and me in the projection."

"I wouldn't have a clue how you build a plan like that," Lori lamented.

"We didn't either, but it's not that hard if you understand the Three Secrets," Kate said.

"The Three Secrets for Increasing Profit," Lori recalled. "I really liked that part of the workshop. Whenever I've heard economists or finance people talk, they either put me to sleep or made me feel stupid. This morning was different. It made sense. It seemed so simple. Actually, it seemed *too* simple. I was thinking, what's the trick?"

"There's no trick. It *is* simple, but that doesn't mean it's easy," Chris offered, turning his head to look at Lori and then back to the road. "The hard part for me wasn't learning the Three Secrets. The hard part was accepting that just about everything I thought I knew about success in ranching was wrong. But the numbers don't lie. I had to let go of a lot of outdated thinking before I could embrace the changes we're making."

Lori wasn't smiling. "I've never been very good with change," she said.

"How good are you with the way things are?" Kate asked gently.

"Touché," Lori said. A moment later she added, "What the teacher said about the Three Secrets made sense, but I don't understand them well enough to build a plan around them."

"You want to go over it together?" Kate asked. "How about opening your notebook up to the Three Secrets graph?"

Lori opened her notebook. "I'm there," she said.

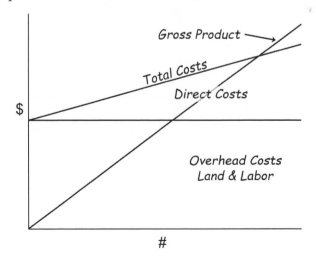

"Let's start with overhead costs. Those are the costs we listed on the napkin." Kate explained that overhead costs include all land and labor costs. Land overheads include rent, repairs and maintenance for buildings, roads, pipelines and water troughs, fences, corrals, and all the other things attached to the land. Labor costs include salaries and benefits, equipment, machinery, and working horses and dogs. In short, labor costs include all costs that involve work.

"At the bank they call these fixed costs, but this morning the teacher insisted that they aren't fixed," Lori said. "He really emphasized that point."

"Right," Chris said, looking at Lori in the rearview mirror. "At the school they don't use the 'F' word. The word 'fixed' implies they can't be changed. I don't think the teacher likes the notion that there's something you can't change."

"I thought you were just going to drive," Kate nagged, playfully.

"So," she asked, "what is it about an overhead cost that makes it an overhead?"

"There are three rules," Lori began. "First, if it's a land or labor cost, it's an overhead. Second, overheads usually don't change very much as the units in an enterprise change." She paused, then added, "Like when we destock because of the drought, our liability insurance doesn't change and we still have to make the full payment on the pickup, even though we have fewer cows than we had last year. But the teacher said there are some overheads that *do* change. I didn't understand that. How can some change and others not?"

"It's actually pretty simple," Kate said. "Think about the lease we have with my uncle Phil. We pay a flat fee for that. It doesn't matter if we have one cow there or a hundred, we pay the same thing every year. Then there's our government lease. That lease is on an animal unit basis. We pay for the two leases differently, but in both cases we are renting land, and *all* land costs are overheads. Now, what's the third rule?" Kate asked.

"If you are in doubt about what kind of cost it is, it's probably an overhead," Lori said. "The teacher said that overheads account for somewhere between 60% and 80% of all the costs on most ranches. I guess it's a good thing they aren't fixed."

"Any questions about overheads?" Kate asked.

"Yes. The teacher said that even if you own the ranch, your livestock have to rent it. Chris brought that up at lunch too, but I'm still a little confused. Why do we have to rent the ranch if we own it?" Lori asked.

"That's the opportunity rent," Chris said turning to look at Lori.

"I thought you were going to keep your eyes on the road," Kate said.

She continued, "At the school they told us to consider the ranch as two entities: the land investment and the operating business. Whether you own the land or someone else owns it, the operating business has to pay rent for the land it uses. It's the only way to know if the livestock operation is subsidizing the land or the land is subsidizing the livestock operation. In Ranching For Profit, they want each to be viable on its own."

"So, do you figure out what you could rent the ranch to someone else for and charge that to the operating business?" Lori asked.

"Exactly! There are a lot of other reasons for looking at it that way too," Kate said. "We met one guy who attended the class over 15 years ago. He was probably 60 and was repeating the school with his daughter and his son-in-law, who were taking it for the first time. They had separated the operating business from the land business. She and her husband rent the land from her folks. The rent is her folks' retirement income. They said it made both the succession plan and the estate plan a lot clearer."

"Their estate plan?" Lori asked.

Kate tried to recall the conversation at the school about this. "In their estate plan they are leaving the land in an undivided interest to all their kids — I think there are four of them. They have a strict buyout agreement. The couple running the ranch will own the operating business and pay rent to themselves and their siblings as landowners. If any of the kids want out, they get their shares bought at a steeply discounted rate by the others."

"That doesn't seem fair," Lori observed.

"A minority share of a family business isn't worth very much. Besides, no one is forcing anyone to sell anything they don't want to sell," Kate said. "If the folks leave the ranch with the caveat that it's got to stay intact or in the family unless everyone wants to sell, well, that's their right. Parents don't owe their kids an inheritance."

"Okay, okay. I see your point." Lori held up her hands in mock surrender.

"Of course, just because that's what they did doesn't mean it's the right thing for someone else," Chris said. "Like any option there are positives and negatives. They were determined to keep the land intact. It's pretty hard to put something back together once it's split up."

"Any other questions on overheads?" Kate asked.

"I think I've got it," Lori said. "The other kind of costs the teacher talked about were direct costs, right? Direct costs change as the number of animals change. They include feed, vaccines, ear tags, and trucking."

"Right. One more cow, one more vaccination," Kate said. "Any questions about that?"

"Yeah, a couple," Lori said. "First, feed is a direct cost, but pasture rent is an overhead, even though the pasture is providing feed. What about things like grazing crop residues or corn stalks? Is that a feed cost or a land cost?"

"I had the same question myself," Kate said. "Here's the rule: If you're bringing the cow to the feed, it's a land cost. If you're bringing the feed to the cow, it's a feed cost. So, bringing cows to residues ..."

"That's a land cost. It's an overhead. That's simple enough," Lori said. "Okay, second question. When you buy an animal, is that a direct cost?"

"No, it's not," Wayne said, opening one eye. "It's a capital expense."

Chris looked over at him. "I thought you were sleeping."

"With all this noise and your driving? I've got bruises on my forehead. Are you aiming at the ruts? You've hit every single one so far."

"I don't get it. How is buying the cow not a cost?" Lori asked.

"It's one of those economics versus finance things Chris was telling me about," Wayne said. "When you buy a cow, it's a trade. You have money and you trade it for a cow. Your business is out the money, but now you have the cow. You didn't gain or lose any value. You just changed the form of the asset."

"It's the same if you buy a truck," Chris explained. "The truck is a capital expense. It's the interest payment, depreciation, repairs, and fuel that are the costs. Those costs are overheads because the truck helps labor. With the cow, the purchase is a capital expense, but the interest, vet bills, and feed are direct costs because they change as the number of cows change."

"Okay, I think I've got it," Lori said. "When you buy something like a cow or a truck it's a capital expense. It's the depreciation, interest, repairs, and fuel that are the costs."

"Right. Anything else on direct costs?" Kate asked.

"No, I'm good for now," Lori said.

"The next line is gross product," Kate said. "That's the total value the enterprise produces."

"We don't use gross income because we need to include the change in inventory value, right?" Lori asked.

"Right, and it's super easy to figure. All you do is add your sales to your closing inventory value and subtract your purchases, like any bulls or replacements you buy. Then you subtract your beginning inventory value. The process for calculating it is called a trading account. Here's how you do it." She took the notebook Lori had been using and wrote:

```
Trading Account
   Closing Inventory Value
  + Sales
  - Purchases
  - Beginning Inventory Value
   Gross Product
```

"So, let me make sure I've got this," Lori said as she organized her thoughts. "Overheads are land and labor costs. They don't change much as the number of cows you carry increases or decreases, but they aren't fixed. There are things you can do to change them. Direct costs are costs that increase or decrease as the number of cows increase or decrease. Gross product is the total *value* an enterprise produces."

"You got it!" Kate said. The emotions at the restaurant and the lethargy everyone had felt after lunch had been replaced by enthusiasm.

"So, this zone here," Kate said, as Wayne contorted his body to face the back seat so he could see what she was pointing to, "the area between the gross product and total costs, that's profit."

"It's not very big, is it?" Lori said.

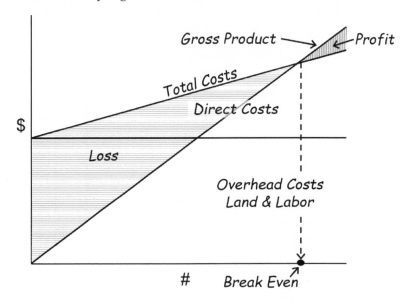

Kate continued, "This zone, where the total costs are greater than the gross product, what do you call that?"

"Normal," Wayne laughed. He quickly added, "That'd be a loss." A moment later he said, "Geez, that's a whole lot bigger, isn't it?"

"So, what's this point right here where the total costs and gross product meet?" Kate asked as she pointed to that spot on the graph.

Lori drew a line from that point down to the X axis of the graph. "The break-even point?" she said, with some hesitation.

"That's right!" Kate confirmed. "The break-even point." She was genuinely happy to see Lori and Wayne understanding this. She knew it could open doors for them, as it had for Chris and her. It was also a kick to realize how much she herself had learned. She continued, "If you are on the right side of the break-even point you are making a profit and ..."

Wayne cut in, "If you are on the *wrong* side of it you are making a loss."

Wayne looked over to Chris and said, "I was curious about that. In the workshop the teacher only referred to the break-even point once. Most other people who talk about this stuff seem a lot more concerned with the break-even point. Our banker always asks about the 'break-evens.'"

"It's the Ranching For Profit School, not the Ranching For Breaking Even School," Chris said. "The goal isn't to break even."

"Fair enough," Wayne nodded.

"Now for the Three Secrets," Kate said. "See if you can find them on the graph."

"Well, the first is to cut the overhead costs." Lori drew a dashed line below the original overhead line. Then she redrew the direct cost line in the same way. "If we can cut our overheads it will move the break-even point back, and if we were making a loss before, we might make a profit now. So, the first secret is to cut the overhead costs."

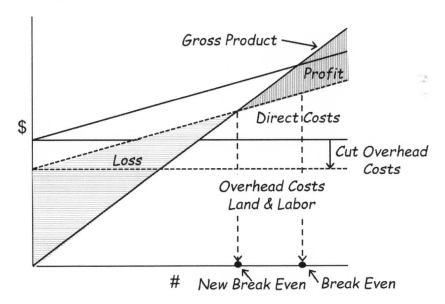

45

"What's the second secret for increasing profit?" Chris asked.

"Before this morning I would have said it's to reduce the direct costs, especially feed costs, or to get more for my calves," Wayne explained. "But if I cut my feed costs, that could impact my productivity and gross product could go down. If I try to increase gross product by increasing the conception rate or weaning bigger calves, it could increase direct costs. Even doing things to get a higher price like preconditioning, or spending more on genetics or marketing might result in higher direct costs." He turned, looked at Kate, and concluded, "So we have to look at gross product and direct costs, together."

"Exactly!" Kate said. "So, if the second secret to increasing profit isn't reducing direct costs or increasing gross product, what is it?" She was impressed with how Wayne was connecting the dots.

"Was that gross margin?" Lori asked. "That was just the gross product minus direct costs, right?"

"Right, that's how you calculate gross margin," Chris said. "You guys will be teaching this before long."

Lori wrote in the notebook:

$$\begin{array}{l} \text{Gross Product} \\ \underline{- \text{Direct Costs}} \\ \text{Gross Margin} \end{array}$$

"So, the second secret for increasing profit is increasing gross margin?" Wayne asked.

"Not quite," Kate corrected. "There are two ways to increase the total gross margin. One is to simply have more units in the enterprise. If I have 200 cows my total gross margin will be double what it is if I only have 100 cows. The other way to increase the total gross margin is to increase the gross margin per cow. Gross margin per unit measures the efficiency of the unit. You need to take the total gross margin and divide it by the number of animal units. Improving the gross margin per *unit* is the second secret for increasing profit."

Wayne repeated, "So the second secret is to increase the gross margin per cow?"

"Almost," Chris confirmed. "Not all cows are created equal. Your cows average, what, maybe 1,200 pounds? The cows on the Davis place average at least 1,400 pounds."

"I'll bet they're even bigger than that," Wayne said.

"Probably, but either way, his bigger cows eat more than yours, so they'd better produce a higher gross margin. What the gross margin per unit really measures is the economic efficiency with which different animals graze," Chris said.

"You couldn't very well compare the gross margin for a steer you have for only six months to a cow you have for a year," Kate explained. "You just have to make sure you use a unit that works for the comparison. For farming we use gross margin per acre. For livestock enterprises we usually use gross margin per animal unit."

"How do you figure out what's what? How many animal units to a steer or a cow?" Wayne asked.

"They show you in the school.[1] It's really simple," Chris said.

"Okay, so we can lower the overheads or improve the gross margin per unit. What's the third secret for increasing profit?" Kate asked, getting things back on track. Home was less than 10 minutes away and she knew there would be too many distractions to continue once they got there.

"Well, the last one would be to increase the number of cows," Lori said.

"Right," Kate confirmed, "except it might not be cows. It might be stockers. It might even be adding a whole new enterprise. Do you remember what the teacher called this in the workshop?"

Lori was stumped. Wayne offered, "Turnover?"

"Right. Turnover. Turnover measures the total number of units in the business, whether it is cattle, or timber, or hunting, or farming," Kate explained.

"So those are the only three things in any business you can do to increase profit?" Lori asked.

---

1 Instructions for determining animal units are provided in task 7.3, Livestock Enterprise Gross Margin per Unit.

"That's right," Kate confirmed. "Lower the overheads, improve the gross margin per unit or increase turnover."

"So, these apply to the bank or the hospital as much as the ranch?" Lori asked skeptically.

"I guess so." Kate had to think about this. "At the hospital they certainly have facility and infrastructure costs, and I don't work there for free, so they have land and labor overheads. We have all sorts of different procedures and processes. I don't know what they charge, but they aren't cheap. And we go through supplies like crazy, so I know there are direct costs. There must be a margin on each procedure. The number of patients would be the turnover."

"Don't forget the pharmacy and the physical therapy unit, and optometry. Wouldn't those be other enterprises that add to the turnover?" Chris offered.

Nodding, Kate said, "Sure. So, I think all Three Secrets apply."

They turned into the driveway. "So, there are three ways to increase profit," Wayne said. "That's great, but what do we do with this? How do we apply it to our place?"

Chris eased the truck to a stop in the yard. A hundred yards away, in a pasture, they saw Sally and Robyn. The kids had spotted them too and started running to meet them. "I'd like to continue going through this with you. Working through this would help us too," Chris said.

"Help you?" Wayne asked.

"Absolutely," Kate confirmed. "Going over these things with you reinforces them for us. Besides, you said it yourself earlier, sometimes when someone else looks inside your operation they see things you don't. We've found that when we look inside someone else's operation we see things they could do that we could do too. But we would never have thought of it for ourselves if we hadn't seen it for them. So yes, it would help us."

Wayne joked, "Well, you'll owe me big time for letting you help us."

Lori rolled her eyes. "It's clear we have a lot to learn. Let me call you tonight when we can look at our schedule. I'd like to set another time to talk about this." She was eager to learn more but also anxious to get home.

"That'd be great," Chris said enthusiastically. "I think it'd be helpful if next time you brought some numbers with you, like your gross product and your direct costs. I think if we can calculate a gross margin for a couple of your enterprises, that would be a successful start. How's that sound?"

"It sounds great," Lori said.

"Are you clear on what we're calling an enterprise?" Chris asked. Without waiting for an answer, he explained, "An enterprise is a part of the business that can stand on its own. Cows, stockers, hay. Those are all separate enterprises. Let's just look at the cows and the stockers when we get together. I'll send you an email with what we'll need."

Wayne wasn't sure how he felt about sharing his numbers with his neighbor. He was even less certain about being able to assemble all his numbers. There was something else causing him to resist the idea of meeting again to discuss the application of these concepts to their ranch. He knew if he agreed to do this with Chris and Kate, he'd have to spend time preparing. He didn't like homework in school as a kid and he didn't like the idea of it now. He didn't want to agree to something and then not follow through. He realized that he didn't want to be held accountable.

Sensing Wayne's resistance, and remembering his own uncertainty, Chris added, "The numbers don't have to be perfect, just close. The thought that goes into coming up with the number is more important than the number itself."

Lori, who liked to get things down to the penny, said, "I'm sure we can pull out receipts and reconstruct last year."

"Last year is over," Kate said bluntly. "You can't do anything about what already happened. How would you feel if Chris drove us home looking only through the rearview mirror, looking at the road he'd already driven down instead of the road up ahead? No. Let's look ahead through the windshield and project into the future. Besides, this year you have a lot fewer cows than last year. Last year's numbers won't be relevant to what's happening this year."

"We'll try," Lori said.

Kate, sensing Lori's discomfort, said, "I'll send you an email tonight with some notes about what to do to prepare. It won't be bad.

Trust me. You can do this. Call me when you can look at your calendar and we'll pick a time to meet, okay?"

"I'll do that," Lori said. Then she gave Kate a hug. "Thanks so much. Both of you. I think today might be one of the most important days I've had in a long time."

Kate, concerned about promising results they might not be able to deliver, spoke softly, "It was a good day. We'll see if we can help you find some answers."

Giggling as they ran, Robyn and Sally arrived in a cloud of dust. Allison, who often babysat the girls for Chris and Kate, was close behind. Robyn hugged Chris's right leg while Sally proudly displayed a necklace she had made from weeds.

Over the commotion Chris shook Wayne's hand and asked, "So Wayne, this morning, the workshop ... worth your time?"

After a moment's pause Wayne admitted, "It got me thinking."

Chris's grin grew. "Good. Next time then."

Lori got in their car from the driver's side since the passenger door did not open. She gave Chris a wave. "Thanks so much," she said.

As Wayne and Lori drove off, Chris turned to walk toward the house. He walked stiff legged with one girl clinging to each leg. As he approached the screen door, he whispered to himself, "It got me thinking." Then with satisfaction, "That was the point." He suspected that some big changes were in store for Lori and Wayne.

SUMMARY OF CHAPTER 5
CONCEPTS

- Separating the land from the operating business can help with managerial succession and estate planning.

- An enterprise is a part of a business that could be run as a separate business.

- Gross product measures the value an enterprise produces. It includes sales, purchases and the change in inventory value.

- A trading account is the tool used to calculate gross product.

- Direct costs are costs that change directly as the units of production increase or decrease.

- Cutting direct costs may reduce gross product. Increasing gross product may require spending more on direct costs. Gross product and direct costs must be considered together (gross product minus direct costs equals gross margin).

- Gross margin per unit measures the economic efficiency of the production unit.

- The unit can be an animal unit (livestock) or an acre (farming).

- Gross margin of all the enterprises minus overhead costs equals profit or loss.

- There are only three things that anyone in any business can do to increase profit:
  - Reduce overhead costs
  - Improve the gross margin per unit
  - Increase turnover

- Turnover refers to the total throughput of the business. It is measured by considering all of the enterprises in the business and the number of units in each enterprise.

- Test your plan by running various scenarios.

- Last year is over. You can't do anything about the past. Project into the future.

Chapter 6
A Good Day: Projecting the Stock Flow

Yesterday had been a good day. It was almost always a good day when Wayne was out on his own or with the boys working with the cows. It was spring break and the boys, out of school for the week, had come with him to help. At 13, Justin was turning into a pretty good hand. It wasn't that long ago that the combined effort of Wayne and Justin was a lot less than Wayne could do by himself. Justin loved being out with the cows and Wayne imagined that one day, 20 or 25 years from now, Justin would be running the place. A troubling question occurred to him: *Is knowing how to raise livestock enough to be able to run a business that raises livestock?*

Justin is capable, he thought. *But what about Matt? What if he wants to be part of things?* Wayne hoped that both kids would want to be part of the ranch, but he knew there wasn't enough income to support the two families that depended on the ranch now. *Actually,* he corrected himself, *one family depends on the ranch — Dad — and one family depends on my wife.* He frowned.

Wayne thought about the arguments he'd had with his brother about the ranch. *When was the last time I talked to Sam? Around Christmas?* Sam had wanted to be part of things, but there wasn't room and Sam was too young to take things on when Dad needed help. Wayne felt guilty about the opportunity he'd had. *Opportunity or obligation?* He felt both grateful and resentful but wasn't sure toward whom or for what.

Wayne's brother, Sam, now 30, worked for AgCo selling livestock pharmaceuticals. *My brother the drug dealer,* he chuckled. At least Sam and he were on speaking terms now.

So, Matt and Justin running the place … how is that going to work? He looked at the brightening reflection on the thin clouds in the east and took a deep breath. *In 20 years, Matt will be 29. Justin will be 33. Just three years younger than I am right now! How is that possible? How will we work together? Will it be like me and Dad? I hope not.*

A sliver of sun crept over the horizon. *Will I be ready to let go? What would I do if not this? This place isn't big enough. Will Dad still be here? Will he have passed? Did Dad ever finish his will like he said he would? He said he was leaving the ranch to me. Did he tell me that because he thought that's what I wanted to hear, or because that's what he was really going to do? He's going to feel like he needs to leave Sam something. 50/50? Would he really split the ranch? I'd never be able to buy Sam out. Would he even want to be bought out?* Wayne shuddered as he tried to clear the thought from his mind. He wanted today to be a good day.

Is Matt 9 or is he 10 now? Wayne realized he wasn't sure. Matt tried to help, but he would rather dig holes, fill them with water, and throw dirt clods in them, pretending they were bombs exploding. Matt had a passion for the outdoors but not for work.

Yesterday they had checked the cows and mended fence. At least he and Justin had mended fence. Matt spent most of the afternoon collecting last year's cow pies, tossing them as high as he could, then throwing a rock, like skeet shooting, trying to make them explode. It did look pretty cool when he hit one, which wasn't very often. Wayne laughed thinking about it.

They were almost through with calving and, while it had been dry and it was still cold, at least the weather was consistent. Not like last year where one day was cold and the next warm. Then two days later it would snow. They weren't having the scour problems this year that they'd had last year. What a mess that was.

So far this year's calving had gone well. He had only pulled two calves. One of them had been stillborn. Even so, things were going more smoothly than last year. *It's too bad we've had to destock so drastically,* he thought, as he looked up at the sunrise. *Another glorious day. Another dry, glorious day.*

His routine was to check the cows twice each day. He would check late at night — actually early morning — and he would stay out until after sunrise. That was his favorite part of the day. He would check again at 3 or 4 in the afternoon and be back at the house by 6 or 7 in the evening, assuming everything was okay.

He'd barely talked to Lori last night. He wasn't trying to avoid her, it's just that their schedules didn't match very well, especially at calving. By the time he'd get back to the house, Lori would already have left for work and taken the kids to school.

Steam escaped from his thermos as he poured himself a cup of coffee. He took a scalding sip and enjoyed what was left of the sunrise.

Lori had taped a note to the thermos. It said that Chris and Kate were going to help them work on the numbers Saturday morning. He considered Chris a good friend, maybe his best friend. It wasn't a long list to choose from. And he really liked Kate, but he wasn't looking forward to their meeting. He knew they needed to get the numbers better organized, but working on the numbers made him worry *about* the numbers. *You can't control the future. What happens is what happens. Balance sheets, cash flows, and plans are for bankers.*

Along with Lori's note was a copy of an email Chris sent to both of them. Wayne had his own email account, but he hadn't checked it since the start of calving season. Lori knew that Wayne would never see the one Chris sent him, so she'd printed the one he cc'd to her. In his email Chris listed some things he wanted Wayne and Lori to do before their meeting. Wayne took another sip as he read it in the bright morning light.

It looked doable. Chris had just asked for the opening and closing inventory numbers and sales and purchases for the coming year for each class of stock in the cow/calf enterprise. He wondered how he was supposed to know how many calves they would have to sell, what the sale prices would be, and what the closing inventory numbers would be. *Do I just guess? Lori's not going to like that.* Chris also asked him to project the direct costs for the cows and the stockers for the coming year. *Projecting is just a fancy way of saying guessing, isn't it?*

He took another sip and spent a few minutes looking through the cows. Nothing happening here, he concluded, and he headed back to the house a little earlier than usual.

He entered the mud room and smelled sausage cooking. Wayne loved the smell of sausage almost as much as the taste. He heard the sharp sound of it sizzling in the pan the moment he walked in the kitchen.

Lori looked like a juggler, with the cell phone between her shoulder and her ear, a spatula in one hand and the coffee pot in the other. She cocked her head toward the pot as she raised it. He grabbed a cup and she poured. He mouthed, "Thank you."

With the kids home for spring break, Lori was able to leave a little later than normal. He was grateful when their schedules overlapped, even briefly, especially when it meant a hot breakfast.

"Yes, I'm still on hold," she said. Wayne heard an elevator version of *The Girl from Ipanema* coming through the phone. Lori leaned over to him. "I think Matthew has an ear infection. Can you …" She spoke into the phone now, "10:30? Yes, fine, we'll make that work. Thank you." She put down the phone.

Wayne, unaware of the implications on his day, said, "He hasn't had an ear infection in …"

Lori finished for him, "… in more than two years. I know, but he's got to get seen and get something for it or it's going to get worse. Can you …"

Wayne's body language showed his lack of enthusiasm for dealing with this. Then he saw Lori's look. She stood, spatula in hand, the way the guy holds the stop sign on a road crew at 3 p.m. Her head was cocked to the side, her mouth open. Without a word her message was clear, "Really, do I have to do everything around here?"

"What time?" he asked, though he already knew.

"10:30. Probably ought to be there by 10:15," Lori confirmed, relieved that she wasn't going to have to push the issue.

"Okay. If we're still there close to noon, you want to grab lunch?"

"Ahhh, sure." The suggestion caught her off guard. "That'd be nice. You want to come by at noon?"

"By the time he gets seen and we get the prescription that'd probably be about right," Wayne said.

"You saw my note?" Lori asked. She placed a plate with eggs, sausage, and toast on the table in front of him. "I talked to Kate a little while ago," she said, as she sat down across from Wayne with her breakfast. "She said they can do it this Saturday or next. What do you want to do?"

"Might as well get it over with," Wayne said. When he looked at Lori, he saw that she wasn't amused. "I didn't mean it that way," Wayne apologized. "I know we need this and I'm glad they are going to help us, but I know I'll feel stupid. I'm not sure how I'll figure out the costs we haven't had yet or how to figure out what our closing numbers are going to be. I'd just be guessing."

It was unusual for Wayne to accept that he didn't know how to do something.

"Maybe I can look up what we spent on things last year," Lori offered.

"They said not to do that," Wayne remembered, "but I don't know another way."

"I'll do it tonight," Lori said. "Maybe you can do the inventory numbers this morning?" Wayne knew this was more a request than a question.

Suddenly the assignments didn't seem as abstract as they had yesterday, or even earlier that morning. He was actually going to have to sit down and figure this out.

Once Lori was off to work, Wayne grabbed a pad of paper and a pencil and sat down at the kitchen table. *This won't be so hard. I'll knock this thing out and get it over with.*

A half hour later he had listed the opening inventory, but nothing else. He wondered what he would tell Lori at lunch. *I can't tell her it was too hard.*

He reluctantly called Chris. "How am I supposed to know how many animals I'm going to be selling or have in my inventory at the end of the year, let alone what prices are going to be?" He tried to hide his frustration by joking, "I don't have a crystal ball."

Chris realized he should have given Wayne more guidance in his email. "Sorry. Yeah, the hardest part of the process is coming up with good estimates." Knowing he couldn't teach him the stock flow process that he'd learned at the school over the phone, he suggested another approach. "Remember the mind map the teacher drew at the workshop, where one thing led to another and another? Use that. Start with your opening inventory of cows, and from there show how many might die. Whatever doesn't die will live, right? So, draw that in too.

"Then show how many of those that live you don't expect to wean a calf. Write in that as the number dry."

Wayne was writing as fast as he could. "Okay, dead or alive, then drys. Then what?"

"Okay, whatever isn't dry will be wet. Those are the ones that will wean calves."

Chris was drawing this out on a notepad as he explained it to Wayne.

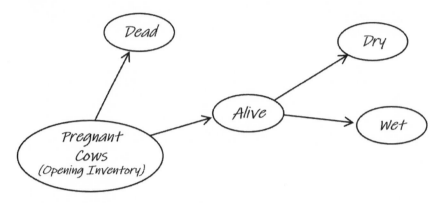

He continued, "There will be some cows that are too big, too sickly, or too crazy to keep. That one that broke Justin's collarbone … you gonna keep her?"

"No. I ought to shoot her," Wayne retorted. "But, that's right. There are going to be some animals that, even if they wean a calf and get pregnant, I won't want to keep. That's what you're saying, right?"

"Yep. Too big. Too ugly. Too old. Too mean. Any reason you might get rid of her other than reproductive performance," Chris confirmed. "Label those 'culls.' Oh, and if you destock some more because of drought like you did last year, those get added to the culls."

"Really?" Wayne questioned. "But they were good cows."

"Yeah, but I'm guessing they weren't your best cows," Chris justified. "They were probably your worst. In fact, when you think about it, those drought sales probably helped you improve your herd."

"Yeah, I see that. So, any cow I sell for non-reproductive reasons gets called a cull. Got it," Wayne said.

"Now, the ones you don't cull, those will all get exposed right? Some of those will be open. What kind of breed up do you usually get?"

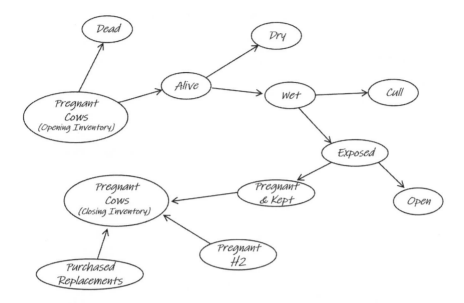

"Okay, I see where this is going." Wayne was a visual person, and this was making sense. "So, I'll figure that 10% are open. That means that 90% are pregnant. And that's my closing inventory, right?"

"Almost," Chris said. "You'll probably be bringing some pregnant replacements into the herd. You'll need to add them in to get the closing number of cows."

"Okay. Then I'm going to have to run through this same process for my replacement heifers too, aren't I?" Wayne asked.

"Right." Chris hadn't thought of that, but Wayne was right. "In fact, it'd be best to start with your H1s. Those are your weaned heifer calves. Once an H1 is confirmed pregnant it becomes an H2. So those bred heifers will end the year in your closing inventory as H2s. The H2s will have their first calf and get exposed a second season. When they are confirmed pregnant, they'll be cows. So, yeah, draw a mind map for your H1s. Then do another for your H2s, and finally, do it for the cows. You'll also have to make some guesses about how many of your calves you'll keep for stockers and replacements."

"Okay. I think I've got it." Wayne had drawn a similar diagram to Chris's. "I'll need to do this for bulls too, right?"

"Yeah, but that'll be simple," Chris said. "You'll just show what you start with, what dies, what you'll sell, and what you'll buy." Chris paused to give Wayne time to make notes. "You have questions about any of this, just call. I'm pretty much available all day."

"Wait a minute. What about prices?" Wayne remembered one of his big frustrations. "How am I supposed to predict the prices I'll get for my calves and culls?"

"You can't know what they are going to be, so guess. Be realistic but conservative," Chris advised. "Don't take the worst market that has ever existed, but don't be a wild-eyed optimist either.

"You'll need to value your inventory too. Again, be conservative. Take each class of animals you have at the beginning of the production year and ask, if I had to sell these animals in a hurry, what would they bring? It won't be the replacement cost, but it won't be the salvage value either. It'll be somewhere in between. It'll probably be closer to the salvage value than the replacement cost. Does that make sense?"

"Okay, I can do that. What about valuing the closing inventory?" Wayne asked.

"Like you said, none of us has a crystal ball, so use the same value per head on each class that you used in the opening inventory."

"That's simple enough. I'm going to work on this right now. Thanks. See you Saturday," Wayne said, relieved.

Wayne went to work. Twenty minutes later he had finished the mind map.

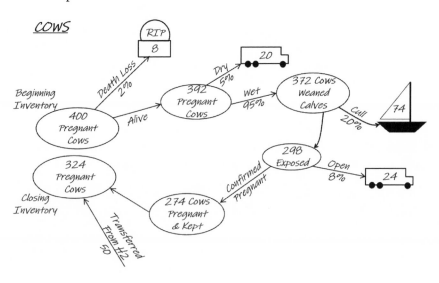

His projection showed that the closing inventory would be 324 cows. *Gee, closing inventory is down 76 cows from the beginning inventory. If we get decent moisture this spring, we really ought to increase our numbers. Of course, if this spring is like last spring we might need to cull more heavily. Where could I find some short-term custom cattle if we wind up getting some extra grass? Extra grass, that'd be a nice problem to have. People are going to want grass. Should I be trying to pick up another lease? What if I tried to feed my way through this? Yeah, right, what if I do that and it doesn't rain?*

Something the teacher had said at the workshop came back to Wayne. "The process is more important than the result." He realized this was what he was talking about.

Pleased with what he had done, he looked up at the kitchen clock and panicked. 9:40!

"We got to get!" he shouted. "Matt, Justin, you ready?"

They were. Lori had seen to it before she left. "Let's roll, boys!"

SUMMARY OF CHAPTER 6
CONCEPTS

- The stock flow is a tool for projecting deaths, births, sales, purchases, and class transfers in an enterprise. It starts with the beginning inventory of stock in each class and ends with a projection of the closing inventory in each class.

- By knowing your inventory numbers through the year, the stock flow assists you in projecting direct costs (vaccines, ear tags, supplements, etc.).

- Use conservative prices in valuing livestock for the livestock valuation.

- Use the same per head value for each class in the closing inventory that you used to value the beginning inventory.

- The thought process through which you arrive at the numbers is more important than the numbers themselves.

Chapter 7
Crunching Numbers

Chris and Kate had asked Allison to watch Sally and Robyn for the morning. Kate felt a little guilty about having someone else take care of the girls when she and Chris were home, but she knew that with Allison watching the kids, there'd be fewer distractions. Chris had said, "We pay her so we can do our $100-an-hour work." He was right. Their planning time was too important to the future of the ranch and their family. Without it she knew she wouldn't be able to cut back at the hospital. That would have a much bigger impact on the quality of their lives than hiring Allie for four or five hours every couple of weeks.

Wayne and Lori showed up a little late. Sometimes Lori felt like getting Wayne and the boys in the car all at the same time was like trying to push a wheelbarrow full of rabbits.

Wayne and Lori had spent a frustrating night. Chris and Kate had suggested they project the coming year and not try to reconstruct last year. In spite of that, both Wayne and Lori agreed that they had to look at the previous year's numbers if they wanted reliable cost figures. Lori spent hours looking through the checkbook for everything they spent.

They were frustrated with the assignment and with one another. They'd shared some harsh words. Now, on the drive over, they weren't sharing anything at all. Early the night before Lori said through her tears that she didn't want to come. It was too embarrassing. Wayne had put the pressure on, saying, "This was your idea. You're the one that wanted to do this." Earlier this morning Wayne almost refused to come. But here they were.

When they arrived, Matt and Justin sprang from the back seat like freed prisoners. They didn't normally play with girls, but Robyn was a tomboy, and, for a girl, she was okay. Justin, who had started to notice girls, liked Allison, who was two grades ahead of him in school. He was too shy to say anything to her, but he'd been looking forward to today.

Chris came out on the porch with his usual grin. He held a "World's Greatest Dad" mug in one hand as he waved at them with the other. "Mornin'. Come on in," he called cheerfully. He saw through Lori's pretend smile. Wayne didn't try to pretend.

Kate came out of the office with her laptop, a pad of paper, and some forms. She laid the forms on the kitchen table as Chris led Wayne and Lori into the house. Kate welcomed them. "Good morning! We thought we'd be more comfortable in here where we can spread out. Coffee, anyone?"

Lori nodded. Wayne said, "I'll take some Johnnie Walker in mine."

Focused on the papers and coffee, Kate hadn't picked up on the tension and asked, "So, how'd it go?"

There was no masking their frustration. "I've never been so lost. This is hopeless," Lori said. At least she and Wayne were on the same page about that. "I've just gone around in circles. None of this makes sense."

Chris didn't see what was confusing about the assignments he'd asked them to complete. He thought they must be doing something to make it harder than necessary. "I'm sorry it was frustrating. Was there anything in particular that was confusing?" he asked.

"Everything," complained Wayne. Wayne had a heart of gold, but he was definitely a glass-half-empty kind of guy. Rather than ask Wayne to specify, Chris turned and asked, "Lori?"

"I just couldn't find everything I needed." She avoided looking at either Chris or Kate as she spoke.

"Find everything? You tried to put together last year?" Chris asked.

"I know. I know what you said, but those numbers are real," Lori said defensively.

"Yeah," Chris sighed. "We felt that way the first time we tried to put things together too. We tried to recreate the previous year and we really struggled."

"It was awful," Kate agreed. "We have a hard time remembering yesterday, let alone 15 months ago, don't we, Hon?"

"Yeah. We were both frustrated with it. And that was in a classroom with a teacher available to help us when we got stuck," Chris remembered.

"Tell you what," Kate said. "I know you're frustrated with that, so let's put it off for now. I have a hunch that we'll be able to sort it all out pretty fast when we get to it, but we have some work we have to complete for our board meeting. We'd wanted to work through that first anyway to show you how we do it. Then we can talk you through the process with your numbers. Why don't we start with that? Come on, have a seat."

"What's this board meeting?" Lori asked.

Kate explained, "Ranching For Profit has a graduate support program called Executive Link. We call it EL. Remember how we were saying it's always easier to solve someone else's problem than your own? In EL you participate on a board with four or five other ranches. Our board meets three times a year. At each meeting we spend a few hours reviewing each board member's business. We look inside the other businesses and make recommendations, and then they look inside our operation and tell us what they see."

"You leave each meeting with a plan that shows what you commit to accomplish, who's responsible for each action, and deadlines for getting it all done," Chris said.

Kate excused herself from the room while Chris continued, "If we didn't have to report on our progress at our next board meeting it'd be really easy to find other things to do, and we'd probably never get to the big-ticket items. In fact, when we left the school, Katie and I had a long list of important things we were going to do. We were positive that we would knock one thing after another off the list."

"It didn't quite work out that way, did it?" Kate shouted from the other room.

"No," Chris agreed. "When we got home, we did one or two small things but then we fell back into our old routines. It didn't take but a month to realize that if we were really going to make big changes, we needed ongoing support and accountability. Our EL board holds us accountable to do what we say we're going to do."

"How do they do that?" Wayne's tone was skeptical.

"You got the assignments done that we asked you to do, right?" Chris asked.

"Well," Lori said, "we did our best."

Would you have done them if you hadn't had to come over here today?" Chris asked. "If there wasn't a deadline and someone to hold you accountable, would you have done it?"

"No. I would have put it off, or just quit when it got hard," Lori confessed.

Chris pointed down the hall. "At our first meeting our board asked us where we did our planning work — what we call WOTB, or Work On The Business."

From the other room Kate said, "They saw the mustard stains on our planning forms."

"Yeah, they told us we needed an office," Chris continued. "We knew they were right, but without their push, we'd probably still be trying to do our $100-an-hour work at the kitchen table. Even though that wasn't cutting it for us, we wouldn't have set up our office without their push." Pointing again down the hall he added, "Having an office has made a big difference."

"It sure has," Kate agreed, as she walked in with a sheet of paper at least two by three feet and taped it on the wall with masking tape. "This is our plan from our last board meeting."

CCR Ranch – Chris & Kate 2/17			
I/U	Action/Result	Who	When
5/5	Negotiate longer term on Dixon lease (>3 years)	Chris	3/30
50/3	Calving Season Decision • Compare GM of calving seasons • Identify marketing alternatives • Evaluate impact on OH • Determine ideal replacement strategy (replacement cows?) • Consider Drought implications	Chris	7/31
50/1	Implement plan to insulate biz from absence of key person	Kate	6/30

"The first item here is to renegotiate our lease with Phil Dixon into something longer," Chris said. "The security of our leases has been a big worry for us. Last month we met with Phil and found out what he needed. Turns out there was more than money on his mind."

"He didn't care about the rent?" Wayne asked.

"Well sure, he wanted a fair rent," Chris said, "but there's a lot of folks out there who will pay that. I'm sure some will pay more than what we pay now. There were things like the condition of the perimeter fencing and a patch of spiny clotburr that's growing next to the highway. He can't get around to take care of some of those things the way he used to, and I think it's hard for him to come to grips with his limitations. He's still hoping that his son, Peter, will come home to ranch, but Pete isn't ready for that. We mostly did a lot of listening."

"But we talked about our need for security too," Kate added. "When we came home, we drafted a proposal to take care of his concerns that also met our needs. We gave it to him the following week and last month we signed a new three-year lease."

"Three years isn't all that much security," Wayne observed.

"That's right, but it includes a provision to automatically add another year to the lease once a year is completed. There's a price adjustment for that year tied to the rate of inflation. This way when one year is done, we get a new year added. If he wants to renegotiate or kick us out and rent it to someone else or sell the property, we have at least two years notice. If he needs to make a change before the two years he can buy us out, but he pays a big penalty for that."

Wayne thought it was an interesting idea. "It renews for another year, every year? I've never heard of anything like that," he said.

"Neither had we," Chris explained. "We got the idea from someone in the EL who was doing it. It wasn't even someone on our board. At the start of the last meeting we just asked if anyone in the EL had any ideas on ways to negotiate increasing the security of leases. Several members did so we got together one evening after our board meetings to pick their brains."

Kate pointed to the second task on the sheet. "Calving Season Decision. This is the one we were working on this morning. And the last one has to do with options to protect ourselves if something were

67

to happen to Chris or me. We have an appointment to meet with the insurance people next week to discuss options on that.

"It's funny," Kate said, smiling, "these are all things we know we ought to do. In fact, they are things we actually *want* to do, but without the accountability of our board, we probably wouldn't do them. We'd get bogged down in the daily grind or distracted by the crisis du jour."

Wayne nodded. He related to the situation.

Kate continued, "As far as accountability, no one jumps down anyone's throat if a task isn't completed. Accountability isn't about beating people up when things don't get done. Accountability in EL is about finding out what prevented someone from successfully completing an action and helping them figure out how to overcome those obstacles so they can be successful next time. We *want* our board members to succeed."

"And they want us to succeed," Chris added. "It's a pretty cool deal."

"What are the numbers?" Wayne asked pointing at the numbers in a column on the left of the chart labeled "I/U."

"That's how we score the priority of each task," Kate explained. "The first number is the importance. It's scored on a scale of plus or minus 1, 3, 5, or 50. One is small potatoes. Three has a moderate impact. Five is a really big deal. And a 50 is a game changer. A negative 50 could wreck the business. A positive 50 is a potential breakthrough. It could take the business to a whole new level. The second number is for urgency. We score that on a 1, 3, 5, 7, 9 scale. One is not urgent, it can wait a year. Nine means it's a crisis, it needed to happen yesterday."

"At our first meeting," Chris recalled, "we scored everything on our proposed agenda a 50 in importance and a 9 in urgency. The board helped us be more rational about recognizing that not everything that seemed urgent was really all that important. And the most important things …"

"… weren't very urgent," Kate said. "Since the things that were going to determine our long-term success weren't urgent, we never got around to working on them."

"We were driven by crisis," Chris concluded. "If something was important but not urgent, we just didn't do it."

"Important but not urgent? Like what?" Lori asked.

"Like the planning we are going to do today." Kate sat down next to her friend.

Lori nodded. She knew all too well what it was like to be driven by crisis.

"Who are the people on your board?" she asked. "Are they from around here? Are their ranches like yours?"

"No, we have board members from four different states. One's in desert country, another is in the mountains at pretty high elevation. They're from all over," Kate answered.

"And they have way different operations," Chris added. "There's one other cow-calf outfit. They have a conception to consumption grass finishing/direct marketing program. There's a seed-stock operation, one that's mostly stockers and custom grazing, and another that's primarily sheep. There's even a bison operation. One's a first-generation outfit, another is in the fifth going on to the sixth."

"I wouldn't think that the bison or sheep operations would be able to relate to the issues y'all have as well as other cow-calf producers could," Wayne said.

"This isn't a cow-calf board. This is a business board," Chris explained. "It doesn't matter what enterprises they have. We all have to watch cash flow and be smart with capital allocation and debt. We all have to build a team and hold people on that team accountable. The diversity is an asset because they bring fresh eyes to our situation. I don't think we'd get nearly as much out of it if everyone on our board had similar operations."

Kate added, "I remember the instructor saying, 'If we all think the same thing, then only one of us is necessary.' I think we learn as much looking inside their operations as we learn from them looking at ours."

"Definitely," Chris agreed.

"Our board will be coming here this summer," Kate added. "We'll have a field tour before our board meeting. The meeting will be board members only, but we'd sure like you to come to the tour. You'd really enjoy meeting our board. It's in a couple of months. I'll send you an email with the details."

"I imagine we'll do some kind of barbeque," Chris added. "You'd really like these people and we'd really like you to come."

Wayne was nodding, but Chris thought he looked anything but eager.

"We've got a lot of ground to cover," Kate pointed out. "If we're going to get something done we'd better get started." She took out the forms she'd been working on earlier that morning.

Chris brought the pot over and topped off coffee for Lori and Wayne as Kate began. "Here are the changes we're thinking of making. First, we've already decided to change the calving season. We just aren't sure if we're pushing it six or eight weeks later."

"That'll be mid-May to June. You'll never get the cows bred in the heat of the summer," Wayne warned.

"That's something we definitely want to take a look at," Kate said, "and we'd like you to challenge some of our assumptions on this in a bit. On the scenario we ran this morning Chris knocked the conception rate down to 85%."

Wayne nodded. He thought an 85% conception rate might be plausible.

"By calving later, we'll cheapen up the cost of running a cow by at least $200 and maybe as much as $400. But even if it's only $200 cheaper, it's still a game changer for us," Chris said.

"Cutting direct costs like hay, that's what you're thinking, right?" Wayne asked.

"Yeah, hay is huge," Chris confirmed, "but there are other costs too."

"Wait a minute," Wayne interrupted. "How is hay a direct cost? You grow your own hay. You don't have to buy it. How will you save money when you don't buy it in the first place?"

"We do buy hay," Chris said. "If we didn't feed the hay we make to our cows, we could sell it." Wayne nodded so Chris continued, "Since our hay enterprise could sell it to someone else, our cow enterprise has to buy it from our hay enterprise and has to pay the hay enterprise whatever someone else would have been willing to pay."

"It's the only way to know if the hay enterprise is subsidizing the cows, or the cows are subsidizing the hay enterprise, or if each is able to stand on its own," Kate explained. "And we don't want one enterprise to subsidize another. They all need to be able to stand on their own."

"That's another thing we are thinking of doing," Chris added, "or more precisely, not doing. Maybe we shouldn't be putting up any hay. Maybe we ought to just buy what we need."

"Or maybe we ought to hire someone else to put it up for us," Kate said.

"There are several options we want to look at," Chris said, "but the only way we'll be able to know which of these options is best is for our cows to buy the hay at what we could have sold it for."

"Okay," Wayne nodded. "That makes sense."

"Part of this change may include changing our replacement strategy," Chris continued. Our projections show that we'll save over $200 per cow on hay. But by buying older cows, rather than raising our own replacements, it looks like we may be able to reduce annual depreciation by about $200 per cow. Even if we wean fewer calves, if they're smaller and we get a little less for them, the gross margin improves by almost $300 per cow in this scenario. That alone would increase our profit by over $100,000!"

"Right. But every number is wrong," Kate reminded him.

"There you go again," Wayne's tone had no humor in it. "On the drive home last week you kept saying, 'Every number is wrong.' But if your numbers are wrong, won't your conclusions be wrong too? At some point your numbers have to be right, don't they?"

"It's a fair question, but close enough *is* good enough," said Kate. "It's not like we only run the numbers one way and we stop. We ran a scenario with 85% conception and another with 80%. We ran one with prices where we think they'll be and another with where we're afraid they might be.

"Remember what the teacher asked us after class one night?" Kate reminded Chris.

"Sure," Chris recalled. "We were back in the classroom one evening trying to project the numbers on shifting the calving season and I was worried that our guesses were just that — guesses. The teacher was helping folks apply the processes that we'd learned that day to our own situations. When he got to us he could tell we were frustrated. When he asked us what the problem was, Kate said something like, 'Garbage in, garbage out.' We didn't have confidence in our guesses."

Kate picked up the story. "So, the teacher asks us, 'Do you have a $100,000 mistake?' Chris says, 'No, I'm not off that much.' The teacher asks if there's a $50,000 error. Again, Chris says he doesn't think so. Then the teacher asks if we've made a $20,000 mistake. This time Chris tells him that there could very easily be a $20,000 mistake in our projections. The teacher nods and asks us, 'Will $20,000 one way or another change your conclusion?'"

"That was a breakthrough for us," Chris said. "Our projections showed that this new strategy could increase our gross margin by more than $100,000. And we were worried that we might have made a $20,000 mistake? On whose planet does that make sense?"

Kate said, "We try to get our numbers as close to being right as we can. But knowing they are wrong, we run different scenarios. Our estimates for calving later show it'll be $100,000 to $200,000 better than what we're currently doing. If we're off by $100,000, and I don't see how we could be, but if we are, the worst outcome is that it would be no worse then what we do now."

Chris said, "We used conservative numbers in the projection that showed calving later would be more profitable. Then we ran a worst-case scenario, with even lower conception rates, lower prices, and higher costs. That wasn't any worse than what we currently get. That made it a no-brainer. We need to change."

"And depreciation?" Wayne asked. "You said something about depreciation on cows a minute ago. Where's that come in?"

"Good question," Chris said. "It took me a while to understand this, but depreciation is the biggest direct cost in a lot of conventional cow-calf operations. It's neck and neck with feed costs in ours. We don't list it as a direct cost because it's automatically accounted for in the trading account. The depreciation is calculated when we enter purchases or transfers of high value bred replacements in the trading account and then transfer them to the cow herd. Remember, we are valuing the cows pretty conservatively. We have these high value H2s that go into the cow herd, and four or five years later, what are they worth?"

"Not as much," Wayne admitted.

"Not as much by $400 or $500, maybe more, and those are the ones that make it that long," Chris said. "Do you remember in the workshop what the teacher said about the number of calves a typical cow has in her lifetime?"

"Yeah. It was a lot lower than I thought it'd be." Wayne had wanted the teacher to say more about that. "I thought it'd be six or seven calves, but he said it's three! That's a little hard to believe."

"I felt the same way when I first heard the teacher say that," Chris admitted, "but then I did the math."

Kate slid the notepad to Chris. "Start with 100 cows," she suggested. "That'll make the math easy."

```
100 Pregnant Cows
- 20 (Cull, Open Dry, Dead)
  80 Pregnant & Kept (Year 1)
- 16 (Cull, Open Dry, Dead)
  64 Pregnant & Kept (Year 2)
- 13 (Cull, Open Dry, Dead)
  51 Pregnant & Kept (Year 3)
```

Chris began, "Assume we sell everything that does not wean a calf. If we have 2% death loss, 5% drys, 5% culls, and 8% opens, that's a 20% replacement rate. We lose 20% of the original 100 cows." Subtracting 20 from 100 on the notepad he announced, "At the end of the first year we wind up with 80 of our original 100 cows. Second year we'll lose another 20%. Twenty percent of 80 is 16." He talked as he calculated. "80 minus 16 is 64. At the end of the second year there'd be 64 of the original 100 cows left." He did the math for the third year and said, "At the end of our third year only 51 of our original 100 cows are left." Circling 51 on the notepad he concluded, "Half of the cows in the herd had three calves or less in their lifetime."

"But that's not the way it happens," Wayne protested.

"Right, that's not the way it happens," Chris admitted. "It's front loaded. If you keep your own replacements the H2s will probably fall out faster than any other class. But on average, it's right."

Chris continued, "Let's go one more step. Take the value of a pregnant replacement, subtract the value of a cull, and divide that by the number of calves the average cow has in her lifetime. That will give you a rough estimate of the average annual depreciation of your cows. For us it's over $250 per cow, per year, in a down market. In a strong market it can be over $400 per cow per year."

"Depreciation is more when cattle prices are high?" Wayne questioned.

"Yeah," Chris confirmed. "Maybe that's why we never have any money even when cattle prices are good." He paused for a moment before explaining, "We think we'll be able to buy open or late calving H2s cheaper than raising our own replacements. We might even look at buying older cows."

"I sure wouldn't want to do that," Wayne responded reflexively. "Who knows what genetic or health problems you'd bring in?"

"That might be an issue," Chris conceded, "but according to the research I've looked at and what I've been told from other EL members who've done this, young, open cows are more a result of mismanagement than genetics. Besides, I'm not talking about going to the sale barn to buy these." He looked up at Wayne. "We figure we'll buy them from producers we know and trust. Maybe we ought to buy them from you. But even if there are some problems, if I can knock enough cost out of the replacements, it might still make sense."

"And it'd be nice not to worry about calving out heifers," Lori said, glancing at Wayne.

Kate looked at her watch. "We'd better push on," she suggested. "Let me walk you through the whole process." She pulled out the first form. "The first step is to complete the breeding herd statistics chart. We use it to make projections about deaths, conception, weaning rates, and to record our intentions for culling. We haven't put any heifers on this one because we thought we'd simplify this and see what it looks like if we buy our replacements rather than raising them ourselves."

Breeding Herd Statistics

Enterprise: *Cow/Calf - Buy Replacements*

Class ⟶	Mature Cows		H2s First calf Heifers		H1s Virgin Heifers	
Activity ↓	%	#	%	#	%	#
Pregnant & Kept count inventory (preg. After weaning at start of year)		384		0		0
Deaths projection (Death loss expected this year)	2	8				
Number Live calculation (# Preg. & Kept - Deaths = # Live)		376				
Expected Dry projection (# Live that won't wean a calf)	5	20				
Number Wet calculation (# Live - # Dry = # Wet)		356				
Expected Culls projection (for reasons other than poor fertility)	5	18				
Number Exposed calculation (# Wet - # Culled = # Exposed)		338				
Expected Open projection (% exposed that will not be pregnant)	15	51				
Pregnant & Kept calculation (# Exposed - # Open = # Preg. & Kept)		287				
Bulls count inventory (Total number of bulls)		15				
Calves Weaned calculation (# Wet Cows + # Wet H2s = # Weaned)		356				

Chris looked at Wayne, "You think breeding in the summer might be a problem? You might be right. With our current program our breed up averages 93%. We're projecting that, if we calve six weeks later, our breed up might only be 85%. I don't think that's too optimistic. I wanted to run this as a conservative scenario. How bad do you think the breed up might be?"

"It won't be very good I can tell you that," Wayne answered. "I suppose 85% would be close."

"Let's stick with the 85% conception rate for now," Kate suggested. "So, 15% will be open.

"Now let me show you the stock flow. That's the second step," Kate said as she pulled out another form. "We start with the opening inventory we used on the breeding herd statistics chart and put that here." Kate pointed to the left-hand columns on the stock flow form. In the first column she'd listed the classes of animals in the enterprise. The next column showed the opening inventory for each class. Kate explained, "We apply the performance estimates from the breeding statistics chart to this opening inventory to project the closing inventory. This is how we estimate what we'll be selling and the number of replacements we'll need. Since we now know our inventories, it also makes it possible to come up with a good guess about how much supplement we'll need and how many ear tags we'll have to buy. And we know all of that, or at least we have a good guess of all of that, six months to a year before we need it."

Stock Flow

Enterprise: _Cow/Calf - Buy Replacements_

Class of Stock	Fiscal Year Open	Born	Purch.	SALES			Dead	Class Transfers		Fiscal Year Close
				C	O	D		Out	In	
Bred Cows	384	na	90	18	51	20	8			377
Heifer Calves	0	178		178						
Steer Calves	0	178		178						
Herd Bulls	15	na	3	3			1			14

Analysis of Sales

Projected Sales:	Class of Stock							
	Open Cows	Dry Cows	Cull Cows	Steer Calves	Heifer Calves	Cull Bulls		
Number Sold	51	20	18	178	178	3		
Avg. Weight	1,200	1,250	1,300	480	450	1,800		
Price ($/lb.)	--	--	--	1.65	$1.60	--		
Income per Animal	$700	$1,100	$950	$792	$720	$1,500		
Total Income	$35,700	$22,000	$17,100	$140,976	$128,160	$4,500		

"This is what I did in that mind map you had me draw," Wayne realized.

"That's right," Chris confirmed. "On this stock flow, we've applied the performance estimates we made on the breeding herd statistics chart for calving later. We projected births, deaths, sales, and transfers."

"Transfers?" Lori questioned.

"A transfer is when animals change classes," Kate explained. "When a heifer calf is weaned and kept as a replacement it transfers out from the calf class to the H1 class. A steer calf you don't sell transfers into your stocker program."

"And here, down at the bottom, that's where you work through your projected sales?" Lori asked, pointing to the bottom of the stock flow.

"That's right. And then to get the closing inventory you simply do the math for each row," Kate explained. "Start with the opening inventory of cows, add the purchases, subtract the sales, the deaths and the transfers out, and add the transfers in. That's how you figure your closing inventory."

Kate explained that the projections made in the stock flow gave them the information they need to project a cash flow. "Projecting the cash flow is the third step. Since I have an estimate of our inventory numbers through the year, I can make a pretty good guess about how much supplement we'll need, and ear tags …"

"That's where I got stuck," Lori said. "I spent hours trying to dig up last year's receipts and I know I didn't find them all."

"That's what we tried to do the first time we tackled this," Kate said, "but rather than looking things up, we learned we'd be better off thinking things through. What something cost last year may not be the same this year." Kate pointed to the stock flow. "Since we know how many animals we have through the year, we know how much feed and vaccine we'll need. And we know it months ahead of time. Chris and I look at alternatives for each of the inputs we use and spend a few minutes online researching costs.

"The cash flow shows when our income will come in and when we will have expenses. We can see when there will be deficits and we can figure out how to get through them *before* there's a crisis."

"We used to do the cash flow for the bank," Chris said, "now we do it for us."

"Okay, let me show you our cash flow." Kate opened her laptop and pulled up the cash flow forecast she'd worked on earlier that morning. There were columns for income, direct costs, and overhead costs. There were four rows for each month.

Cash Flow

	A	B	C	D	E	F	G	H	I	J	K	L	M	N	O	P
		Cattle	Crop	Other	Total		Direct Costs					Total		Overhead Costs		
		Income	Income	Income	Income		Feed	Health	Trucking	Marketing	Twine	Direct		Rent	Insurance	Fuel
3	Jan. Budget	12,000	0	0	12,000		0	0	430	120	0	550		0	0	150
4	Actual	10,000	0	0	20,000		0	0	400	100	0	600		0	0	160
5	Difference	-2,000	0	0	-2,000		0	0	30	-20	0	10		0	0	-10
6	Cumulative Diff	-2,000	0	0	-2,000		0	0	30	-20	0	10		0	0	-10
7	Feb. Budget	0	0	0	0		0	0	0	0	0	0		0	8,500	120
8	Actual	3,000	0	4,000	7,000		950	0	120	60	0	1,130		0	0	90
9	Difference	3,000	0	4,000	7,000		-950	0	-120	-60	0	-1,130		0	8,500	30
10	Cumulative Diff	1,000	0	4,000	5,000		-950	0	-90	-80	0	-1,130		0	8,500	20
11	March Budget	0	0	4,000	4,000		0	0	0	0	0	0		0	0	150
12	Actual	0	0	0	0		180	0	0	0	0	180		0	8,550	125
13	Difference	0	0	-4,000	-4,000		-180	0	0	0	0	-180		0	-8,550	25
14	Cumulative Diff	1,000	0	0	1,000		-1,130	0	-90	-80	0	-1,300		0	-50	45
15	April Budget	0	0	0	0		0	2,200	0	0	0	2,200		0	0	200
16	Actual															
17	Difference															
18	Cumulative Diff															

"This first row, 'budget,' is where we make our projection for the month. I record the actuals in the next row. I do that as soon as the credit card statement comes in."

She explained that the third row showed the difference between what they budgeted and what they actually received or spent that month.

"The fourth row shows the cumulative difference. It's for tracking how far off course we've gone since the beginning of the year," she said. "Sometimes one month will seem way off because a bill got paid or a check came in a week late and got posted to a different month. It's this cumulative difference that we pay the most attention to."

Turning from her screen, Kate looked at Lori and Wayne, who'd been peering over her shoulders, and said, "We prepare the budget for the coming year right after we've weaned the calves and preg-checked the cows, because at that point we have a good handle on our closing inventories for the year."

"And the closing inventories for this year are the opening inventories for next year," Lori realized.

"That's right," Kate confirmed. "Chris and I have a meeting to thoroughly review where we are every four months. If conditions have changed, or we're way off on something, we revise the forecast. Take this fall and winter. Things have been drier than normal, and the long-term forecast doesn't look promising. If things don't improve soon, we'll start destocking."

"Or try to find some more grass," Chris added.

"Either way, it wasn't something we anticipated when we drew up the plan, so we'll need to make some revisions. Of course, when I enter the monthly actuals, if it looks like something has gone completely haywire, we don't wait for our four-month meeting. We'll deal with it right away."

"When we were at the school the teacher called the cash flow 'the minutes of the meeting written in dollars,'" Chris said. "That's actually a perfect description. Kate and I think through the production year and what we're going to do, or might do, and then translate that into the impact on animal numbers in the stock flow, and translate that into the impact on income and expenses in the cash flow."

Kate closed her laptop. "Okay, let me show you the rest of this." Wayne and Lori leaned in to see the forms in front of her.

Kate showed them the livestock valuation form where she'd calculated the value of the opening and closing inventories. "Valuing the animals is the fourth step."

Livestock Valuation

Enterprise: Cow/Calf – Buy Replacements

Class of Stock	A Value / Head	B Beginning Number	A x B Beginning Value	C Closing Number	A x C Closing Value
Bred Cows	$1,250	384	$480,000	377	$471,250
Bulls	$1500	15	$22,500	14	$21,000
Total:			$502,500		$492,250

"You use consistent, conservative values on breeding stock," Wayne remembered from his call earlier in the week with Chris. "What about growing stock? What about the calves?"

"It's simple on the calves," Kate answered. "Make your planning year start sometime after weaning and before calving. That way you won't have any calves in your opening or closing inventory to value. It doesn't matter what your fiscal year is when you do this. Remember, this is economics, not finance." She looked up at Wayne to see if he was satisfied with her answer. Seeing Wayne nod, she added, "And if you do have growing stock in your inventory, use a conservative estimate of market value."

"The trading account is the fifth step," Kate said as she showed them the trading account she'd completed earlier that morning. "I don't know why, but I had the hardest time understanding trading accounts. It is so simple. It's just the closing inventory value, plus sales, minus purchases, minus the beginning inventory value. It's how you calculate gross product — the value an enterprise produces."

> ### Trading Account
> Closing Inventory Value
> + Sales
> + Transfers Out
> - Purchases
> - Transfers In
> - Beginning Inventory Value
> = Gross Product

"What do you do with the calves that get transferred into your stocker program?" Wayne asked. "The cows have to get credit for producing them, don't they?"

"Absolutely," Chris said. "It's simple. Think of the transfer out of the cow-calf enterprise as a non-cash sale and the transfer into the stocker enterprise as a non-cash purchase. Use your best guess as to what the market price might be when you assign a value to the animals transferring."

"That's just if animals are transferring from one enterprise to another, right?" Wayne asked.

"That's right. When animals transfer from one class to another within an enterprise, you don't enter anything on the trading account," Chris said.

"The sixth step is to calculate the gross margin," Kate said. "You get the gross margin by subtracting the direct costs from the gross product. We made estimates for most of the direct costs in the cash flow, but there are some direct costs that aren't in the cash flow. For example, our cows buy hay from our hay enterprise. It's not a cash purchase, but we still need to include it as a direct cost in the cow-calf enterprise."

$$
\begin{array}{l}
\text{Gross Product} \\
\underline{- \text{Direct Costs}} \\
\text{Gross Margin}
\end{array}
$$

Chris showed Lori and Wayne the direct costs he'd projected. In addition to the hay, he had included supplements, vaccines, ear tags, pregnancy testing, and trucking. All of the direct costs were based on the inventory numbers in the stock flow. The first direct cost on the chart was opportunity interest. The value entered on the chart was $50,250.

"Opportunity interest, $50,000? That's the money you could make if you sold the herd and invested it somewhere else, right? That doesn't seem like a real cost to me. I don't see why we should put that in. I'm not going to sell the herd, so there won't be any money to invest," Wayne said.

"That's the traditional way to look at it," Chris agreed. "But that's not the way we learned to use it at the school. Think about it this way: If my gross margin per unit is good, what should I do?"

It had been a week since the workshop and seeing Wayne's blank look, Chris clarified, "If every cow I have makes money, what's one way I can make more money?"

"Get more cows?" Wayne asked.

"Exactly! And I know it will work because I've already included the cost of financing the purchase of the additional cows in the calculation. The opportunity cost I'm using here isn't the money I could make somewhere else if I didn't have my money in cattle. It's what it will cost me to expand the herd." He thought for a moment then said, "If I include the interest I'd have to pay to borrow money to buy more animals, it tells me whether expanding the herd is a profitable opportunity. If I don't include the opportunity interest, I'd have to do a separate calculation to figure that out." As he explained this to Wayne, Chris realized he hadn't really understood this unusual use of opportunity costs until just now.

"But you used 10%. I can borrow money a lot cheaper than that," Wayne protested.

Lori didn't say anything, but given their debt load, she doubted they could borrow any more money at any rate.

"Yeah, you can borrow money cheaper than 10%. So can we," Chris agreed, "but remember, we'll be borrowing money to buy replacements. The opportunity cost is based on the conservative value of the whole herd. Ten percent on that conservative value is going to be close enough to what actual interest would be on the replacements, especially once you add in points and other loan fees."

"What about seasonal enterprises like stockers? If you don't have animals for a full year it doesn't seem like you should charge 12 months of interest," Wayne said.

"You're right, but this is simple too," Chris said. "If you have animals for half the year, charge half the interest. If you have them for four months, that's one third of the year, so charge one third of the interest. Of course, that's if you own the animals. You wouldn't charge any interest in a custom grazing enterprise, because you don't own the animals."

"Remember, every number is wrong," Lori said.

"Right," Chris laughed. "They are all wrong, but if we think this through, they are going to be close enough to give us the information we need to make some big decisions."

"And make them with confidence," Kate interjected. Looking at Wayne, she asked, "Does that make sense?"

Wayne didn't answer right away. He was still processing this unusual way of using opportunity costs. When Wayne didn't answer, Chris prodded, "How's about telling us, in your own words, what you think we said?"

"Okay," Wayne agreed. "If my gross margin per cow is good, it tells me I should get more cows."

"Right," Chris said.

"And since I've included opportunity interest in the gross margin calculation, it tells me I can go to the bank and borrow money to do it. Is that right?" Wayne asked.

"That's it! I think you described it better than Chris," Kate said.

"So far we've done the breeding herd statistics, the stock flow, the cash flow forecast, a livestock valuation, a trading account, and we calculated gross margin. There is one more step," Chris said.

"One more step?" Wayne sighed. He was starting to feel overwhelmed again.

"Uh-huh," Chris confirmed. "The seventh step is to project profit or loss for the coming year. To do that we need to look at what our overheads are likely to be. We estimate the cash overheads on the cash flow. But there are some overheads that don't involve cash ..."

"Like depreciation on equipment?" Lori asked.

"Like depreciation on equipment," Kate confirmed. "We use the depreciation on the financial statement we get from our accountant to get that. Opportunity rent and deferred wages are other overheads that aren't on the cash flow. We deduct the total overheads from our total gross margin in the profit and loss account."

"That's the process," Chris concluded. He saw Wayne's concerned look and added, "It's a lot of steps, but each step is simple."

Wayne and Lori looked at one another. Kate saw the "yeah, right" look of skepticism in their eyes. "The process is simple," Kate insisted. "That doesn't mean it's easy. The hard part is making decisions about what our culling criteria are going to be and thinking through how to market our culls more effectively, or how we should supplement the cows to hit our performance estimates."

"But that's also the fun part," Chris added.

"This is fun? You have to be kidding me!" Wayne said. "This seems like a lot of work."

"Maybe exciting is a better word for it," Chris said. "This is how we found a way to turn our place around to the tune of a couple hundred thousand dollars a year. It's how we found a way for Katie to be full time on the ranch. So, yeah, exciting ... and fun. I like thinking about husbandry and production issues and I know you do too. We talk about it all the time. This is just translating it into dollars and cents."

"There are a lot of steps," Lori said, flipping through the forms on the table.

"There are. There are seven steps. And each one is simple once you know how to do it," Kate reassured her.

"The teacher told us that the first time you do this it's a little like trying to drive a car when you've only read the driver's manual," Chris said. "You won't really learn it until you get behind the wheel and start driving."

Wayne looked up from the forms and said flatly, "When we started driving this, I think we totaled it." Lori looked at Wayne and started laughing.

"Is this starting to make sense?" Chris asked.

"I'm following it. I'm not sure I can do it on my own yet, but I'm following it," Lori nodded.

Chris looked at Wayne. "What about it?"

"Yeah. We shouldn't have tried to reconstruct last year," Wayne said.

Kate said, "You know, you can put together last year's numbers, but it is so much easier when you have the projected plan to compare the actuals to."

"This is a lot to absorb in one day. It's gorgeous outside. I don't think it's too cold — let's have lunch on the porch," Chris said.

"That way we won't get mustard on your forms," Wayne joked.

SUMMARY OF CHAPTER 7
CONCEPTS

- Executive Link is a Ranching For Profit School graduate support program in which alumni are formed into peer-review boards.

- Each EL member leaves each meeting (three meetings per year) with an action plan showing the task and result the task will produce, the person who is accountable for producing the result, and the completion deadline.

- Accountability in EL focuses on removing barriers to success.

- EVERY real business needs an office for WOTB (Working On The Business).

- The average beef cow in North America has 3.2 calves in her lifetime.

- Depreciation is often the biggest cost of keeping a cow.

- If you grow hay and feed it to your livestock, the livestock must "purchase" the hay at the hay's market value. Add this non-cash value to the hay trading account and deduct it as a non-cash direct cost in the livestock enterprise gross margin calculation.

- Every number in your projection will be wrong. However, the difference in the profitability is often many times the likely error in the estimates that produced the projection.

- When you have doubts in the precision of estimates, run several scenarios, including best, most-likely, and worst-case scenarios.

- RMC's Seven Step Profit Planning Process is:
  1. Breeding Herd Statistics Chart (performance estimates)
  2. Stock Flow Plan (uses the breeding herd statistics chart estimates to project births, deaths, sales, class transfers, and closing inventory)
  3. Cash Flow Forecast (projects all cash income and expenses by month)
  4. Livestock Valuation (using inventory numbers from the stock flow)
  5. Trading Account (to calculate gross product)
  6. Gross Margin (= gross product – direct costs)
  7. Profit or Loss Statement (total gross margin – overhead costs = profit or loss)

Chapter 8
Farming, Divisions, and Profit or Loss

They talked about kids, cows, and the neighbors over lunch and enjoyed the shade of the porch on what had become a very nice day.

Allison and the kids were having lunch under the big cottonwood tree across the yard. Sally was on her belly in the tire swing. Matthew was winding it up. Sally would twirl, squealing as it unwound.

"My turn!" Robyn slid into the swing after Sally stumbled out, making a futile attempt to walk.

"Eat your lunch," Kate yelled unconvincingly.

"Good Lord," Lori laughed. "Eat your lunch? That makes me sick just watching it."

After lunch Kate, Chris, Lori, and Wayne went back in the kitchen. So far, so good, Wayne thought. The things they had talked about made sense to him, at least more sense than when he and Lori met with their accountant. He didn't like feeling stupid.

"Okay," Chris began. "Let's see where we can get with your numbers." They started with the production assumptions and the stock flow mind map Wayne had made. They discussed what values to put on the cattle inventory.

Chris and Kate helped Lori and Wayne think through likely market prices for the various classes of stock they would be selling and the bulls they planned to buy. With the inventory values they had estimated, and the sales and purchases they had projected, calculating gross product by completing the trading account was simple.

Lori was uncomfortable with some of the guessing they did projecting direct costs. She liked detail and this was anything but precise.

Chris reassured her, "It'll be accurate enough."

With the direct costs estimated, they calculated the gross margin of their cow-calf enterprise. It took a fraction of the time to project the gross margin for their stockers. It took less than an hour to do both.

"How's this compare to yours?" Wayne asked.

"Yours is actually a little better than what ours was," Chris said. Then he cautioned, "But don't throw a party yet. Ours was pretty bad. Better than bad doesn't mean it's good."

"I see your point. So how do you know what's good?"

"We'll get there," Chris said, "but we've got a little more work to do first. We need to calculate your profit or loss."

Lori took a deep breath. "This isn't going to be pretty. Okay, lay it on us."

Chris began. "Y'all have farming."

"Just hay," Wayne clarified.

"Hay is farming," Chris insisted. "Doesn't matter how much you put up, if you put it up yourself, or if you hire someone to put it up for you. If you grow hay you are farming. We need to do the gross margin for that."

"Okay, let's do it," Wayne said with as much enthusiasm as he could muster. "The price we put on the hay is going to be the same whether we sell it to someone else or feed it to our own cows, right?"

"That's right," Kate confirmed. "That shows up in the hay enterprise trading account as a 'transfer out' to the livestock enterprise. It's non-cash income for the hay enterprise and a direct cost to the livestock."

Chris asked, "At some point will you graze the hayfields?"

"Sure," Wayne confirmed. "The cows will graze the residue in the fall."

"The hay enterprise needs to charge the cattle for grazing the residue. That's value the hay enterprise produced and it needs to get credit for it," Chris said. "It's really simple to do. We just figure a fair rate to pay for aftermath grazing. That gets figured into the gross product for the hay and it is a cost to the cattle."

"But that can't be a direct cost to the cattle, because it's rent," Lori said. "The other day you kept telling us that all land costs are overheads."

"That's right." Chris was impressed that Lori caught that. "Leasing the stubble is an overhead and the livestock are going to have to pay for it. We'll get to that in a few minutes. Right now, let's finish up figuring the gross margin on the hay."

"Let me see if I can draw a trading account for hay," Wayne said. "Would there be opening and closing inventory?"

Hay Trading Account	
Closing Inventory	0
+ Sales	
+ Transfers Out	
+ Value of Grazing	
- Transfers In	0
- Purchases	0
- Opening Inventory	0
Gross Product =	

"If you're selling hay to other people, maybe," Chris explained. "If you're feeding it all to your own cows, then no. Normally you'd have your cows buy everything they might use before the end of the year, so your hay enterprise is sold out."

"Sales would be cash sales to other people. We actually did sell a little last year," Wayne said. "Then I add transfers out — that's the value of the hay we fed to our own cows. I add to that the value of grazing the residue. Then I subtract transfers in, purchases, and opening inventory. I can't imagine what I'd be transferring in. My hay enterprise doesn't buy any hay, so I can't see that there'd be any purchases, and since I sell out each year, there isn't any closing or opening inventory, is there?"

"Not usually," Chris confirmed. "Most people will never enter anything but zeros in those rows."

"Okay, now what about direct costs?" Chris asked. "Those are the costs that change as the number of units change."

"What's the unit in a hay enterprise?" Wayne asked. "In a livestock enterprise it's an animal unit, right? But what's the unit in a farming enterprise? A bale?"

"No," Lori said. "It's got to be an acre. It's like with a cow-calf enterprise, the calf isn't the unit of production. It's the cow, because the cow produces the calf. It's the same thing here. It's the acre that produces the bale. The unit of production in farming enterprises has to be an acre, doesn't it?"

"That's exactly right," Kate said. "We couldn't have explained it better!"

"Here's why this is important," Chris said. "If we're talking about livestock, all land and labor costs are overheads. Things like fertilizer and herbicide are overheads in livestock businesses. I mean, you aren't putting fertilizer or herbicide on the cows. You're putting them on the land, and land costs are overheads, right?"

Wayne and Lori both nodded. Lori saw where this was heading and said, "So, if an acre is the unit of production, and the more acres we have, the more herbicide and fertilizer we apply, then those costs are direct costs in farming enterprises. Is that right?"

"Yes," Chris confirmed. "Irrigation water, fertilizer, herbicide, seed for annual crops, all of those things are direct costs in a farming enterprise. And of course, things like baling twine."

"Custom harvest?" Wayne asked. "Is that a direct cost too?"

"You would ask that," Chris smiled. "That's a good question. It's a gray area. When you hire someone to harvest your crop, you're paying for fuel, which goes up the more acres you have. But you're also paying for interest on the tractor, the labor to drive the tractor, and other things that are still overheads. Unfortunately, when you're crunching the numbers you can't have gray areas. It's either got to be this or that. The teacher told us to make custom harvest a direct cost."

After Chris and Kate walked Wayne and Lori through a rough projection of gross product, direct costs, and gross margin for the hay enterprise, Wayne asked, "How do you know if it's more efficient to hay an area or graze it? Would you just compare the gross margin per acre of each enterprise?"

"That's where you'd start," Chris confirmed, "but there's something else you have to consider." He started writing on the notepad. "Let's say we've got stockers with a gross margin of $100-per-animal unit and, to make the math simple, we can carry two animal units per acre. That makes the gross margin for livestock $200 per acre, right? Now let's say our hay gross margin is $250 per acre."

Stockers		Hay	
GM/SAU	$100	GM/Acre	$250
SAU/Acre	2	-Overheads	??
GM/Acre	$200		
-Overheads	$0		

"Hay is a more profitable use of that acre," Wayne concluded.

"We don't know that yet," Chris cautioned. "Are there some overhead costs that we'll have if we hay that ground that we won't have if we graze that ground?"

"There could be," Wayne realized.

"This is something Kate and I are taking a hard look at," Chris explained. "We're thinking of having someone else come in and cut our hay. We're also considering not making hay at all and buying whatever we need. Either way we'd be able to get rid of a lot of equipment costs. Our repair bill last year was a killer. Once we factored in the overheads it became clear to us that hay is a big part of the deadwood in our business."

"Overheads aren't included in the gross margin calculation. Where exactly do they come in?" Lori asked.

"That's an important question," Kate said. "An enterprise is one part of your business that could be run as a separate entity, right? Cow-calf is an enterprise. Stockers, custom grazing, a feed lot, they can each be enterprises. Each crop you grow can be an enterprise. Now, there may be some enterprises or groups of enterprises that have overheads that are unique to them. For example, if I have a feed lot, a cow-calf enterprise, and a stocker enterprise, there might be some equipment and labor that are unique to the feed lot that have nothing to do with the grazing enterprises."

"Or farming enterprises," Chris interjected. "There might be some labor and machinery costs because of the farming that you wouldn't have if you didn't farm and only had livestock."

"When that's the case you need to create a division." Kate explained that a division consists of one or more enterprises that share unique overheads. Feedlot enterprises, farming enterprises, grazing enterprises, and recreation enterprises are typically grouped in separate divisions because they have different overheads associated with them.

"Then our ranch has two divisions," Wayne said as he slid the notepad in front of him and started drawing. "We have a livestock division with the cow and stocker enterprises and a farming division with just the hay enterprise."

"You forgot the feedlot in Spring Valley," Lori said. "That's definitely going to have overheads that don't apply to anything else. It's got to be a separate division."

"That's right," Wayne sighed. "I don't know what we're going to do with that. Buddy thinks we ought to run it ourselves. If that's the case it'd definitely be a separate division. But I'm thinking we ought to lease it to someone. If we don't have any costs associated with it, we wouldn't call it a division, would we?"

"If you run it yourselves, it is definitely a separate division," Chris said. "If you lease it out, you won't have any overheads, so I'd just call it 'other income' to the business and I wouldn't create a division for it."

"It's the same with a couple of our board members," Kate said. "One has a big recreation division. They guide hunts, do trail rides, and have cabins and do ranch-stay vacations. For them, recreation is definitely a separate division. Another board member just leases the hunting on his ranch to a hunt club. He just calls that 'other income' on his profit or loss statement."

"Not that it applies to y'all right now, but if you were grass finishing and direct marketing beef in a conception to consumption operation, you'd probably have cow-calf, stocker, and grass finishing enterprises in your grazing division. You'd make a separate meat division for processing and sales," Chris said as he drew on the notepad. "If you're selling at farmers markets or making online sales you'd have a retail enterprise, and if you sell to butcher shops and restaurants you might have a wholesale enterprise too."

Cattle Division			Meat Division		
Cow-Calf	Stockers	Grass Finishing	Processing	Wholesale	Retail

"Let's bring it back to our ranch," Kate said. "If we have an overhead that is completely unique to our hay operation, we call it a division overhead and assign it to our farming division. A while ago you asked about the rent that the cattle pay to graze the hay fields. That's charged as a livestock division overhead."

"What happens when an overhead is shared?" Lori asked. "What about a tractor we use in the hay enterprise that we also use to feed the hay to the cows?"

"Don't allocate it," Chris and Kate warned in unison.

Kate looked at Chris as she began. "This is something the teacher emphasized in the class, and it's one of the big differences between the way the Ranching For Profit people do the numbers and the way everyone else seems to do them, even the universities. Everyone tells you to allocate shared overheads. At Ranching For Profit, they insist that you should not. Here, I'll show you where they go."

Kate took the notepad from Chris and started to draw as she explained, "Here's what you do. First, you've got to identify your divisions and the enterprises in those divisions.

"Second, estimate the value each enterprise produces by projecting gross product.

"Third, estimate the direct costs that you anticipate for each enterprise.

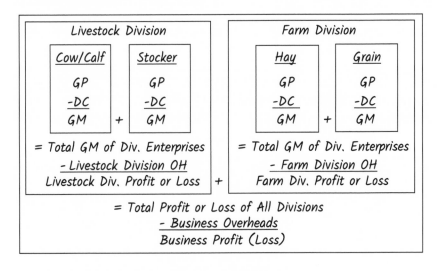

"Next, do the math. Subtract the direct costs from gross product to calculate the gross margin of each enterprise.

"Fifth, add together the gross margin of each enterprise in the division. That's the division gross margin.

"Sixth, subtract the division overheads. Those are the overhead costs that you wouldn't have if you didn't have that division. The result is your division profit or loss.

"Seventh, add the division profit or loss of all your divisions.

"And last, subtract the business overheads. Those are the shared overheads. Those are the overheads that you would not completely lose if you stopped doing a division. What's left after subtracting those overheads will be your business profit or loss." Kate looked up from the notepad.

Lori concluded, "So, it's all or nothing. If eliminating the division would eliminate the overhead, you should allocate it to that division. If you wouldn't lose the cost completely, you shouldn't allocate it at all. It's a business overhead."

"That's exactly right," Kate said, smiling.

"But that can't be right," Wayne protested. "If I use my tractor 50% for hay and 50% for livestock, shouldn't I split that cost in half? Shouldn't I allocate 50% to cattle and 50% to farming?"

"I fought this too," Chris empathized. "On the surface, allocating everything makes sense. It's the way everyone else will tell you to do it. But let's say we have livestock and farming," he said as he began writing on the notepad. "The livestock gross margin is $25,000. The farming gross margin is $20,000. We rent pasture for $15,000. If we didn't have the cattle, we wouldn't rent the pasture. We rent our farm ground for $15,000 too. If we didn't farm, we wouldn't rent that ground either. So, it's appropriate to allocate those. But what about the truck?" Chris asked rhetorically. "Between repairs, interest, depreciation, and everything else, it costs me about $14,000 a year. I use it 50% for livestock and 50% for the farm, so you'd have me allocate that 50/50, right?" Chris looked at Wayne.

"Well, that's how everyone I've ever heard talk about this stuff says to do it," Wayne said.

"Well let's see if everyone is right," Chris continued. "Let's split the cost in half, $7,000 for cattle and $7,000 for farming. Total overheads, rent plus the truck, comes to $22,000 for cattle, making the division profit $3,000. The overheads for farming are $22,000 too, so that division makes a loss of $2,000. The total business profit is $1,000." Looking to Wayne and then to Lori he asked, "So give me some advice: How can I increase my profit?"

	Livestock	Farming
Gross Margin	$25,000	$20,000
Overhead Costs		
Rent	$15,000	$15,000
Pick-Up	$7,000	$7,000
Total Overheads	$22,000	$22,000
Division P or L	+$3,000	-$2,000
Business P or L	+ $1,000	

"It's obvious," Wayne concluded. "The farming division is losing money. Stop farming."

"That's what these numbers tell us to do," Chris agreed. "So, let's see how this decision works out for us. Now that we aren't farming, we don't get the $20,000 gross margin. We got rid of the rent payment too." He crossed out the $20,000 farming gross margin and the $15,000 rent payment. "But what about the pickup? Is your banker going to say, 'Golly Wayne, since you're only using the pickup half the time now, I'm going to cut your payment in half'? I don't think so! That whole cost comes over to the livestock side." He crossed out the $7,000 he had allocated for the pickup to farming and wrote $14,000 in the cattle column. "Now our total overheads are $29,000 and our business makes a $4,000 loss instead of a $1,000 profit." Chris put down his pencil. "By doing the numbers the way we've been taught by everyone else, the obvious decision made our situation worse by $5,000!"

	Livestock	Farming
Gross Margin	$25,000	~~$20,000~~
Overhead Costs		
Rent	$15,000	~~$15,000~~
Pick-Up	$14,000 ~~$7,000~~	~~$7,000~~
Total Overheads	$29,000 ~~$22,000~~	~~$22,000~~
Division P or L	+~~$3,000~~	~~$2,000~~
Business P or L		(-$4,000) +~~$1,000~~

Wayne still wrestled with the idea of not allocating everything. "Everyone everywhere tells you to allocate everything," he protested.

"I know," Chris agreed. "But remember, everyone else is focused on breaking even. This isn't Ranching For Breaking Even. This is Ranching For Profit." He continued, "I heard an ag economist advising people to allocate all costs, direct costs, and overheads so that you can compare the efficiency of cattle enterprises on different ranches. But think about the pickup truck in this example. If I allocate it to 200 cows, the cost per cow would be double than if I have 400 cows. The economist said that means the cows got more efficient. But he's wrong. Having more cows didn't make my cows more efficient. It made my pickup more efficient!"

"That makes sense," Wayne said slowly. He paused before continuing, "The hardest part about this whole thing isn't learning it." He looked at Lori. "It's unlearning what I thought I knew."

"Exactly!" Chris agreed.

"Let's push on," Kate suggested. "I imagine y'all are going to need to get going soon and it's been a long day already."

"What's the next step?" Lori asked.

"The next step is to figure out what your overheads are going to be. We made some rough guesses about your overheads on the way back from the workshop last week, but you'll want to come up with estimates that are more precise," Chris explained. He paused before adding, "But I'm kind of wiped out right now. I think you probably are too. It'd be helpful for you to review your cash flow. And you'll need to make some decisions about rent and what you ought to be paying yourselves. You'll want to look up some things like depreciation and take some time to figure out which overheads to allocate to divisions and which should be business overheads. You want to pick up where we left off next Saturday? Same time? It won't take as long as we took today."

"I didn't expect to be taking up as much of your time as we have today. I do have some work to do before it gets dark," Wayne confessed.

"What do you call what we've been doing? "Lori asked cheerfully.

"Work," Wayne admitted. "I'm exhausted."

"That's why they pay you the big bucks for it," Kate quipped. "It's $100-an-hour work."

SUMMARY OF CHAPTER 8
CONCEPTS

- In farming enterprises an acre is the unit. Therefore, costs that change as the number of acres change are direct costs (e.g., seed, fertilizer, herbicide, etc.). These costs are overheads in livestock enterprises.

- In farming, rent is still an overhead.

- A division is one or more enterprises that share unique overhead costs.

- You should only allocate an overhead cost to a division if that cost would be completely lost if the division were discontinued.

- Allocating shared overheads makes it more difficult to evaluate the profitability of enterprises.

- All overheads shared between divisions should be considered business overheads and not allocated to any divisions.

Chapter 9
Overheads

Wayne and Lori didn't say much on the drive home. They were exhausted. At one point Wayne said, "I never realized how much hard work thinking is."

They agreed to take the evening off. There were cows to check, kids to feed, and there wasn't much point in trying to do $100-an-hour work when they weren't worth even $10 an hour. They also agreed to pick it up the next morning. Lori had to go to work, but Wayne thought he would be able to project the overheads on his own. "Every number will be wrong," he promised Lori.

"That's okay. At least we won't have to kill ourselves looking things up," she said.

"Maybe at the end of the day we can sit down and go over them," Wayne suggested. "You can hold me accountable."

"You usually have another word for that," Lori mused.

Wayne looked at her, confused.

"Nagging," she said.

"It's hard for family members to hold one another accountable, isn't it? I guess that's one of the advantages of having a board," he observed. "First things first. I'll have the overheads put together by noon and we'll go over it together tomorrow night."

Wayne usually liked to linger in the morning when he checked the cows, but this morning he was eager to finish so he could get to work on the numbers. *Imagine that, me in a hurry to work on our business. Who would have thought?*

By the time Wayne got back to the house Lori had left for work and taken the kids to school. He poured himself a fresh cup of coffee, sat down at the kitchen table, got out a notepad and a calculator, and began.

He started with land. He wondered if he should charge cows rent for the rangeland and the farm division rent for the land they hayed. He remembered advice Chris had given him: "Be a lumper, not a splitter. When in doubt, DON'T split it out." He decided to err on the side of simplicity and made all rent a business overhead. He asked himself, *What would this place rent for? How can I figure it out?* "I'll ask Dr. Google," he said aloud, and looked up rents in his region. He came up with what he felt was a decent estimate.

What other land costs do we have? He listed maintenance and repairs of buildings, fences, corrals, pipelines, machinery, and vehicles. He decided to call all the repairs on things attached to the land, like fences, pipelines, roads, and buildings, land overheads. He categorized the repairs on things that labor used, like machinery and equipment, as labor overheads.

He asked himself if there was anything about to break. *This is a ranch, of course there's something about to break.* He looked at a map of the property and thought through unit by unit what, if anything, needed to be done. He realized that they needed to do a lot of work on the pipeline on the south side. He wondered what that would cost. He remembered talking to someone who had laid a pipeline last year. He called and left a message.

What about depreciation? He decided to call depreciation on infrastructure a land overhead and depreciation on machinery a labor overhead. He went to Lori's filing cabinet to look it up. He pulled out the red folder with the year-end financial statements their accountant prepared. *Maybe we ought to change the color of that folder from red to something else,* he mused.

Since he had the financial statements out, he looked up what they spent on insurance and professional fees. He was surprised that professional fees were so high. Then he remembered the work they did with the lawyer on an easement. He estimated that professional fees this year would be several thousand dollars less than last year.

Salary. He looked up what they paid John last year, then thought, *Last year is over. What about John next year? John hasn't had a pay increase in a while. We ought to at least make some kind of cost-of-living adjustment. He'll probably work the same number of days. We gave him a half a beef. What's that worth? A side of beef ... that's compensation for labor, so it's another labor overhead,* he concluded.

What about me and Lori? I'm full time, she's maybe a quarter time. I'm the hired hand, mechanic, and CEO. What does a CEO make? I'm not a very good CEO, so probably not much.

He was tempted to use $50,000, the number Chris had used on the drive home from the workshop. It would be a $50,000 raise. Before writing it in he decided to think it through.

What would I have to pay to replace myself? Should I base my salary on the work I've been doing or on the work I will be doing if I step up and really start running the place. His stomach got a little queasy as he wondered if Buddy would give him enough authority to really manage things. He sat back and looked at the ceiling tiles. Suddenly he shook his head, the way their dog shook its head every morning, slapping its ears from side to side. *Can't do anything about that right now. Focus!*

He asked himself how much work Buddy did and how that should be compensated. He decided that, at best, Buddy was a half-time employee and only did physical work. *He doesn't do any planning. What's fair for the work he does?* He listed wage, housing, utilities, a vehicle, beef. He asked himself, *Would that be enough to live on?* Then he realized that what Buddy needed and what was fair were unrelated issues. Buddy's salary should be for what the work he did was worth. If Buddy needed more, he could take it out of profit as an owner's draw. "If we make a profit," he muttered.

He went through each piece of equipment used in the livestock division. *If we didn't have livestock would we have this?* Yes, on the pickup. No, on the stock trailer. He did the same for everything used in farming. *If we didn't grow hay would we have this?* No, on the baler and a half dozen other implements and one of the tractors. Yes, on the other tractor.

An hour later Wayne couldn't think of any other overheads. I've probably missed something, he thought. Maybe Lori can spot it when she looks this over.

Satisfied with the job he'd done, he poured himself another cup of coffee. The house was quiet. He stared out the window and thought, *I wonder how Buddy will react when I tell him that I want to go to that school?*

Lori had had a rough day. By the time she got home that night she was beat. They had installed new software at the bank and there were glitches. The technician kept saying, "That shouldn't happen."

"Good Lord, I almost had to call you to bail me out. I was about to strangle that guy," she told Wayne. On a more serious note, she said, "I'm probably worth about 10 cents an hour right now. I don't think I can do $100-an-hour work tonight."

They agreed to look at Wayne's projections in the morning. Wayne would check the cows early and be back at the house before Lori left with the kids.

Two calves were born that night. No problems. Wayne wondered how many calves he saved by checking. *If I had to pay someone to do this, would it make us money or cost us money?* He didn't know. He enjoyed checking the cows at the beginning of the season. It was a great feeling to see new life, to watch a baby calf wobble to its feet and nurse for the first time. He no longer weighed each calf like Buddy used to. What good was all that data if you never used it for anything? Buddy just about went ballistic when Wayne told him that he wasn't doing that anymore. Wayne still tagged all the calves at birth, but he was starting to question whether it was worth the time, effort, and risk. He had almost been mauled by an overprotective cow a couple of days earlier. He wondered if they ought to be tagging them at branding, figuring it wouldn't be that hard to see who goes with whom.

Wayne wondered, *Am I working on the business right now? Is this WOTB?* He decided that it probably wasn't unless he followed the train of thought all the way through and made a decision to do something or stop doing something. He smiled, thinking, this was probably WATB: Worrying About The Business!

He tagged the second calf, checked the time and came back to the house a good 45 minutes before Lori had to leave.

"You want to take a look at the numbers I put together?" Wayne asked as he poured himself a cup of coffee.

"Yeah, let's do that," Lori said as she put on an earring. "I'm sorry I was so beat least night."

"That's nothing to be sorry about," he said. "You usually aren't as worn out as you were yesterday, but it's gonna be hard to do $100-an-hour work together. You spend your $100-an-hour time at the bank. I wonder if this is a chicken and egg thing."

"What do you mean?" Lori asked.

"I wonder if we can find the $100-an-hour time we need to figure out how to make the ranch profitable enough so you can quit the bank if you don't quit the bank so we can have the $100-an-hour time. If we're going to figure this out, it's going take some $100-an-hour time together," Wayne said.

"I know," Lori said. She paused before suggesting, "Maybe that's something we need to ask Chris and Kate about. Kate is still working full time. She's planning on cutting back soon and then quitting altogether, but right now, she's still full time."

"Will you remember?" Wayne asked, wondering if he should start a list of things to discuss.

"I'll remember," Lori said with certainty. "Let's look at the numbers." She took a seat at the kitchen table. "It would be nice to have an office, wouldn't it?"

"Yeah, but unless we make the boys share a room, I don't see where we'd be able to squeeze an office into this house. There's room in Buddy's house, but I don't think that'd work. Can you imagine?" Wayne looked out the window at his Dad's house across the yard.

Lori shook her head, "No."

"A trailer?" Wayne wondered out loud.

"Another issue for another day," Lori said. "Let's focus on this right now."

Wayne laid out his work, showing Lori the land-related overheads, the labor-related overheads, and his decisions about which were division overheads and which were business overheads. Lori followed along, impressed by Wayne's thoroughness and his explanations.

When she saw the wage he had assigned himself, she asked, "Isn't that low for a CEO?"

"I'm only a part-time CEO, and a piss-poor one at that," Wayne justified. "Don't worry, when I start producing results I'll give myself a raise."

She pointed to Buddy's salary. "How's he going to react to that?"

"I don't think he needs to know," Wayne said. "It's not about hiding anything. It's just that these are the economic figures. This is what I think we'd have to pay someone to do the work that Buddy currently does. It doesn't mean that he won't continue to take a draw."

Lori nodded, "Okay." She looked up at Wayne. "It all seems logical to me."

"It was simpler than I thought it'd be," Wayne said, sitting back in the chair. "The other night I was worried about it. I barely slept. I'd convinced myself it was going to be an impossible task. But once I sat down and focused, it wasn't that hard." He paused. "I can't help feeling like I've missed something."

Lori scanned the pages again. "It looks complete to me. Maybe it's because it hasn't gone all the way to the profit or loss projection," she said.

"Maybe. I was wondering if you'd mind if I did that today," Wayne said. "I know we'd planned to do it together, but we don't have $100-an-hour time together and I'm kind of antsy to see what it says."

"Good Lord, no, I wouldn't mind!" Lori was surprised, relieved, and impressed. "I'd better get going, but we can take a look at it tonight. I'd like to see it too."

"Or tomorrow morning, either way," Wayne offered.

"That'd be great," Lori said. She turned around and yelled, "Kids, we gotta skedaddle."

A moment later Matt and Justin were out the door with their backpacks, shouting, "Bye Dad," as the screen door slammed behind them.

"Love you Babe," Lori said as she gave Wayne a quick kiss on the top of his head. "Gotta go. Good luck with the numbers."

Wayne stood up and waved goodbye from the doorway. *I can do this, can't I?* He sat down, took out the gross margin calculations they had done at Chris and Kate's and went to work.

That evening when Lori pulled into the driveway, Wayne was in a foul mood. Lori saw it as soon as she stepped out of the car. "What's wrong?" she asked. She'd been excited to see the results of Wayne's work.

"Either we're broke, or I've done something wrong," Wayne grumbled.

"Kate told me that if something looks too good or too bad to be true, it's probably not true. There's probably a mistake," Lori said.

"I hope there's a mistake," Wayne said, "but if there is, I can't find it."

"Let's have a look," Lori said.

Wayne realized he was springing this on Lori at the end of what had been a long day for her. He hadn't even asked her how things had gone at the bank. "Did you get the computer stuff working?"

"We went back to the old software until they sort out the problem," Lori answered absentmindedly. "Show me what you have."

Wayne's projections showed a loss of over $100,000. "Whoa!" Lori whispered.

"The math is right," Wayne said.

"Every number is wrong," Lori offered as a tentative explanation.

"They ain't *that* wrong." Wayne was trying to hold his frustration in check.

"Okay, let's say it's right," Lori suggested. "If the numbers are right, how come we haven't gone broke yet?"

Wayne looked up at her, "Good question." Suddenly the answer came to him. He slapped the table. "That's it! It's the opportunity rent and my wage. It's also the opportunity interest on the cattle."

"Right, those aren't cash costs, are they? If we take those out," Lori said as she did the calculations on her phone, "we'd do a little better than break even. That seems plausible, doesn't it?" She showed the display on her phone to Wayne.

"Yeah," Wayne said, nodding his head. He felt like he should have realized that as soon as he'd calculated the loss. "I was in such a state of shock I stopped thinking. I just got frustrated."

"It's still not good," Lori said cautiously.

"No," he agreed, "but it's believable. It's better than bad. Actually, no. It's bad. It's just not as bad as I was thinking it was." He smiled for the first time since morning. "The good news is that I'm pretty sure I know how to put the numbers together now. All day I'd been wondering what I'd been doing wrong. I kept thinking it can't be that bad." He paused. "It's bad, but it's not that bad."

It was interesting to Lori that Wayne found some good news in what was clearly a bad situation. Wayne usually focused on the negative and didn't look for silver linings. Pleased that Wayne was feeling better but worried that there were no solutions yet, Lori said, "The big question is, what are we going to do to improve things?"

"That's what Chris and Kate are going to help us with on Saturday." Wayne took a deep breath and released it slowly. "Now that we know our numbers, we need to know what they mean."

SUMMARY OF CHAPTER 9
CONCEPTS

- If something looks too good or too bad to be true, it usually isn't true. It's usually the result of a mistake.

- When it comes to allocating overheads: Be a lumper not a splitter. When in doubt, don't split it out.

- The opportunity rent you must charge your operating business is the rent someone else would pay to lease your ranch.

- Pay yourself what it would cost to replace yourself.

Chapter 10
What Do the Numbers Mean?

It was a cold, drizzly morning and, unlike last Saturday, it would be an indoor day for the kids. Allison was in the family room watching TV with Robyn and Sally.

Kate smiled as she opened the door. "Good morning!" Matt and Justin cautiously entered, navigated around their parents and made their way to the family room. Moments later they were transfixed by whatever was on the tube.

"Chris will be here in a few minutes," Kate apologized. "Last night Phil Dixon called about a broken pipe on the place we rent from him. When we got there, it looked like Old Faithful. We were there past 11 last night fixing it. Chris invented curse words I've never …" Her voice trailed off as she pictured Chris in the three-foot hole he had dug, thigh deep in water, bending down trying to work through the muck with only the light of the headlights. She wished she had taken a picture.

"I've never seen anyone covered with so much mud. I hosed him off before I let him back in the truck. It was either that or ride in the back. He'll probably catch pneumonia," she laughed. "He showered last night, but when he got up this morning, I saw a circle of dirt on his pillow. I think it must have fallen out of his ear! I made him take another shower this morning."

Chris came in drying his hair. "Mornin'."

"Sounds like you had your crisis du jour," Lori smiled.

"That was yesterday's crisis," Chris corrected. "Nothing's exploded today ... yet." He swatted the towel toward Kate. It missed her and almost knocked a cup of coffee off the counter.

Cringing at the near miss, Chris asked Wayne and Lori, "How'd it go?"

Kate poured coffee for their friends. "We were half expecting to hear from you during the week. No news, good news? Everything go okay?" she asked.

"I'm satisfied I got the numbers right, but I about had a heart attack when I saw how horrible things are," Wayne confessed. "I wondered, how can things be this bad? Then I realized that, while the economics are terrible, we are able to cash flow because we own the land, I don't pay myself, and Lori has a real job and actually gets paid for the work she does."

"That's probably the story on most ranches," Chris said. "I'll bet nearly all of them, at least the conventional ranches, operate at an economic loss. They only survive because they inherited the land or they work for free, or at least a lot less than they'd have to pay to replace themselves."

"Or they sell off a piece to keep the rest going," Kate added, thinking of the cabin they had sold.

"Or there's a wife who works in town to subsidize her husband's ranching addiction," Wayne said as he smiled at Lori.

"So maybe Ranching For Profit *is* an oxymoron," Lori said dejectedly.

"It doesn't have to be," Kate said confidently as she sat down next to Lori. "We have members on our EL board who are profitable. We've seen their numbers. They are making an economic profit," she said.

"We are too," Chris interjected, "or at least we will be. We've projected that we're actually going to make a small economic profit this year."

"Really?" Wayne was impressed. "Well, we need to figure it out. Now that we know our numbers, we need to know what they mean."

"This is where things get interesting," Chris said. "But we should warn you, we aren't experts at this. We've taken what we've learned and applied it to ourselves and looked at the numbers in our EL board members' businesses, but it's not like we know this stuff inside-out yet."

"You're light-years ahead of us. We don't know it at all," Lori admitted. "We calculated our gross margins. We projected that the ranch will make an economic loss. Now we need to know what to do about it. Can you help us figure out what the numbers mean?"

Chris hung the towel on the back of a chair and sat down next to Wayne. "Let's have a look."

He and Kate reviewed the enterprise gross margins that they calculated a week ago with Wayne and Lori. They looked at the overhead, division profit or loss, and business profit or loss projections that Wayne had made. Chris asked a few questions about Wayne and Lori's assumptions and seemed satisfied that their thinking was sound.

"The math all looks right," Chris concluded.

"It may be right, and it may barely cash flow, as long as I don't pay myself and Lori keeps working at the bank." Wayne touched Lori's knee. "But I don't want to keep doing what we're doing knowing what I know now. I want to find out what will work. I want to know how to figure that out from all of this," Wayne said, gesturing at the papers on the table.

"This is where the key performance indicators and the Ranching For Profit benchmarks come in," Kate explained. "The key performance indicators, we just call them KPIs, are vital signs that measure the health of a business, like blood pressure and body temperature are vital signs for people. The RFP benchmarks are the targets for those indicators. The benchmark for a person's temperature is 98.6, right? Well, there's a benchmark for gross margin and overheads and other indicators."

"How'd they come up with the benchmarks?" Wayne asked.

"Over several years, Ranching For Profit averaged the KPIs of the most profitable businesses in their Executive Link program. The average return on assets for those businesses is usually about 10%. So, the benchmarks show how we stack up to some really profitable ranch businesses. They help us figure out if the problem is overheads, gross margin per unit, or turnover. They help us find the profit drivers and the deadwood."

"The what and the what?" Wayne asked.

"Profit drivers," Kate said. "Those are the things that are working. They are the things you want to do more of. Deadwood is the exact opposite. Those are the things that aren't working, the things that either need to be radically changed or cut out entirely."

"It might be helpful to look at two KPIs in particular," Chris said. "The gross margin ratio and the overhead ratio."

"The gross margin ratio tells you if direct costs are out of whack relative to the productivity of an enterprise," Kate explained. "You calculate it by dividing the enterprise gross margin by the gross product. You want your gross margin ratio to be greater than, or equal to, the benchmark, 70%.

$$\frac{\text{Gross Margin}}{\text{Gross Product}} > 70\%$$

$1.00 GROSS PRODUCT
- 30¢ DIRECT COSTS
70¢ GROSS MARGIN

Kate wrote on her notepad as she talked. "If the ratio is 70% it means that, out of every dollar of gross product the enterprise produces, you spend 30 cents on direct costs and keep 70 cents as gross margin."

Kate pulled out her phone and opened the calculator app. Looking at her notes from last week she pointed to the gross margin they calculated for Wayne and Lori's cow-calf enterprise. "Divide the gross margin for your cows by the gross product," she paused to enter the numbers and held her phone up to show Lori and Wayne the result. The display read 0.571899.

"Fifty-seven percent. That's not good," Wayne said.

"No, it's not," Chris confirmed. "Out of each dollar of value you create …"

$1.00 GROSS PRODUCT
- 43¢ DIRECT COSTS
57¢ GROSS MARGIN

"We spend 43 cents on direct costs and make a gross margin of only 57 cents," Lori said.

As bad as the gross margin was, Lori felt as though the clouds were lifting.

"This is telling us that we shouldn't get more cows until we improve the gross margin." She looked at Kate for confirmation.

Kate nodded, "That's what it tells me."

"So, we know the cow gross margin is bad. Is there any way to know *why* it's bad?" Wayne asked. "I'd like to know what I can do to fix it."

"There are a couple of things we could look at," Chris said. "The first is feed costs. That's probably your biggest direct cost. The KPI is feed cost as a percentage of gross product. The benchmark is 16% or less. Feed costs should be less than one sixth, or 16% of the enterprise gross product."

$$\frac{\text{Feed Costs}}{\text{Gross Product}} < 16\%$$

Lori added up the hay transfers and the supplement purchases for the cow enterprise and divided it by the gross product. She held up the calculator displaying 0.310291. "Thirty-one percent. According to this our feed costs are almost double what they should be."

"I don't know how we could feed less," Wayne said. After thinking for a moment, he said, "This is why you're changing the calving season, isn't it?"

"That's part of it," Chris said. "We think we'll be able to stockpile grass in the winter, and with the cows' peak requirement timed to be in sync with the grass, we think we'll be able to drastically reduce what we feed."

"You said there were a couple of things we could look at," Wayne said.

"The other is to break the heifers out from the cows and calculate a gross margin for H1s and H2s as though they were separate enterprises," Chris explained.

"Why don't you just do that in the first place?" Lori asked.

"It's more complicated," Kate explained. "You have to allocate the direct costs figuring out how much hay and supplement and vaccine goes with each group. You have to split up the bulls on your stock flow. It's not hard once you know how to do this stuff, but when you're learning … Besides, if you calculate it all as one enterprise and it turns out to be good, you don't have to break the heifers out. Why do more work than you need to?"

"There are other things we can look at too," Chris said, "but I think we ought to get back to looking at the gross margin ratio."

Nodding agreement, Kate handed Lori her phone and said, "Lori, I think you've got this down. How about calculating the gross margin ratio for your stocker enterprise."

"Sure." Lori looked at the notes from last week. She entered the stocker gross margin and divided by the gross product. "Can this be right?" she questioned as she held up the phone. The display showed 0.732111.

"It looks right to me," Chris said.

$100 GROSS PRODUCT
- 27¢ DIRECT COSTS
73¢ GROSS MARGIN

"Seventy-three percent. So, for every dollar of value the stockers produce, we spend 27 cents on direct costs and get a gross margin of 73 cents. So, the stockers are way more profitable than the cows?"

"That's what this suggests," Chris agreed, "but there's probably more risk."

Wayne said, "We should run fewer cows and more stockers, right?"

"Stockers have a better gross margin ratio, but they are grazing different pastures," Chris said. "You've got your stockers on some really good pastures. Your cows graze some pretty rough stuff. If you put the stockers where the cows are, what do you think would happen?"

"They wouldn't do as well," Wayne realized. "If we put the steers on that range country their gross margin will suffer, won't it?" He didn't wait for an answer before summarizing, "So everything else being equal, we should run fewer cows and more stockers."

"But everything else is hardly ever equal," Chris said. "Let's calculate the ratio for your whole business." Looking at Lori, who was still holding the calculator, he asked her to add up the total gross margin for the cow, stocker, and hay enterprises and divide it by the combined total gross product of those enterprises.

"Sixty-five percent," Lori reported. "Not very good."

"Keep in mind, the 70% benchmark comes from highly profitable businesses," Kate said. "Sixty-five percent isn't great, but it's not a crisis either. If it were much lower, I'd send up a red flag."

"One KPI will never tell you the whole story," Chris said. "The overhead ratio is another important KPI. The overhead ratio tells you if your overheads are too high relative to your productivity. It's simple to calculate. You just take the total overhead costs, including non-cash overheads, and divide by the gross product."

$$\frac{\textbf{Overhead Costs}}{\textbf{Gross Product}} < 40\%$$

"You have to make sure you include *all* of the overheads," Kate added.

"So, even if Wayne doesn't pay himself, we need to include the salary he ought to get?" Lori asked.

"Exactly. Whatever it would cost to replace all the work he does," Chris confirmed.

"And you need to include the opportunity rent you'd have to pay someone else if you didn't own the ranch," Kate added. She paused to let that sink in, then added, "The benchmark for the overhead ratio is 40%. We want overhead costs to be less than or equal to 40% of our total gross product. That means that for every dollar of gross product our business creates, we want to spend 40 cents or less on overheads. When we came to the class our overhead ratio was 71%. Overheads were taking 71 cents out of every dollar of gross product we made."

"Ouch!" Wayne said.

"Ouch is right," Chris agreed, "but we weren't alone. There were some people in the class who had ratios of over 100% ... some were pretty big outfits too."

"An overhead ratio of over 100% would mean ..." Wayne talked slowly as he was thinking this through.

"It means," Lori said, "that for every dollar of value they produce, they have more than a dollar of overhead costs."

"That's right," Kate nodded.

"Good Lord, I wonder what ours is."

"Let's work it out," Kate said.

Lori added up all the division and business overheads and divided by their total gross product as Wayne looked on. When Lori saw the total, she hung her head and glumly reported, "Seventy-four percent."

"Our overhead ratio is 74%? So, for every dollar of value we produce, we are spending 74 cents on overheads," Wayne said. "Since our gross margin ratio is 65%, we make 65 cents of gross margin on that dollar of gross product. Gross margin minus overheads is profit, so for every dollar of gross product we produce, we make an economic loss of 9 cents.

```
65¢ GROSS MARGIN
- 74¢ OVERHEAD COSTS
- 9¢ LOSS
```

"So, overall, our cow-calf gross margin is bad, our stocker margin is good, and our overheads are awful. Our overheads are killing us," Wayne concluded.

"That's what the numbers say to me," Chris confirmed.

"How do I know for sure the problem is overheads?" Wayne asked. "If I've got $100,000 in overheads, but I only have one cow, even a really productive cow, my overhead ratio will be awful. But the problem in that case wouldn't be overheads, it would be turnover. The turnover is too low. How do I know it's overheads and not turnover?"

"That is a really good question," Chris said. "It's actually pretty simple. Do you remember when we drove home from the workshop and we were talking about what profit is for? We talked about setting a profit target. Let's say your profit target is $100,000. On your projections here you have roughly $300,000 in overheads. That means you have to generate a total gross margin of $400,000 to cover the overheads and produce your profit target." Chris looked at Wayne to make sure he was following.

```
$100k PROFIT
+ $300k OVERHEAD COSTS
- $400k GROSS MARGIN TARGET
```

"Okay, I see that," Wayne nodded.

"Now divide your gross margin target of $400,000 by the gross margin per cow."

Wayne picked up the calculator and did the math. The display showed 1,252.372. "That's telling me I'd have to carry 1,250 cows at this gross margin to cover our overheads and hit our profit target."

"Right. Would you be able to increase numbers that much?"

Wayne shook his head. "No. Even accounting for the stockers, that's more than double what we've got now. There's no way we can carry that many."

"Then you have an overhead problem," Chris concluded. "Improving gross margin per unit and increasing turnover will help, but you're going to have to find a way to cut your overheads."

"I can see why you didn't want to call them fixed," Wayne said with a wry smile.

"Your numbers aren't all that different than ours were," Kate told Lori. "Remember last week we showed you our projected gross margin for the changes we are making?" Kate asked as she opened the folder with her paperwork. "Divide our projected gross margin per unit into $400,000."

Lori did the math. The display on her phone read 841.7101. "So, if we get the gross margin up in that neighborhood, it'd take about 840 cows to cover the overheads and hit this profit target." Lori concluded.

"840? That's still a reach," Wayne said

"It'll be closer yet once you get the overheads down," Chris suggested.

"It's kind of a shock to be confronted with this, isn't it?" Lori asked. "I mean, I knew we weren't rolling in dough, but it's a slap in the face to see this in black and white."

"And red," Wayne said.

"So, what do we do now?" Lori asked.

"You start exploring alternatives that could improve the gross margin and reduce the overheads," Kate offered. "We are looking at changing the calving season, changing our replacement strategy, not making hay, and using cell grazing to increase our carrying capacity."

"I don't think our biggest problem is going to be finding a strategy that'll work." Wayne said.

"Really?" Lori asked with surprise.

"No. Our biggest problem is going to be getting Buddy to buy into whatever we figure out."

"That might be a challenge," Chris agreed. "I know Buddy's stubborn, but he's not stupid. If he wants the ranch to stay in the family, he's got to know that things can't keep going the way they are."

"I know," Wayne agreed. "But first we have to figure out something that can work. Do you mind showing us how the changes you're making have changed these ratios for you?"

Chris and Kate looked at one another. Kate said, "Sure, we can do that, but you need to realize that just because something might work for our situation doesn't mean it's right for yours. There is no one-size-fits-all prescription."

Kate went to the office to bring back the binder with their gross margin and profit or loss projections. She opened the binder to the first tab.

"Alright, here's where we started. Overall, our gross margin ratio was 66% and our overhead ratio was 71%." Kate wrote on the notepad as she spoke. "For every dollar of gross product we produced, we paid 34 cents in direct costs, and kept a 66-cent gross margin. Of course, the overheads ate up all of that and more. For every dollar of gross product we created, we made a 5-cent loss.

```
66¢ GROSS MARGIN
- 71¢ OVERHEAD COSTS
- 5¢ LOSS
```

"This year, with the changes we are making, our projected gross margin ratio is 73%. We haven't made progress on the overhead ratio because we haven't pulled the trigger on the calving season and haying decisions, so our overhead ratio is still around 71%. That leaves a 2-cent profit for every dollar of gross product."

```
73¢ GROSS MARGIN
- 71¢ OVERHEAD COSTS
  2¢ PROFIT
```

"What's the projection for changing everything?" Lori asked.

Kate flipped the page in the binder. "We have more work to do exploring alternatives and figuring out how we make the transition, but our conservative projections are that the gross margin will be about the same, but the overhead ratio will drop to about 60%. That means we'll keep about 13 cents of profit for each dollar of gross product we produce."

73¢ GROSS MARGIN
- 60¢ OVERHEAD COSTS
13¢ PROFIT

"The overheads will still be higher than we'd like, but we'll tackle that by increasing our scale," Chris explained. "We've got a strong gross margin now, so if we can increase the capacity of our pastures, we'll be able to increase our turnover without increasing our overheads. At that point, we think we can get the overhead ratio even lower. That's one of the things I want our EL board to help us with at our meeting this summer. We'll be exploring strategies to increase carrying capacity."

"Once we're on that trajectory, I go to part time," Kate said. "This time next year I'll be full time here." She leaned back in her chair.

"Wow!" Lori was happy for her friend and felt more hopeful for herself and Wayne than she had earlier that morning. "Do these benchmarks apply to all ranches everywhere?"

"Yes and no," Chris said. "They apply anywhere because whether you're in Australia or South America, Africa or here, a healthy business is a healthy business and certain vital signs apply. But these benchmarks don't apply to every business because different business models have different vital signs. People anywhere, if they are healthy, should all have similar vital signs, but," Chris pointed to Lefty, their 14-year-old Blue Heeler, who was sleeping on a rug in the mud room, "you wouldn't expect a healthy dog to have the same vital signs as a healthy person."

"Take Kevin, on our EL board," Kate said. "He hardly owns anything. It's all custom grazing on leased land. I think he even leases his pickup. His business model is way different than ours. Different business models require different benchmarks."

"Exactly," Chris confirmed. "The benchmarks Kate used here apply to a business like ours where we own all of our cattle."

"We're further out of whack than you were," Wayne said as he got up and stood behind his chair. "What if we can't figure out how to hit the benchmarks?"

"Then you look for another way," Kate said, looking up at Wayne. "We may never hit the overhead benchmark but, with the changes we're making, our gross margin ratio is better than the benchmark. The benchmarks aren't a straitjacket."

"It goes back to the profit target," Chris added. "You don't need to be as profitable as a benchmark business. You just need to be as profitable as you need to be."

"The benchmarks give you guidance as to where your profit drivers and deadwood might be," Kate explained, "but if you made a $100,000 profit would you really care if you hit every benchmark?"

"No, I guess not," Wayne said.

Chris stood and stretched. "I wish we could tell you what enterprises you ought to have and when you ought to calve and whether you should be putting up hay. We can't. But you can use these tools to figure it out for your place."

"You have done so much for us already," Lori said gratefully. "This feels overwhelming right now, but we need to learn this so we can do it ourselves."

"That's why you and Wayne need to go to the class," Kate said firmly. "We will help you all we can, but you need to go."

Lori, looking up at Wayne, said, "*We* need to go to the class."

Wayne looked her in the eyes and said, "Up to now I was wondering how we could afford to go, but now I'm thinking maybe we can't afford not to go. But I don't think we can both get away at the same time. Which one of us …"

Kate cut him off. "You both need to go. It would be best if you go to the class together. Chris and I can help fill in while you're gone, but if for some reason you can't both get away at the same time, you both still need to take the school."

Wayne nodded. He knew she was right.

SUMMARY OF CHAPTER 10
CONCEPTS

- The RMC benchmarks are based on statistics drawn from highly profitable businesses.

- Benchmarks are guideposts to help identify deadwood and profit drivers.

- The gross margin ratio [(gross margin/gross product) x 100] measures the efficiency with which an enterprise employs direct costs to produce gross product. A gross margin ratio of 70% or higher is considered very good.

- Separating a cow-calf enterprise into H1, H2, and mature cow enterprises is one way to find the deadwood in a breeding enterprise.

- According to the feed efficiency benchmark, feed costs should be no more than 16% of gross product.

- The overhead ratio [(overhead costs/gross product) x 100] measures the efficiency with which overhead costs are used to produce gross product. An overhead ratio of 40% or less indicates a very lean, efficient operation.

- By subtracting the overhead ratio from the gross margin ratio you will determine the business profit or loss as a percentage of gross product.

- Most ranches produce an annual economic loss. They only survive because they are subsidized with cheap family labor, inherited wealth (land), and off-ranch income.

Chapter 11
Working On The Business

"That didn't take as long as I thought it would," Wayne said, looking at the kitchen clock. He had figured that sorting through their numbers would take at least until noon. It was just 10:30.

"Speaking of time, that reminds me of something we wanted to ask you," Lori said. "I come home from the bank beat. Wayne is going flat out 7-days a week. At the end of the day we aren't worth 10 cents an hour. How do you find time to do your $100-an-hour work? It's hard to imagine adding another thing."

"It's challenging," Kate agreed. "But we'd been stuck and we knew that if we wanted to get unstuck we needed to make working *on* the business *the* priority. Once we started scheduling blocks of time to work on the business, we started finding things we were doing that we didn't need to do. That made it easier."

"People talk about 'making time' for this or that. But you can't *make* time. You can only use the time you have, so you have to use it smarter," Chris said. "I take a couple of mornings a week to work on projections, analysis and planning. The challenge has been to have blocks of time together. Given Kate's schedule, that pretty much means Saturday mornings."

"We tried to cram this planning in at the end of the day," Kate admitted. "But you can't do $100-an-hour work when you are dragging."

"Even with the things we've stopped doing we've been working at an unsustainable pace ... especially Katie."

"But it's a short-term thing and it's leading to a big pay-off ... a simpler more profitable business and a better life," Kate said. "That motivates us to keep going and get it done."

"Maybe that's part of the problem right now," Lori said. "We don't really have a clear picture of the pay-off, at least I don't. And if I was to sit down to work on the business, I wouldn't know where to start. If it hadn't been for the assignments you gave us ..."

"We were in the same spot a year ago," Kate said.

Chris excused himself, saying that he needed to check something in the office, and he asked Kate to help him. They were back in the kitchen within a minute.

"We've got an idea," Chris announced. "Kate and I had scheduled a WOTB meeting for this morning. We bumped it to tomorrow so we could help you. I'm not wild about having our WOTB meeting on Sunday and since we finished early, we have time to do it now. We think it would be helpful to have your input and it could be useful for you to see how we hold a WOTB meeting. These meetings have been the key to all the changes we are making and to turning the ranch from a job into a business. What do you think?"

"Sure," Lori said tentatively, looking at Wayne "We'd love to watch."

"No, not watch — participate," Kate corrected. "One ground rule. In any business meeting we have with anyone, we ask that they agree to keep anything they hear or any materials they see in confidence."

"What happens in a WOTB meeting stays in the WOTB meeting?" Wayne asked.

"Something like that," Chris said.

"It's one thing to understand how to crunch the numbers and how to use the benchmarks to make decisions," Kate explained. "It's another thing to have the discipline to actually do the work and make the decisions. These WOTB meetings are how we do that. We do one each month. We tackle one topic at each meeting."

"Topics like?" Lori asked.

"Our very first one was about our decision to join Executive Link. Actually, there were two things on the agenda at the first meeting, weren't there?" Kate asked, turning to Chris.

"Yeah. We also did the assignments that led to our mission statement," Chris said over his shoulder as he walked out of the kitchen and into the office.

"Assignments? Agenda? There's an agenda?" It sounded like overkill to Wayne.

"Uh-huh. There's a reference manual they give you at the school that has agendas for something like 10 or 12 meetings," Kate explained. "The structure helps make sure we have effective meetings that produce the results we need."

"That result will either be a decision or a list of questions we need to answer to make a decision," Chris said as he returned from the office with an easel and a flip chart. There was an action plan on the flip chart.

"It may seem formal," Kate said, "but our ranch is a business. This is a business meeting and Chris and I have to be businesspeople. That doesn't come naturally to either of us. Without the formality I don't think our meetings would be as effective." She walked out of the kitchen and into the office.

"Used to be we'd bring something up when we were both being pulled in a dozen different directions," Chris said. "We'd toss the issue around for a while and never get any resolution. Even if we made a decision on something there was no plan. There was no follow-through. A month or two or six later the same thing would come up again. We'd wrestle around with it again, and again, and again. Unless it was a crisis, we'd never completely work it out. The formality provides structure so that things get resolved. So, you want to help us with our meeting?"

Wayne looked at Lori. When she nodded, he said, "Sure. What's the topic?"

"We are going to decide our herd replacement strategy," Chris explained.

"Replacement heifers," Wayne said. He thought that this might be interesting.

"Well, that's one possibility," Chris acknowledged. "We actually realized that it's not heifers we need to replace. We need replacement cows. Growing heifers into cows is one option."

Kate returned with some papers in her hand. She gave one to Wayne, another to Lori, and kept the last one for herself. "Here's the agenda." Turning to Lori, she said, "We start every meeting reading our mission and vision. It's a good reminder of what we're trying to accomplish. Reading it is like flipping a switch that turns off all the distractions and turns on the meeting." She took her cell phone out, "Speaking of which, do you mind putting your phones on silent?"

Wayne turned off his phone, but he wondered if his friends weren't going a little overboard.

Chris read, "Mission: Healthy, productive livestock from healthy, productive land, supporting healthy, happy people. We aren't done until we've gone the extra mile for our customers, our community, and our family. We aim high and shoot straight."

Chris continued, "Vision: Cottonwood Creek Ranch is a highly profitable, financially stable, family-owned and managed livestock business. It is a simple place to run with enterprises that fit the ecosystem and produce gross margins that meet or exceed applicable benchmarks. The ecosystem is diverse, productive, and resilient. We produce these results with management, not purchased inputs. CCR is led by a highly effective management team that is always looking for ways to improve. Challenging the status quo is our status quo. Everyone on the CCR team is on the same page. They know the substance of the strategic and annual operating plans. Team members know their roles and how those roles contribute to CCR's success. Performance is measured against objective targets. CCR is a great place to work. We invest in our employees, compensate them well, and expect a lot from them. CCR creates opportunities for employees and family to have rich meaningful lives on and beyond the ranch."

Wayne was impressed. "That's quite a description. I didn't know you had an employee."

"Other than Chris and me, we don't," said Kate. "Not yet. Our vision doesn't describe the way things are now. It's a description of where we want to be five years from now. We obviously have a lot of work to do."

Wayne and Lori nodded.

"Okay, report on progress on the action plan from the previous meeting," Chris continued. He read the first action on the flip chart. "Project gross margins for replacement alternatives. I did that. I've got the gross margins for the four options we identified," he said as he held up a spreadsheet he'd printed.

"Second action," Chris continued, "determine bred heifer and cow price trends. Did that. I summarized prices and trends from the last several years of market reports from the three biggest auctions within 300 miles."

Nodding toward the flip chart, Kate said, "Third task on the chart is to contact two order buyers to see if we can get the replacement heifers or cows we need when we need them. That took some doing, but I contacted three. I got conflicting messages from the first two, so I thought I'd better break the tie. Had a great conversation with Jimmy Lane about it. He explained some context that made me realize that the first two weren't as far apart as it seemed. We can get into that in a bit."

Turning to Wayne and Lori, Chris said, "Our objective at this meeting is to make a decision on our replacement strategy and how and when we will implement it. We thought the best way to do that would be to use a decision grid."

"A decision grid?" Wayne asked.

"One of the things about EL is that you learn several planning and decision-making tools for identifying options and thoroughly evaluating the alternatives," Kate explained. "We use them in our EL board meetings, but we also use them ourselves when we're working through things here. Most of them are really simple. They give structure to our discussions so that we don't waste time going over ground we've already covered and so we don't miss anything that might be important. You'll see."

Kate got up and turned to a blank page on the flip chart. Turning to Chris she asked, "What are the criteria we are going to use to make this decision? What outcomes do we need?" She started writing as she answered her own question, "It's got to improve the gross margin." She wrote "Gross Margin/Unit."

"Right," Chris agreed, "and it needs to help us simplify things. I think that can probably be captured with the heading 'Labor Overheads.' And while we're at it, you might as well put turnover on the list. We need to consider how this will impact the number of productive animals we're able to carry."

As Kate wrote "Turnover," she said, "We need to consider the cash flow implications of buying something versus raising something." She added "Cash Flow" to the list.

After a few moments Chris said, "I'm not coming up with anything else." Turning to Wayne and Lori, he asked, "If you were thinking of changing your replacement strategy, is there anything else you'd want to consider?"

Before they could answer, Chris said, "Wayne, you said that you'd be concerned about bringing health problems into the herd. Maybe we should add that."

"Isn't that already covered by gross margin?" Kate asked. "If there are health issues, won't they show up there?"

"Yeah, they would," Chris agreed. "It would also add to overheads if we have to spend extra time dealing with sick animals. Let's add it anyway just to make sure we address those concerns."

"Anything else?" Kate asked as she wrote "Herd Health."

"What about market risk?" Lori offered. "You said you checked into whether you'd be able to get what you need when you need it. I'd be concerned about what it might cost you."

"That's an important one," Kate agreed as she wrote "Market Risk" on the chart.

"Anything else?" Kate asked.

Chris shook his head. "I can't think of anything."

"I can't either," Wayne added.

Chris pointed to Gross Margin/Unit on the first row on the flip chart and asked, "Should we give any of the criteria more weight than the others? I think gross margin is the most important."

"That and labor," Kate added. "I think that anything that makes the operation easier is every bit as important."

"Give each of them a weight of two then?" Chris suggested. Kate nodded and drew two stars next to Gross Margin/Unit and Labor Overheads.

"Should we turn to the options?" Chris asked.

"Sure. The first is to raise our own replacements like we do now," Kate said as she started writing.

Chris offered the next one. "Buying bred heifers from someone who has a program we like." He paused as Kate wrote, then added, "Another alternative is to buy older cows, say six or seven years old, that have most of the depreciation out of them."

"And the last one we want to consider is buying other people's late-calving cows," Kate said. "Since we'll be calving later, their late-calving cows might fit our program perfectly."

"Alright, gross margin. What'd you find out?" Kate asked.

"You know, I should have printed out another copy for Wayne and Lori." With that Chris sprinted to the office.

"This is a decision grid?" Lori asked Kate.

"Uh-huh. We list the decision-making criteria in a column on the left. If we think some things are more important than others, we can give them two or three stars. We show the alternatives we want to consider across the top. Then we have a discussion as to how each option measures up against each criterion. We give each option a score of -10 to +10 on each criterion. If something has two stars, it doubles the score. Three stars it triples the score. We add up the scores to see what wins, but the discussion that leads to the score is more important than the score itself. Sometimes we don't even add them up."

Chris came back with the pages he'd printed. "Okay, so here's what I found. I did the gross margin for the H1s and H2s. Without the replacement heifers, the cow gross margin comes in just above the benchmark."

Chris continued, "The H1 gross margin is bad. On an animal unit basis, it's $150 less than the cow margin. The gross margin ratio for the H1s is 55%. The H2 gross margin is even worse. The gross margin ratio for the H2s is 46%."

Kate considered the numbers for a moment before saying, "Since the heifer margins are way worse than the benchmark and are drawing the cow margin down, I think we ought to give the gross margin for raising our own heifers a negative score on the grid. It could be worse, so I wouldn't go all the way to -10, but I think it's a solid -5."

"I'm good with that," Chris agreed. "Now, this next one, we'd be buying bred heifers. There's really no difference between this and our H2 enterprise. The gross margin ratio came to 45%. The only advantage, if you can call it that, is that since we don't have any H1s, we free up some capacity so we could carry a few more cows. But the margin is terrible. And we'd still be calving out H2s."

"We'll get to the other things in a few minutes. Right now we're just scoring the gross margin," said Kate, wanting to keep things focused.

"You're right," Chris nodded. "Okay then, if the gross margin of raising our own H1s and H2s was a -5 and this is just the H2s, which was worse, I think this is a -10."

"That's probably a deal killer for that option," Kate said as she wrote "-10" in red on the flip chart.

"The next option is to buy older cows that fit our program. These would be six- to seven-year-old cows," Chris explained. "I went back eight years into market reports to look at prices. Six- and seven-year-old cows were consistently a lot cheaper than three- and four-year-old cows. You can see how that improves the gross margin. The gross margin is better because we aren't taking such a big hit on depreciation. The breed-back is a lot better than it would be on the H2s too. I ran several price scenarios. In every case the gross margin ratio on the cow herd was over 73%."

"And you wouldn't have to calve out heifers," Lori observed.

"Good point, and we'd be able to carry more cows because heifers that aren't going to give us a calf for another year wouldn't be eating up our grass," Chris noted.

"I'd be a little concerned with how you'd source these," Wayne said.

"Hey guys," Kate interrupted, "good points, but we aren't there yet. Let's stick with the impact on gross margin for now. We'll get to the other things soon enough. So, I think this gets a big score. I'm inclined to give it a 10."

"That's what I'd give it," Wayne said, as Lori nodded.

"Yeah, I don't know that the gross margin could be much better. Give it a 10," Chris agreed.

Chris led the discussion on the gross margin for late-calving cows. After they scored it, they focused on the next criteria, labor overheads. As the discussion continued, Wayne and Lori got more involved and brought up several good points. When they finished the scoring, an hour later, Kate tallied the scores at the bottom of the grid.

Replacement Strategy				
	Raise Our Own	Buy H2	Buy Older Cows	Buy Late Calving Cows
Gross Margin/Unit**	-5 x 2 = -10	-10 x 2 = -20	10 x 2= 20	10 x 2 = 20
Overheads (Labor)**	-3 x 2 = -6	-5 x 2 = -10	5 x 2= 10	3 x 2 = 6
Turnover	-3	1	3	3
Cash Flow	0	-1	5	8
Risk (health)	10	0	-1	-3
Risk (market)	0	-5	-3	-1
TOTAL	-9	-35	(34)	33

"These scores are pretty subjective, so there may not really be any difference between the last two strategies," Kate explained, "but we find that this process helps us have good discussions and make better decisions."

"If it'd been me, I could see how I might be married to one idea or another," Wayne observed. "This makes it easier to look at all the options and give each one a fair shake. It takes a lot of the emotion out of the process." He wondered if something like this could help frame a discussion with Buddy. "So, what are you going to do?"

Chris drew a circle around the score for buying older cows and said, "I think we ought to go with this. It should radically cut cow depreciation. It dramatically improves our gross margin without increasing any overheads. It doesn't lock us into anything long-term. If it turns out that there's a better way, we can always change. It got the highest score. I feel good about it."

"You won't be calving out first-calf heifers," Wayne noted.

"And you won't be wasting grass on heifers that won't produce a calf for another year," Lori added.

"I agree," Kate said. "The margin is terrific and there are three or four sources, so we ought to be able to get replacement cows when we need them at a price that works. So, what are we going to do with the heifer calves we have now? Should we sell them when we wean or hold them, breed them, and then sell them as bred heifers?"

"Good question," Wayne said. "Maybe it should depend on where we are in the cattle cycle. If people are expanding, maybe you should breed and then sell them. If we're in a contraction phase, then maybe it'd be best to sell them at weaning."

"That sounds good, but I got to tell you, I'm spooked by the ugly H1 margin I calculated," Chris confessed. "Remember, I had our H2 enterprise buying them at what I could sell them to someone else for and it wasn't good. I'd need to be pretty darn sure prices are going to be at the top end of what I was seeing in the market reports. I think we ought to sell them when we wean them. That frees up capacity for a higher margin enterprise too."

"Then maybe put them in your stocker program," Wayne suggested.

The discussion continued and ultimately led to an action plan showing the things Kate and Chris would do to implement their decision.

"Anything on your mind that we need to spend some time on?" Kate asked Chris.

"Nothing right now. You?"

"I'm a little worried about prepping for the meeting this summer," Kate answered. "It's a ways off, but I think we need to put our heads together about lodging and where we'll actually have the board meeting. There's likely to be 10 or 11 people. Can we schedule some time to talk about it next Saturday?"

"I'm good with that. You want to ask Allie if she's available next Saturday?" Chris asked.

When Kate nodded, Chris turned to Wayne and asked, "How you feelin'?"

"What do you mean? About what we just did?" Wayne was caught off guard.

"Uh-huh. We always end our WOTB meetings with two things. First, we check in with one another to see if anyone has anything on their mind that they're worried about. If there is, we either deal with it right then or, like now, we schedule time to work on it. The other thing is to check in to see how people are feeling about the process, about the decision, and about one another. Better to get things out in the open than have someone uncomfortable and resentful. This meeting was pretty straightforward, but sometimes we deal with some pretty emotional stuff."

"I can imagine. Okay, well, I'm feeling ..." Wayne searched for the right word. "Impressed? Yeah. Impressed. It's clear that you're running a business here. You aren't flying by the seat of your pants. You have a well thought out plan because you have a process for thinking things through. I'm impressed."

"Lori? How are you feeling?" Chris asked.

"To be completely honest, overwhelmed," she said. "There I go with that word again. I'm impressed too, but I look at Wayne and me and try to visualize us having a meeting like this." She looked at Wayne. "This is so different from anything we've ever done. Can we do this?" Then she looked at Kate. "This seems so effortless for you and Chris."

"Effortless? Oh gosh no!" Kate did not want to dismiss her friend's concern, but their WOTB meetings were anything but effortless. "I didn't believe it when the teacher told us that holding regular WOTB meetings would be the single most important *and* most difficult thing we would do if we were going to implement the things we learned in the class. But he was right. I would find an excuse not to meet, or Chris would. When we would hold one, we'd fumble around. We wouldn't use any of the tools. We'd get frustrated. That made it easy to get busy with other things and put off holding another for a couple of months. There's no point in having a meeting if you aren't going to get anything done." Kate paused for a moment before adding, "It wasn't until we got in EL that we started getting our act together. There's nothing like working with people who have been there and done that, and struggled just the way we were. Just the way you will."

"Lori, I can see how concerned you are, but you're worried about something you haven't even tried to do yet," Chris offered gently. "You haven't had any training in how to do this yet." As Lori nodded, he added, "You and Wayne *can* do this."

"I guess it's stupid to assume we'll fail at something we haven't even tried yet. But I'm still feeling overwhelmed," Lori said. "But I'm hopeful too."

"Do you think it would help if either Chris or I sat in on your first meeting or two?" Kate asked. "We'd have to make sure the agenda topic was something you'd be okay talking about with us. You need the training first, but we can help you get started."

"Yes! That would be amazing," Lori said.

"Kate, how are you feeling?" Chris asked.

"I feel good. I feel really good. I'm grateful that Wayne and Lori were here and helped. It's easier when it's not just the two of us. It was so much easier having the four of us, and I feel good about our decision. How do you feel?"

"I feel hungry," Chris said, then added, "I feel good. I am confident in our decision." He looked at Lori and added, "I also feel grateful that you and Wayne were here. This is easier with more minds than just ours. This all got a lot easier once we started having some success, because we both knew that these meetings are where that success came from." A moment later, he said, "I really am feeling hungry too. Let's eat."

Wayne and Lori were about a mile down the road. Justin and Matt were in the back seat playing I see something red, or green, or some other color. Lori spoke softly so the kids wouldn't hear,"You know how I'm feeling?"

"How are you feeling?" Wayne looked at her.

"I'm feeling scared," she confided.

"Scared? Of not remembering this stuff and not being able to work through the numbers?"

"No. I'm actually feeling hopeful about that. I'm scared that I'm going to get my hopes up for us becoming profitable, for me being home, for the success that Chris and Kate seem to be having, and then nothing will change." She let the thought sink in. "It's been a long time since I've felt hopeful about the future." She took a deep breath and let it out slowly before adding, "This is going to sound stupid, but I guess I'm afraid to feel hopeful."

"Afraid to feel hopeful? No, that's not stupid. Things have been pretty discouraging."

"Tell me about it. Every morning when I drive to the bank, every evening when I drive home, I think …" Lori stopped. She knew talk like this didn't help and it made Wayne feel guilty.

Wayne didn't know what to say. He thought the meeting with Chris and Kate had been a very positive experience. He also knew, between the ranch and work, Lori was paying a heavy price. What was it she'd said to Kate the other day? "I'm tired of being tired?" He felt a deep sadness come over him. He said, "I know I've let you down."

"That's not it. I mean, you haven't. You haven't let me down. You came home because Buddy needed you. We stayed because, well, you love the work. I love the ranch too. I can't imagine living somewhere else. I don't want to live anywhere else. It's just that I feel like we have been treading water for years. We've been treating life as though it is something that's going to happen later. We've never even taken the boys camping …" She whispered, trying to hold back tears and hoping the boys wouldn't notice. "If things don't change, we're going to wind up where we're headed. And I'm sorry, but I don't like where we're headed."

"Things need to change," he acknowledged.

"That's not enough. If things are going to change, *we* need to change," she said firmly but quietly through her tears. She wasn't angry, she was resolute.

SUMMARY OF CHAPTER 11
CONCEPTS

- You can't run a sustainable business on unsustainable effort, but sometimes it takes unsustainable effort to build one.

- You can't *make* time. You can only manage the time you have.

- It is impossible to do $100-an-hour work after putting in a full day. WOTB work must be done when people are fresh, energetic, and able to concentrate. Prime time for prime work.

- Your business's mission describes its purpose. It explains why you are in business. It consists of three parts:
    - Customer value (What value does your business create for a customer?)
    - Core principles (What principles guide the way you do business?)
    - Owner value (What quantifiable outcomes do the owners want to produce for themselves?)

- A vision statement is a long-term picture of what the business will look like when fully developed and delivering on its mission.

- Cow-calf producers don't need replacement heifers. They need replacement cows. Replacement heifers are just one way to replace cows.

- A decision grid is a tool for scoring alternatives against criteria for making a decision.

- Holding monthly WOTB meetings is an essential process for transforming a ranch into a successful business.

- Things won't change until you change.

Part II

Boots on the Ground

Chapter 12
The EL Tour

There were eight rigs in Chris and Kate's yard when Wayne pulled in. There were at least a dozen people on the porch. Wayne wondered if he would know anyone other than Chris and Kate. He was uncomfortable in crowds and even less comfortable meeting new people, but he had promised to come.

It had been almost three months since Chris and Kate had helped Wayne and Lori with their numbers. Whatever momentum they'd found working those two weekends with Chris and Kate had been lost. Good intentions had not turned into any meaningful change.

Chris came out with a tray.

"Is that zucchini bread? I love Kate's zucchini bread," Wayne said. Kate wasn't far behind with a bowl of sliced cantaloupe, strawberries, and grapes.

Sally and Robyn were across the yard with two other children he didn't recognize. One was in the tire swing under the big cottonwood. Allison was sitting at the picnic table close by doing something on her cell phone. She looked up, waved, and shouted, "Hello, Mr. Metcalf." Wayne waved back, thinking he should have brought Matt and Justin. He wished Lori could have come too. She had wanted to come, but there was an all-hands-on-deck meeting at the bank this morning. At least she'd be there for the barbeque this evening.

Wayne wasn't clear on the details, but he knew that the tour and dinner were part of Chris and Kate's Executive Link board meeting. Chris told him that the tour was not a "show-and-tell" as much as it was a "show-and-get-critiqued." Wayne also knew that the actual board meeting was something he was not invited to attend. He didn't want to anyway. Wayne was a private person and a little nervous about attending the field tour and meeting the "board."

"Mornin' Wayne." He'd been looking at the kids and Kate surprised him.

"Good morning." He tried to match her enthusiasm.

"Let me set these down. I'll be right back," she said, walking over to a nearby table with a carafe of coffee in each hand.

"You must be Wayne. Chris and Kate said you'd be coming." Turning to see who was talking to him, Wayne recognized the teacher from the workshop he and Lori attended with Chris and Kate months earlier.

As they shook hands, Wayne said, "I didn't know you'd be here. I sure enjoyed that workshop. It got me taking a hard look at a lot of the things I do."

"Thank you. That's the goal," the teacher said, smiling.

"I came to it expecting you to say that you had all the answers. I spent most of the time trying to prove everything you said was wrong, or at least that it didn't apply to me. It was really on the drive home with Chris and Kate that I started to understand what you'd been talking about."

"Chris and Kate are terrific," said the teacher." They've really started to do some exciting things here." He leaned closer to Wayne and said, "You know, your reaction isn't unusual. We all find new ideas threatening. The status quo feels safer. Even if it isn't working very well, at least it's known. Most people find that even a bad situation is more comfortable than the unknown."

"It may be comfortable," Wayne agreed, "but it's exhausting."

"And expensive!" Chris chimed in. "Katie and I wish we'd taken this school 10 years ago. Wayne and Lori are going to take the class this winter."

Wayne and Lori had not signed up for the class. Wayne hadn't even told Buddy that they wanted to go.

Just then Kate returned. "Am I interrupting?"

Wayne was grateful for the opportunity to change subjects. "No, not at all," he said with relief.

His relief vanished when Kate said, "Let's get you introduced to our board." She tapped a bell on the porch to get everyone's attention and shouted, "Everyone this is Wayne ... the best neighbor you could hope for." Kate began the round of introductions. Wayne held no hope of remembering everyone's name.

A stocky man with an infectious smile, stepped forward and vigorously shook Wayne's hand. "I'm Joe Street," he said. Wayne felt like his hand was in a vice grip. "… and this is my first wife, Lynda." He pointed to a tall woman walking toward them.

"First, last, and only wife," Lynda said. She was a couple of inches taller than Joe. "Stop crushing the poor man's hand," she scolded. Lynda replaced Joe's hand with her own. "Good to meet you. You're Chris and Kate's neighbor?"

"Neighbor twice removed," Wayne explained. "There are a couple of places between us. Where are you all from?"

"Near Dickerson. Fourth generation seed-stock outfit," Joe said.

"Street Angus? I've heard of you."

"Nothing too bad, I hope," Joe laughed.

Wayne thought, *Seed Stocky Joe and Lanky Lynda*, hoping that this would help him remember their names.

Chris broke in, "Wayne, this is Mike." A tall, thin man wearing a Minnesota Twins baseball cap shook Wayne's hand.

"I'm Mike Young. Good to meet you."

Wayne repeated *Minnesota Mike, Minnesota Mike* to himself.

Mike introduced his very pregnant wife. "This is my wife, Patty."

Patty extended her hand, "Friends call me Pat. Call me Pat."

"Pat it is. Thanks. What do y'all do?" Wayne asked.

"Everything," Pat laughed. "We have sheep and cattle."

"And kids!" Kate interjected as she joined the group. "Two over there with Robyn and Sally and two in there," she said as she put her hand on Pat's swollen belly. Turning to Pat, Kate asked, "Due?"

"September." Pat confirmed.

"Twins? Was the Twins cap a thing before or after you found out?" Wayne asked.

"Before, but it might have been an omen," Pat laughed.

"You'll have your hands full," Wayne said as he repeated to himself *Pregnant Pat, Pregnant Pat.*

An older couple joined them along with a young man who walked with a slight limp. Chris introduced them. "Wayne, this is Becky and Steve." They have a grass finishing operation around Smithfield. And this is Kevin. Kevin runs stockers in North Carolina."

"North Carolina! You're a long way from home," Wayne said.

Kevin was tall and lean and had shoulder-length blonde hair. "Good to meet-cha."

"Stockers?" Wayne said, trying to be a good conversationalist.

"It's mostly custom grazing," Keven said. "I'm starting to get more into sell-buy marketing, but our bread and butter is custom grazing."

"Kevin adds a lot to our board," Becky said. "If you take conventional wisdom and do the opposite, you've got Kevin's business."

"I'm Vince McBride." Wayne shook the hand of someone who had to be six foot four and looked like an aging NFL linebacker.

As Wayne and Vince shook hands, Chris said, "Vince was a detective in Denver, so watch yourself. He left the department to run his family's ranch near Claremont five years ago. They have bison."

"Bison, really?" Wayne wondered what kind of stories Vince might have from his detective days but figured it wasn't the right time to ask.

"And you know Roger, Jack, and Dan from Daisy Creek," Chris said.

"Sure," Wayne confirmed, as they exchanged handshakes. Although he had never talked to him, other than to say hello, Wayne had always looked up to Roger. Now 70, Roger was fit and very active in community and industry organizations. Daisy Creek had been in his family for over 100 years and had won national awards for stewardship.

Jack was a different story. Jack had been managing Daisy Creek for as long as Wayne could remember. He wasn't family and Wayne didn't find him very friendly. In fact, Wayne felt he could be downright intimidating.

Dan was the opposite of Jack. In addition to being a top hand, he was one of the most kind and generous people you could ever meet. Wayne thought a lot of him.

Wayne shook hands all the way around as he said, "I didn't know that y'all were part of Chris and Kate's board."

"We're not," Roger said. "We were in EL several years ago. In it for five years, I think. We probably ought to get back in it."

"We asked them to come so we could pick their brains. They've been there and done that with some of the things we're thinking of doing," Chris said.

"I don't know how much there is up there to pick," Roger chuckled, pointing to his head. "We're always ready to learn something new." Then he added, "It's been too long Wayne. How's your dad?"

Avoiding the question, Wayne said as cheerfully as he could, "He'll probably be here tonight for the barbeque."

Kate put her hand on Chris's shoulder, "Hon, we probably ought to get started, don't you think?"

"I try not to," Chris joked. "Yeah, we ought to get started. I'll get the stuff." He jogged up the porch steps two at a time and disappeared into the house, the screen door slamming shut with a creak and a bang.

Chris was back in less than a minute, wrestling an easel and a flip chart through the screen door. Kate unrolled a big map and a six-foot wide laminated chart and pinned them both to the wall.

It was 8:30 when Chris rang the bell by the steps. It immediately got everyone's attention. "We're all here, so let's get started."

The porch was a maze of chairs and stools and benches arranged in a semi-circle around the easel, but most folks either sat on the railing around the porch or stood.

"Thank you for coming," said Chris. "Welcome to Cottonwood Creek Ranch. We're excited to have you here. We've been looking forward to getting your input on a lot of things Katie and I are thinking about. We've got some big decisions and big changes ahead.

"Katie and I thought we'd start this morning with a little history. We'll describe the way things have been run and where we'd like to see things five to 10 years from now. Then, we'll head out to see a few things and get your input on the changes we're considering. We should be back here by noon. We'd like to end with lunch and a turn-around session."

Wayne wondered what he meant by turn-around session, but he seemed to be the only one that didn't know, so he didn't ask.

Kate pointed to the map and was about to start when Pat asked, "Shouldn't we start with your mission and vision?"

"Of course," said Chris, handing a paper to Pat. "Pat, would you mind reading our mission and vision?"

Wayne wondered why Chris didn't read it himself.

Pat read the Cottonwood Creek Ranch mission statement and then handed the paper to Mike to read their vision statement. He read the vision slowly as though he was trying to visualize the picture it described as he read.

"Thank you," Kate said. She meant it too. When she or Chris read their mission and vision, they tended to race through it. When someone else read it, they found it much easier to really think about their goals.

"Okay, that's why we're here and what we want," Kate said. "Now let's talk about how we got here." Pointing to various areas on the map, Kate showed them the original ranch her great-grandfather bought over 100 years ago. She explained how the ranch had grown, been divided, and changed over the years.

After Kate's abbreviated history lesson, Chris described how the ranch had been run for the last several years. "Everything has been pretty conventional, but that's about to change. Historically we calved in spring —"

"Don't you mean winter?" Joe challenged. That got a chuckle from the group.

"Right, thanks. We calved in winter." Chris enunciated winter slowly and loudly. "Heifers start about the first of March and the cows by the first of April. Around here we don't really have grass until May, so yeah, that's really still winter," Chris acknowledged.

He continued, "We feed about two tons of hay per cow. Up until now we've put it up ourselves. That's something we want you to challenge us on. The grazing has been pretty conventional. We thought we were rotational grazing. Each herd would graze through four paddocks, but at the school we learned that with fewer than eight paddocks it's really 'rotational overgrazing.' Kate, why don't you pick it up from here?"

"We had heifers separated from the cows and the cows divided into two herds," Kate explained. "The very first thing we did when we got home from the class was to put all the cows in one herd. That doubled the stock density and got us up to eight paddocks for that herd. We would have added the heifers to the herd, but our water system was already maxed out. We are applying for cost sharing to improve water distribution and delivery and to fence."

"Can I ask a question?" Dan asked.

"Sure Danny," Kate answered with a smile. "What do you want to know?"

"I was just wondrin' how many paddocks you were going to take this up to."

"We don't know for sure. We'd like to have at least 16 for the cows," Kate answered. "This is actually something we'd like everyone's input on, especially with the steers. We've been thinking that we might do most of that with polywire. When we get out in the pasture let's talk about this."

Dan nodded, "Thanks."

Kate liked Dan. She had always called him Danny, even though he was probably 20 years older than she was. Everyone else called him Dan, but he didn't seem to mind 'Danny.' He was a good hand and Daisy Creek was lucky to have him. But his question broke her train of thought. She was trying to pick up where she left off. Rather than fight it, she punted.

"Chris, your turn."

"So, results," Chris said. "Well, combining herds made things easier. It takes less time to check one big herd than it does to check two small herds, but if we're going to keep them together this summer, we really need to do something about the water.

"Most of the things we've done so far are behind the scenes, working through the Ranching for Profit Online assignments, describing our mission and vision, projecting the gross margin of each enterprise and alternatives within the enterprises, defining effectiveness areas, and setting targets."

This was new language to Wayne. He wondered what Ranching for Profit Online[1] was and what Chris meant by "effectiveness areas."

"We installed a transect last night to document the current condition of the range. Time permitting, we'll put another one in with y'all at our third stop this morning. Like Kate said, we want to improve our grazing. We'll talk about that at the second stop," Chris said.

"Our numbers show that we ought to be calving later, but before we go all in, Kate and I want to hear from y'all on how we ought to make the transition."

Kate softly interjected, "Don't forget hay."

"Oh, right. If we calve later, it should drastically reduce our need for hay. We want you to help us think through what we ought to do and when we ought to do it. Should we have someone come in and put up hay for us? Should we stop haying all together and graze it with stockers, or stockpile it for the cows? Are there alternatives we haven't thought of? One thing I know is, this time next year, I don't want to be putting it up myself.

"Are we ready? Grab a bottle of water and let's load up. There's 15 of us. We can do that in two rigs if some of you don't mind sitting in the back." Chris loaded the easel and the flip chart in his truck and said, "Let's go."

---

1 Ranching for Profit Online is a follow-up support program available to Ranching For Profit School graduates. It consists of dozens of step-by-step assignments and video coaching tutorials to help RFP grads implement everything they learn in the school to their businesses.

Chapter 13
Stop One: Hay Fields

After a short drive Chris pulled up to a stack yard with about 25 weathered round bales. To the north and east of the stack yard were large flood-irrigated fields with nearly knee-high grass and alfalfa. Wayne looked across the field and thought it looked pretty good.

Chris led the group into the field. "This probably ought to be the last stop, not the first. We can't stop feeding hay until we change the production schedule ¬—"

"But you can stop putting it up," Joe interrupted.

"True, and we've been thinking about that. Our equipment is old, so we don't have a lot of depreciation —"

"Probably means you have a lot of repairs," Joe interrupted again.

"We have our share," Chris nodded. He was a little annoyed that Joe would not let him explain what they were doing. Chris started again explaining that they had a total of 300 acres in hay, all flood irrigated, yielding about two tons per acre.

"This year is pretty typical. We'll take our first cutting in about two weeks. We usually have enough water to give the fields two more irrigations and sometimes that's enough to get a second cutting later in the summer. But it's been too dry and we won't get a second cutting this year."

Chris explained that they planned to put up hay one more season. Next year they would either hire someone to put up the hay on a custom basis or they would stop making hay altogether and buy whatever they needed. Rather than hay the fields, he and Kate were thinking of grazing them with stockers early in the season and then stockpiling forage for winter grazing for the cows.

"So, Mike, Pat," Chris asked, "you don't put up hay anymore, right?"

"Right, we buy whatever we need now," Mike confirmed.

"It's sooo much easier," Pat added.

Wayne had a hard time understanding how anyone could justify taking what seemed to be a productive hay field like the one they were in and not hay it. "Doesn't that put you at the mercy of the market?" he asked.

"I guess," Mike conceded, "but we looked back at hay prices for the last five years and in four of them it would have been more profitable for us to buy it than to make it. We decided it was better to manage for the rule and build a contingency for the exception rather than build the whole ranch around the exception."

Turning to Chris, Mike said, "Chris, it feels like we're walking on pavement here." He stomped his left foot a couple of times on the hard ground. "All the years we were haying we never considered the fertility we were removing. I think you've mined a lot of the fertility out of this soil. I'm not sure how you measure that, but the loss is something to consider."

"I know," Chris said apologetically. He got down on one knee and pushed the leaves back so he could see the soil. "That's another reason to change things up. I never really looked at it before, but there's an amazing amount of bare soil under the canopy. I wonder, if we grazed this, and that filled in, just how much more productive this could be."

Wayne was startled by the amount of bare soil. He'd never looked at his own fields this way and began to wonder how much bare soil he had.

Looking at Joe, Chris asked, "You still put up hay, right?"

"Well, we don't put it up. We *have* it put up," Joe clarified. "The guy we have does it better and cheaper than I ever did. And now, while they're working, I can go fishing." He made a motion like he was casting a line.

Wayne said, "I'd be worried about getting someone when you need them. If they didn't show when you needed them, you could lose a lot of quality."

"You could," Joe agreed, "but the bigger question is, what does it cost to ensure we get that quality? Too much, at least for us."

Lynda added, "We actually avoided the issue. When we decided to stop making hay ourselves and started exploring alternatives, we had a hard time finding a custom operator. It occurred to us that if we

146

couldn't find someone to do ours, then other people probably had the same problem and that might be an opportunity for a new enterprise. We didn't want to do it ourselves, but we knew this kid who'd helped us with haying a couple of summers. He loved it, so we offered to set him up in the custom hay business a couple of years ago. Scotty leases our equipment and we hire him to put up our hay. He's been super reliable."

"It's been a sweet deal for us," Joe added, "because if we sold the equipment, I doubt we'd get anything close to what it's worth."

Looking at Jack, the teacher asked, "You still make hay at Daisy Creek, right?"

"We do," Jack said unapologetically. "It's a stand-alone, profitable enterprise. But we've got the scale to make it work. We hire a couple of seasonal guys to help and our equipment is going nonstop through the season. We don't feed hardly any of it to our cows. It's very good hay. Too good and too expensive for our cows. They don't need that high a quality. We buy whatever hay we feed them, and we don't feed them much. We average less than a quarter ton per cow per year.

"We've handled the fertility issue by doing a couple of things. First, we always leave cover. Just like our pastures, we never have bare soil in those fields.

"Second, we don't use chemical fertilizers. They contain a lot of salt, so we don't use them. When we add calcium or sulfur or phosphorous, we apply them in pure form.

"Next, we introduce microbes. Used to be we thought of soil as dirt. Dirt is dead. Soil is alive. We've brought back microbes by adding compost to some fields, but for us using compost tea has probably been the most effective way to improve soil biology.

"We've also added some micronutrients to feed the microbes and done some things to minimize compaction. Those microbes need air, and that means they need pore spaces. They will not persist in compacted soils.

"Finally, we graze those fields. We graze the residue. And when a field's productivity starts to decline, we will graze it as pasture for a few years to build up organic matter and stimulate soil biology. It's been a steep learning curve, but our yields are up, the quality is up, and we've eliminated the use of synthetic chemicals."

Chris was still kneeling. He pointed at the bare, compacted soil and asked, "If we stop haying and get the grazing right, do we need to do something like that or will this take care of itself?"

"We stopped haying and started grazing our fields three years ago," Mike said. "We made sure we left plenty of cover and gave pastures the rest they needed and we've seen substantial improvement without adding any inputs. There's still a lot of room for improvement, but you will make progress just by getting the grazing right. You'd probably improve things faster with an amendment."

"But would it pay?" Chris asked.

"What's to keep you from running a test?" Roger asked. "You could just lay out a couple of small plots and spray on compost tea with a hand sprayer." He turned toward Jack. "You think you might be able to help Chris with something like that?"

"Be glad to. If not me, Dan," Jack said.

"You bet," Dan said. "You might want to try something else too. Take one of those bales in the stack yard and spread it right here. It'd give you some cover and some organic matter. Couldn't hurt. It could make a difference and it wouldn't cost you nothin'."

Kevin shifted the focus. "So if you stop the haying, are you going to graze stockers?"

"Uh-huh," Chris said. "Whether they'd be our own or someone else's, we don't know yet. Either way, once they go, we were hoping we'd get enough regrowth to stockpile some grass for winter grazing."

"I don't think you'll have much of a feed bank unless you get them out of here pretty early," Kevin said. "Usually with a stocker deal you graze a pasture down and you're done. If you want to create a stockpile you're going to have to graze these pastures up. You're going to have to leave a lot of leaves."

Wayne wondered what he meant by "graze the pasture up" but didn't want to ask. Everyone else seemed to know what it meant.

"I've compared the gross margins of our purchased stockers to the custom stockers we bring in," Kevin said. "Of course, it might be different for you, but there isn't any difference in the gross margin per unit of purchased stockers and custom stockers for us. It's kind of hard to justify tying up capital in owning something when you can make just as much not owning that thing and not putting your capital at risk. And it sure is nice having monthly cash flow and not needing an operating loan.

"If you need a sample of a good custom grazing contract to help put your own together, I'd be happy to send you a copy of what we use. We learned some things the hard way. It's a very good contract now."

"That'd be great," Kate said.

"Any dairies that might be interested in contracting with you to grow out their heifers?" Joe asked. "There's usually a very good margin in that."

"I don't know. It's something we should look into," Chris said.

"If you sold all of your hay equipment, how much would you get?" Steve asked.

"Not that much. It's pretty old," Chris said.

"Yeah, but there's the baler, the rake, I saw two tractors back at the yard. Would you really need both?" Steve questioned.

Before Chris could answer, Kate responded with an emphatic "No. We wouldn't need both. And, conservatively, we'd get $50,000."

Chris nodded.

"So, if I put $50,000 in your hand right now, what would you do with it?" Steve asked.

Neither Kate nor Chris had an immediate answer, so Steve offered, "It's just something to think about. How can you take the money currently tied up in fixed assets and put it in something that will actually make you money? That should probably be part of the discussion."

"Why don't you do it now?" Joe asked.

"Do what? Sell the equipment?" Chris asked.

"Well, maybe, but why don't you have someone come in and put your hay up for you this season? You could keep your equipment for a couple of months as a back-up just in case you can't find someone. But why not have someone else do it this year? What would you do this

149

summer to improve your business that you wouldn't be able to do if your butt is stuck in a tractor seat all summer?"

"We don't have time to find someone," Kate said.

"How long does it take to make a phone call?" Vince asked, challenging the notion. "What's the downside of exploring that?"

Joe added, "Whether there was time to get someone wasn't my question. My question was, what would you be able to do this summer if you weren't working yourself to death making hay?"

Chris quietly answered, "I don't know."

"It's something you might want to think about," Lynda suggested.

Kate made a note on her notepad.

"If you were to graze this, how would you fence it?" Mike asked, wanting to take the discussion in another direction.

Chris talked about how they had been thinking they'd use temporary electric fencing to divide the field. They talked about the number of paddocks they'd need and where they'd put water. They discussed the stock density they should shoot for, how long the recovery periods should be, and how they might change over the course of the summer as growth slowed. When the discussion turned to whether they should use fiberglass rods or tread-in posts, the teacher asked, "What's the next stop?"

Chris realized the discussion had devolved to operational detail. He didn't want to waste their limited time on minutia. "We're going to drive up to a place where we're thinking of putting a cell center. We want some input on cell design from y'all up there. Let's load up."

As they walked back to the truck, Wayne caught up with Chris. "That was intense," he said. "I wouldn't have thought of half of that stuff."

"They probably wouldn't have either if they weren't looking at my situation," Chris answered. "It's always easier to see how someone else ought to do things. When I'm looking at their stuff, I come up with things that never would have occurred to me to do on our place, until I saw the opportunity for them."

"Steve and Becky sure are interesting, and Lynda, she's the real deal, isn't she? Interesting idea about setting up the kid with a new enterprise."

"They aren't just thinking out of the box, I think they blew up the box!" Chris agreed.

"The teacher hasn't said much," Wayne noted.

"No, he doesn't really need to," Chris said. "At the school he said that teaching wasn't about cramming stuff in your head, it was about pulling stuff out of us. In fact, he kept telling us 'the answer is in the team.' He's not here to tell us what he thinks — he's here to help facilitate the conversation."

"Doesn't seem like you need facilitation," Wayne observed. "Everyone just jumps right in. They don't pull any punches, do they?"

"No, they don't," Chris agreed. "It's interesting, a year ago if I'd hosted a day like this and got this kind of feedback, I'd have gotten real defensive. I would have deflected their suggestions, defended what I was doing, and I wouldn't have learned a thing." Chris shook his head. "It's remarkable what a difference it makes to trust that everyone has your best interests at heart. It makes it much easier to hear what people have to say."

Turning toward the group, Chris shouted, "Let's load up."

SUMMARY OF CHAPTER 13
CONCEPTS

- Old or new, machinery is expensive.
- Manage for the rule. Build a contingency for the exception.
- The cost of doing something includes the time it takes away from other things you could be doing.
- If you can't find someone to provide a service, there may be an opportunity for a new enterprise to provide that service to others.
- It's hard to justify tying up capital in owning something when you can make as much, or more, not owning something.
- The money currently tied up in equipment (fixed assets) can probably be redeployed into something that would make your business more profitable.
- A healthy soil is alive. Dead soil is just dirt.

Chapter 14
Cell Grazing

Wayne climbed in the bed of the pickup with Joe, Steve, Becky, Dan, Roger, and the teacher. He turned to the teacher and said, "Chris said that if you had fewer than eight pastures you weren't rotational grazing, you were rotational overgrazing. What'd he mean by that?"

"How much time do we have before the next stop?" the teacher asked. "This could take a few minutes. First, we have to be on the same page as to what overgrazing is. There's a difference between overstocking and overgrazing." He turned to Dan. "Dan, why don't you explain it?"

"Sure," Dan said. "I used to think that overgrazing happened when you had too many animals in a pasture and they grazed the grass too short, but that's *overstocking*. Overstocking means you have more livestock than you have grass to support them — the demand for grass is greater than the supply.

"Overgrazing is different. It doesn't have anything to do with how many animals you've got. Overgrazing happens when a plant is grazed before it has recovered from the last time it was grazed. That begins an ugly chain of events. When plants are overgrazed it weakens their roots. That reduces the organic matter in the soil. That makes the soil less fertile, reduces the water holding capacity, and makes it more prone to compaction. That leads to more runoff and more erosion. We might as well lay out a welcome mat for bare soil, weeds, and less desirable grasses. Of course, productivity drops. In short, overgrazing is bad.

"But most ranchers overgraze all of their pastures every year. They will tell you they don't, but they do. They get overgrazing confused with overstocking. Overstocking isn't good either, but it's different." Dan shook his head, "How can there be a whole gol' darn industry with livestock on hundreds of millions of acres, and they don't even know what overgrazing is?"

"Geez Dan, I didn't realize you brought your soapbox with you today," Roger laughed.

"Well, it ticks me off," Dan said. "You want me to keep going?"

"Absolutely!" the teacher said. "You're doing great! Don't stop now."

"Before you go on," Wayne said, "let me throw another question at you. I read somewhere that a lot of rangeland is *understocked* and *overgrazed*. Is that possible? What are they talking about?"

"It's not only possible, it's the normal state of affairs on a lot of rangeland," Dan said. "See, overgrazing doesn't happen to a pasture, it happens to a plant. Say you've got two grass plants side by side. A cow walks by and grazes one but doesn't touch the other. Now it's a week or 10 days later. The one that got grazed has started to recover. The regrowth is delicious and nutritious. The one that didn't get grazed is a week older and has become less nutritious and less delicious. Here comes the cow. Which one is she gonna eat?"

"She's gonna eat the one with the regrowth — the one she grazed a week earlier," Wayne said.

"Bingo," Dan agreed. "She's going to graze that plant again. Here she comes two or three weeks later and it's the same story, only more extreme. One plant gets grazed repeatedly while the other gets over-rested. That repeated grazing, before the plant has fully recovered from the previous grazing, is overgrazing. You wind up with a lot of overgrazed plants and over-rested plants in the same paddock, side by side. The paddock is understocked because there's a lot of grass that went to waste in those over-rested plants."

"And what will happen to those over-rested plants?" the teacher asked.

"They'll eventually die," Dan said bluntly. "These grasses here evolved with grazing animals. They need periodic grazing to stay healthy."

He didn't want to admit it but, by Dan's definition, Wayne realized he was overgrazing every pasture on his place, and a lot of his rangeland probably was understocked and overgrazed.

"You ready for more?" Dan asked. When Wayne nodded, Dan said, "Alright, I'll let loose with both barrels. There are two ways to overgraze. You can keep stock in a pasture too long, or bring them back too soon."

"How do you know how long you can keep them in and how long you need to keep them out?" Wayne asked.

"You guess!" Dan laughed. "It's actually pretty simple. When things are growing fast you don't need much rest. If Chris grazes that hay field when things are growing fast, he'll probably need to give it 30, 35, maybe 40 days to recover before coming back. Later in the season, when growth is slower, he'd want more like 45, 50, maybe 60 or even 70 days between grazings. It depends on how severely he grazes a pasture too. Graze it severely and it'll take longer to recover. Leave a lot of leaves and it'll recover faster."

"That's irrigated pasture. What about out here?" Wayne asked, gesturing to the rangeland on either side of the truck.

"You'd want more rest," Dan said. "Whether it's fast growth or slow growth, growing conditions aren't as good and it's going to take plants longer to recover. Watch the grass, it will tell you. We have some pastures like this at Daisy Creek that we graze just once a year."

"So, what's the deal with needing more than eight paddocks?" Wayne asked.

Dan took a pencil out of his pocket and started writing on the flip chart Chris had laid in the bed of the truck. "Okay, look here," he said enthusiastically. "Let's say things are growing fast and you have four paddocks, and one herd. If the herd is in one of the four, that means that three are resting, right?

"Now, things are growing fast and we decide we want to give paddocks 30 days to recover before we bring the animals back. Thirty days rest divided by three paddocks resting is 10, right?" He struggled to keep his hand steady as he did the math on the flip chart. "So, animals would have to graze each paddock for 10 days to give this first paddock 30 days to recover."

He looked up at Wayne and asked, "You think there'll be some regrowth in 10 days?"

"Sure," Wayne answered, "if things are growing fast."

Dan nodded and continued, "So staying in a paddock for 10 days will cause overgrazing, right?"

"I guess so. What about if things are growing slow?" Wayne asked.

"Okay, let's make the math easy," Dan said as he started to write again. "Let's say we want 90 days of rest now. With three paddocks resting, how long do we need to stay in those pastures?"

HERD		4 Paddocks

4 Paddocks
-1 Herd
_____
3 Resting

Fast Growth:
30 Days Rest ÷ 3 = <u>10 Day Graze Period</u>

Slow Growth:
90 Days Rest ÷ 3 = <u>30 Day Graze Period</u>

"Ninety days rest divided by three pastures resting is 30. The graze period will be 30 days," Wayne said. "In 30 days you're going to have some regrowth, so the stock are going to overgraze, aren't they?"

"Uh-huh," Dan confirmed. "Okay, what kind of graze period would we get if things are growing fast and we have eight paddocks? With the herd in one, that'd leave seven paddocks resting. Divide 30 days of rest by the seven paddocks resting and that gives us just a little over four. We'd need to stay in each paddock about four days to give each of the others 30 days of rest. There won't be much regrowth in just four days. So, with eight paddocks we stopped the overgrazing."

"What about slow growth when we wanted a 90-day rest?" Wayne asked. "What's 90 days divided by seven paddocks resting?"

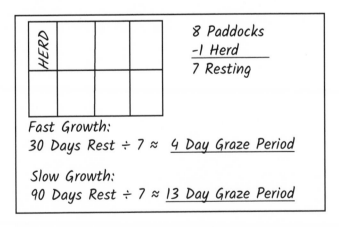

8 Paddocks
-1 Herd
_____
7 Resting

Fast Growth:
30 Days Rest ÷ 7 ≈ <u>4 Day Graze Period</u>

Slow Growth:
90 Days Rest ÷ 7 ≈ <u>13 Day Graze Period</u>

Dan did the math and said, "It's about 13 days. If things are growing slow, we won't have a lot of regrowth by then. So, fast growth or slow growth, eight paddocks pretty much stops overgrazing."

"But we still have a problem, don't we Becky?" The teacher asked, "What's going to happen with eight paddocks?"

"Why call on me?" Becky pretended to complain.

"Because you know the answer. You had this problem, didn't you?" the teacher asked, knowing that she and Steve had serious problems when they'd used an eight-paddock rotation.

"We sure did," Becky said. "Eight paddocks will stop the overgrazing, but there's more to this than just the grass. You need to consider the animals' needs too. Each day animals are in a paddock the quality of forage available goes down."

"Not only that, but the quantity of poop and plants that get trampled goes up," Steve added.

"The result is, that each day the animals are in a paddock they eat a little less than they did the day before," Becky explained. "Even if there's still plenty of grass out there, they will eat less, and when they eat less, performance drops. When we only had eight paddocks during slow growth we'd have cows grazing a paddock for a week or more before we'd move them and their condition really dropped."

"And when the body condition dropped, the conception rate dropped too," Steve added. "And it wasn't just a problem with the cows. When we had our steers in a 10-paddock rotation they only gained a pound and a half a day. The following year we split the paddocks so they rotated through 20 paddocks. We were able to cut the graze periods in half, from four days to two days. Once we did that, they gained over two pounds a day."

"Closer to two and a half," Becky said. "Bottom line is, if you want animals to perform you need to move them more often. And if you move more often with eight paddocks, you'll cheat your recovery periods. That's why eight paddocks isn't enough. You need more. We use 20 paddocks for our stockers when things are growing fast. But we split the paddocks in half when things slow down so that we give the pastures the rest they need and can still move the herd every couple of days. We move our grass finishers every day. Counting the breaks we make with polywire, we probably use 40 or more paddocks for them."

"40 pastures? Man, that's a lot of pastures," Wayne said. "That sounds like a lot of work."

"It's actually less work," Becky said.

"That's been our experience too," Dan said. "Our cells average 25 paddocks, but sometimes we will split paddocks in half or in thirds. So sometimes we have upward of 50 paddocks. Before we did this, we had five guys at Daisy Creek, plus Jack, so actually six guys," Dan said. "Now there's four of us, including Jack, and none of us work as hard as we used to. The biggest time-saver was combining herds. It takes less time to check one big herd than three or four small ones. And we feed a small fraction of the hay we used to feed. It's a lot less work."

"Any other benefits of having that many paddocks?" the teacher asked.

"You mean density?" Steve asked. When the teacher nodded, Steve explained that stock density is the number of animals in a pasture at any particular moment. When stock density is high, the uniformity of grazing increases.

"On range like this, when you push the density up, you are going to get animals to graze areas that went untouched before," Steve said. "And regardless of where you are, increasing stock density will improve the quality of the pasture."

"How do you know when you've got stock density high enough?" Wayne asked.

"The uniformity of grazing will tell you," Becky assured him. "If it's patchy, it's too low. Higher is always better."

"How high is too high?" Wayne asked.

"When you have to start stacking animals on top of one another," Joe joked. "You won't get it too high. There are people who use stock densities of three or four hundred head per acre. I haven't seen it, but I've heard of places where the stock density is over a thousand head per acre. You have to make sure you don't leave 'em on a spot too long, but you won't get the density too high."

"I would think that the really high density would stress the animals and create more health problems," Wayne said.

"It hasn't been an issue for us, at least not so we've noticed," Steve explained. "As with anything, there's an adjustment period — I think more with the people than with the cows. But we didn't have any stress issues. And health, heck, the animals are always moving to fresh, clean pastures. We've had fewer health issues, not that we had a lot before."

"And if you do have a problem you catch it sooner because you are seeing the animals more often. The poor doers tend to be the last ones through the gate," Dan added.

"Okay, I get why rotating through less than eight pastures is rotational overgrazing," Wayne said. "And I get that with only eight pastures, animal performance won't be very good. Becky said they use 20 pastures for their stockers when things are growing fast and 40 for their grass finishers. Dan said they use 25 and sometimes as many as 50! How do you know how many pastures you need in your rotation?"

"I'm afraid this is one of those, 'it depends' answers," the teacher said. "Are we looking at seasonal or year-round enterprises? What's the class of animal? What's the configuration of the property? There are a lot of considerations but, in general, eight to 10 paddocks can stop the overgrazing. You need at least 15 to 16 to support decent animal performance. But if you really want to see rapid improvement in the land, you will probably need at least 25 paddocks per herd."

"That's still a lot of fences," Wayne said.

"You don't need fences to do this," the teacher said. "In some places it makes more sense to do this with herding. There's people who are able to move animals to an area and settle them so that they will stay there for a couple days until the people come back and move them to the next area. You have to be a good stockman, but I've seen it done with great results."

"Rotational grazing without fencing? That's something I might have to see to believe," Wayne said.

"Wayne, it'll be helpful if you don't think of this as rotational grazing," Roger said. "A rotation is a system. Two days here, two days there, two days in the next pasture, lockstep, one after the other. This isn't that. Rotations don't work in nature. What we are talking about is called *cell grazing*. In cell grazing you don't rotate around in a circle. You go wherever you need to go, whenever you need to be there."

"Is that what that big chart Kate hung up next to the map is for?" Wayne asked. "To figure out where you are going to graze and when?"

"Uh-huh," Dan said. "We use the same chart to plan our grazing too. We have one for each cell. There's a row for each paddock and a column for each day of the year.

"We use it to help us figure out where we want the herd and when we want them to be there. Maybe more importantly, we use it to figure out where we don't want them. I prepare a plan for the growing season and another for the dormant season. Jack reviews it. If he's happy with it, which he usually is, then I run with it. If there's a problem, we usually make the revisions together. The chart shows everyone where the herds are, where they've been, where they're going next, and when they'll be coming back. The chart is a great planning tool but it's an even better communication tool.

"Every time you move the herd you write in the number of days they actually grazed the paddock you took them out of," Dan explained. "It's really pretty simple."

"The grazing chart is a little like the cash flow then," Wayne said. "On the cash flow you show your projection for each month. Then at the end of the month you write in the actual."

"It's exactly like the cash flow," the teacher said. "Think of it as a grass flow."

"There's three things in our inventory that we need to manage," Dan said. "Livestock, money, and grass.[1] We use a stock flow to manage the inventory of livestock, the cash flow to manage our money, and a grazing chart to manage our inventory of grass. And like the stock flow plan and the cash flow forecast, you don't follow the plan blindly. Things change and you make adjustments as you go."

"People want a recipe," the teacher said. "Graze for two days, rest for 30, season with a salt block, and you have it. Cell grazing isn't that. Cell grazing is a set of principles that can be applied in any grazing environment. We apply those principles differently in

---

1 Bud Williams told students in his marketing schools that ranchers have three things in their inventory to manage: money, grass, and animals. Bud said, "You'll never go broke having too much grass or money, but you can sure have too many animals at the wrong time."

humid environments than in arid areas, but all the principles still apply. In either case, humid or dry, the principles support good animal performance and improve the health of pastures. Cell grazing has helped many of our graduates increase their carrying capacity, reduce input costs, and increase profit."

"Many of your graduates?" Wayne asked. "Not all of them?"

"Not everyone has adopted these practices," the teacher said with a smile.

"If it can increase carrying capacity and reduce costs, why doesn't everyone do it?"

"You know how hard it is to get a lease of any size around here?" Dan asked him.

"Sure. People wind up with 30 animals here, another 40 over there. Some guys have a half-dozen or more leases 50 miles apart," Wayne said.

"Can you imagine what it would be like if they set up 20 or 30 paddocks on every one of them and had to check every herd every day?" Dan asked. "They'd be driving all day long."

"There's no substitute for doing the numbers," the teacher explained. "Whether it's a question of what enterprise to have, what production schedule to use, or whether someone ought to be using cell grazing to manage their pastures, the gross margin and the overheads will tell them."

Wayne nodded and said, "Let me see if I have this right. You've got to keep the graze period short enough and provide a long enough recovery period to keep animals from overgrazing plants. When things are growing slow, they need a long recovery period. When things are growing fast, it can be shorter."

"Yes. The recovery period depends on the growth rate," the teacher said. "Too short a recovery period is the biggest mistake people make in grazing management, especially in arid environments."

"Okay, then we need short graze periods to support good animal performance," Wayne said.

"That's right," the teacher said. "You want the shortest graze period possible consistent with the required rest. The key is the number of paddocks per herd. We generally need at least 15 or 16 paddocks per herd to support good performance."

"Okay, then we want the highest stock density we can get," Wayne said. "That improves the uniformity of use in a pasture and the overall quality of the pasture."

"Right," the teacher said.

"Is that it?" Wayne asked. "Is there anything else to cell grazing?"

"There are two more things," the teacher said. "Roger, can you think of one of them?"

"It's been a long time since the class, let me think ..." Roger looked up as though the answer was somewhere in the air just above his head. "Get the rest the plants need, use short graze periods for good animal performance, use high stock density for the pasture ... okay, this is a big one, match the stocking rate to the carrying capacity."

When Roger saw the blank look on Wayne's face, he explained, "Carrying capacity is the total amount of feed you grow, right? Stocking rate is the amount you take. All this principle says is don't take more than what's there. Match the demand to the supply. The problem is that the carrying capacity changes year to year. In a drought year you have a lot less feed than in a good year. So, you need to create an enterprise mix that is compatible with the drought risk. That's been huge for us. That's why we have a keeper herd and a disposable herd. Our keeper herd is our cow herd. The disposable herd, that's our stockers program. If we pass a date by which we know we're in trouble, those stockers hit the road! They're gone!"

Dan continued, "Of course the carrying capacity changes seasonally too. It keeps increasing through the growing season and going down through the dormant season. It really helps when you sync the production schedule of those enterprises to match the forage cycle."

"That assumes that you have the right enterprises for the environment," Roger added. "It won't do any good to have cows calving when the deer have their fawns if you've got snow up to your eyeballs for four months of the year. If that's the case maybe you shouldn't have cows."

"Or maybe your cows need to migrate," Dan suggested. "Deer migrate. Sometimes, in some places, cows ought to migrate too."

"Migrate in an 18-wheeler," Joe quipped.

"Okay, match the stocking rate to the carrying capacity," Wayne summarized. "Match the demand to the supply annually and seasonally. That makes sense. But there's one more?"

"Herd effect," Steve said. "The other principle has to do with creating herd effect."

"Herd effect?" Wayne asked.

"Cattle trails are created by animal hooves, right?" Becky asked. "A few animals every day, day after day after day. What if we had five cows in a paddock for 100 days? The stocking rate would be 500 cow days. But, with five cows for 100 days, we'd probably get some trailing right?"

Wayne nodded.

"Now let's take those same 500 cow days but let's say we do it with 500 cows for one day," Becky said. "Do you think it will have the same effect?"

"Isn't that just changing the stock density?" Wayne didn't understand the difference.

"It did increase the stock density, but just increasing stock density won't create herd effect," Becky said. "Take those 500 cows for 10 minutes and stampede them. What'll the ground look like after that?"

"Not like that cattle trail, that's for sure," Wayne acknowledged.

"It'll probably knock down weeds and old rank grass. It may break the soil surface if it's crusted and capped. High stock density alone won't do that. You do that by having big herds and then creating excited behavior," Becky explained.

"It sounds like something I'd want to do with my neighbor's cattle," Wayne joked.

"You don't have to stress animals to get excited behavior," Dan explained. "It could be the impact around a salt block or a protein tub. On Daisy Creek we never put salt in the same place twice. We always put it in a patch of weeds or someplace where we want to jump-start succession."

"We actually use herd effect quite a bit," Roger added. He described how they had put a couple of old, weathered hay bales in an eroding gully near their headquarters. "We did it on the last day of the graze period, when the cows were just a little hungrier than they might be on the first day."

"We put a little molasses on it to make it a little more palatable, remember?" Dan said.

"That's right. Anyway, we had 400 cows, maybe more, going after those two bales. That was fun to watch. I don't know if they smelled the molasses or what, but they sure knocked the heck out of that gully. Sloped it back nice and left enough hay on the surface to protect the soil. Of course, you have to pick your timing on something like that. You do it at the wrong time of year and it could make it worse."

"And you don't need it everywhere every year," Dan explained. "You pick your spots and you pick your time, but it can be a useful tool."

"And the rule is?" Wayne asked.

"The principle is, use the largest herd possible, consistent with good husbandry," the teacher said. "You can't achieve the same impact with a small group as you can with a big herd."

"How big a herd is too big?" Wayne asked.

"You're going to get my favorite answer on that one," said the teacher. "Everyone?"

"It depends," they all groaned, rolling their eyes.

The teacher smiled. "Right, it depends. It depends on the class of animals, your carrying capacity, your facilities, your stockmanship. Roger, what's your thinking about herd size?"

"It'd be better to ask Jack, but we run herds of 600 to 800 cows without an issue. We've been running 1,500 stockers in one group lately. Once we get the water fixed up at Little Bear Butte, we're planning to increase the herd to 2,000."

"In one herd?" Wayne asked.

"We've got some alumni who run 5,000 to 6,000 stockers in a herd," the teacher explained. "They move the herd two or three times a day. If you have the watering capacity and are a good enough stockman to handle a herd that size, it makes a lot of sense. I wouldn't have recommended building a herd that big, but it seems to be working for them. They've sure stretched my thinking about herd size."

"I've got one more question," Wayne said.

"Fire away."

"You all talk about paddocks and pastures. What's the difference? And cells? What's the difference between a paddock and a cell?"

"Sure, good question." The teacher explained, "Technically pasture is a crop, like corn is a crop or alfalfa is a crop. With alfalfa or corn, the area where you grow the crop is a field. We talk about an alfalfa *field* or a *field* of corn. The area where the crop of pasture is grown is called a paddock. You could say a field of pasture, but we say a paddock of pasture. So, a paddock is just an area of pasture. Most people use pasture and paddock interchangeably to describe that unit. Technically, paddock is the correct term, but it doesn't really matter. A cell is a group of paddocks managed as a unit."

As the pickup slowed down, the teacher said, "Good timing. Looks like we're here."

SUMMARY OF CHAPTER 14
CONCEPTS

- Overstocking occurs when grazing demand is greater than the forage supply.

- Overgrazing is grazing a plant before it has recovered from the previous grazing.

- Many rangelands are understocked and overgrazed.

- There are two ways to overgraze:
  1. Stay in a paddock too long (too long a graze period).
  2. Return to the paddock too soon (too short a recovery period).

- Overgrazing and over-rest can occur in the same paddock.

- Not giving plants enough time to recover after grazing is the biggest problem in grazing management.

- Short graze periods improve animal performance.

- Eight to 10 paddocks can stop overgrazing. It generally takes 14 to 16 paddocks per herd to support good livestock performance. It usually takes 25 or more paddocks to see rapid range improvement.

- In some situations, herding is a practical alternative to fencing to implement cell grazing.

- High stock density improves uniformity of use and pasture quality.

- Match the stocking rate to the carrying capacity (match the grazing demand to the forage supply).

- Herd effect is concentrated animal impact and can be used to jump-start succession.

- Herd effect is not something that should be used in every paddock every time it is grazed.

- Use the largest herd consistent with good husbandry.

- Cell grazing is NOT rotational grazing.

Chapter 15
Stop Two: Building a Grazing Cell

They pulled up on a flat where Chris had built a two-wire high tensile electric fence. Fiberglass rods, about an inch in diameter, served as line posts about 50 feet apart. Chris unrolled a map and laid it on the ground. He put rocks at the corners to hold it down.

"You probably can't see this very well," he said, pointing to the map, "but this is the layout we were thinking of for our cell. We are trying to get up to 16 paddocks here and thought we could do that by putting in a center right here." His gesture indicated that the center would be somewhere around where they were standing.

Turning back to the map he pointed to a spot about two miles away and said, "We'll put another center over here. We'd probably make eight paddocks coming off each center. We thought we'd use two wire fences like the one we have here, and we'll need to put water in the cell center."

Wayne was standing in the back listening. He thought he knew what Chris meant by "a center" until he said he was planning to have two of them. *A thing only has one center*, he thought.

Dan leaned over and whispered in Wayne's ear, "You know what he means by a center?"

"I'm not sure."

"A center is just a place where several paddocks meet," Dan explained. "At Daisy Creek we call 'em hubs. It's like a tiny corral, 'cept you'd never work animals in there. It's too small."

Wayne didn't want to miss the discussion, but he was interested in what Dan had to say about cells. He probably had more hands-on experience running a cell than anyone here, even the teacher.

"Here I'll show you." They stepped back from the group as Dan pulled a small notebook out of his shirt pocket and drew what looked a little like a wagon wheel.

"You don't want to get too many paddocks radiating out of a center, 'cause the approaches would be too narrow," Dan said. "That messes with distribution and you start getting trailing. You never move 'em through the center, or hardly ever anyway. It's too crowded and it messes with the flow. When cows coming in on one side see the cows going out on the other side, the cows coming in turn around. It's better to move them through a gate a long way from the center."

Dan figured he'd better get back to listening to what was going on, so he concluded with, "If there isn't water out in the paddocks, piping water to a center is an efficient way to provide water to all of 'em. But if you make a center too big, you'll get a lot of loafing. You want the poop on the pasture, not in the center. Five yards out from the water trough is what we make 'em. Just big enough for an animal to walk behind another when it's getting a drink, or to drive a rig around."

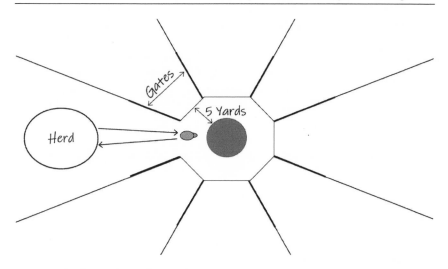

"What happens when they all come in to water?" Wayne asked.

"If you are managing things right, they won't. They'll come in a few at a time and go back out. All day long a few come in and then go right back out. If big bunches are all coming in together or hanging around the center you are either overstocked, you don't have enough flow to the tank, or they're under some kind of stress. Something screwy is going on."

"Thanks," Wayne said. They both stepped back to the group where Chris was talking about the cost of water development and fencing.

"Chris, do you really think 16 paddocks and two water points is enough?" Joe asked. That sparked a lively discussion as they drew alternative designs on the flip chart.

Wrapping things up, Chris said, "Originally we intended to start the project this summer, but I missed the deadline on the cost-share, so we're going to delay the project to next year."

"Chris, do you mind if I ask a question?" the teacher asked.

"Sure."

The teacher turned toward the group and asked, "What do you think about that? What do you think about waiting a year to get on with this project because of the cost-share that will be available?"

"We aren't really waiting. We're going to use polywire for now," Chris said a little defensively.

"Right, how do you feel about that?" the teacher asked the group.

Wayne kept quiet. He wasn't a fan of government handouts, but thought if they're going to give you free money, why not take it?

Dan was the first to speak up. "Polywire is fine for splitting paddocks, but as far as line fences, I'm not a fan. There's a reason it's called *temporary* electric fencing. You're already working your butts off and now you're planning on adding *more* labor to the operation? I wouldn't do it. Besides, what good will having more paddocks do until you fix the water?"

"That's a fair point." Chris knew that water was the limiting factor in managing this area.

Jack said, "It seems to me that getting the hay out, changing the calving season, and cell grazing aren't three different changes, they're all part of the same change. You can't reduce the need for hay until you change the production schedule, but you can't change the production schedule and get the hay out until you have the grazing program to stockpile and ration grass. And whether you use polywire or build a permanent fence, getting the grazing program going is dependent on improving the water system. Do I have that right?"

Chris nodded.

"How much free money do you stand to get?" Jack asked.

"It's a 50% cost-share. The total project will be about $80,000, so the cost-share is about $40,000."

"Once you get the water in so that you can do the fencing, how much will you increase your stocking rate? I mean the first year. How many more cows could you carry right away?" Jack asked.

"It depends on whether we get some decent rain, but we figure that just by increasing the stock density and improving the distribution, we can increase it by at least 20%. That'd be 60 more cows."

"And if you don't mind my asking," Jack continued, "what's the gross margin on your cows?"

"I don't mind. Of course, it depends on prices, but we've conservatively projected $500 per cow with the changes we're making."

Jack did the math out loud. "Gross margin per cow is $500. Times 60 cows, that's $30,000 additional gross margin." Then he asked, "Over the next several years, how much do you expect carrying capacity to increase?"

"We think, conservatively, it could go up another 50%, probably even more," said Chris.

"That's in addition to the 20% this year?" Jack asked.

Chris nodded.

Jack did the math in his head. "So that's a total of 240 more cows," he said. "With a gross margin of $500 per cow, that's $120,000 additional profit, assuming it won't increase your overheads. Do I have that right?"

"We'd also improve the gross margin on the cows we already have by about $100,000. And it doesn't include the changes in our overheads," Kate said. "Without haying, the overheads go way down."

"Sounds like it's going to make a difference of at least $200,000 and maybe closer to $300,000," Jack reasoned. "If that's the case, then isn't delaying the project one year going to cost you at least $200,000? If it takes you another year to get to that $200,000, you'll have one less year of making $200,000. It seems to me that waiting for that free money is going to be awfully expensive."

"I see what you mean," Chris answered tentatively. He had convinced himself that he had to put off developing the cell. Going slow felt more comfortable than rushing into things. "I'm not sure I'm going to have the time."

"If you bring someone else in to put up the hay you'll have time," Vince said.

"Are you thinking about this as the worker who's going to build the fence, or as the business owner who needs the fence built?" Roger asked. "Just because you need it built doesn't mean *you* have to build it."

"You could bring a crew in to build the fence," Vince said.

"Yeah, but ..." Chris couldn't think of anything to add.

"Are you really going to stand there and tell us you don't have time to make $200,000 profit for another year?" Kevin asked. "It looks like low-hanging fruit to me."

"Maybe it is." Chris looked at Kate. This is one of the things they loved and hated about their board. They asked hard questions and challenged them on everything.

Kate, who'd been assuming this would be next year's project, spoke up. "What about the 100% return rule? This doesn't give us a 100% return on our money this year.

Wayne asked, "What's the 100% return rule?"

"It's a guideline that challenges you to demand a 100% return on any capital you invest in an improvement, within a year of your investment," Joe explained. "It's simple, Kate. Put in $20,000 or $30,000 of your money and borrow the rest. Could you put up $30,000 and finance the balance?

"Probably," Kate said reluctantly.

"Well, there you go. That $30,000 gross margin gives you a 100% return on your $30,000 capital investment this year," Joe said.

"And you can probably cheapen up the project a little," Jack said. "I don't want to get too operational here, but I don't think you need two wires on these fences. We use one-wire fences in similar country."

The teacher looked at Chris and Kate. "Where's your resistance coming from?"

Kate's stress had been building as the conversation went on. She had been thinking about all the other changes they were making and how busy they already were. She'd grown comfortable with the idea that this was next year's project and didn't want to add another major project to their to-do list.

"We're already changing so much, and we're already so busy," said Kate. "We'd been focused on the other changes this year. Like Chris said, we figured that we could do what we needed here with polywire for a year."

"That would help us figure out where we ought to put the fences too," Chris added.

Jack shook his head. "You're doing a lot here. But I think you might be kidding yourselves. Sure, putting up and taking down a temporary electric fence is less work than building a fence like this," Jack said, pointing to the two-wire high tensile fence they were standing next to, "but combine that time with the time you'll save by getting off the tractor this summer and you'd have your cell done."

Jack let that soak in, then said, "As far as planning, Chris, we've made about every mistake you can make. If you want, Dan and I can go over the layout with you and share some of the lessons we've learned."

"The hard way," Dan said. "It's kind of fun to mark up a map with fences that I don't have to build."

"We can also put you on to the crew that's doing the trenching for a pipeline project for us," Jack offered. "And we can put you in touch with a couple of guys who can help do the fencing. We've had them do some work for us. They're very good."

Chris and Kate felt overwhelmed with adding this project to their already busy summer. When they didn't respond to Jack's offer, Lynda stepped in, "Look Kate, Chris, I know it'd be more comfortable if we all stood around and agreed with you, and you probably want to kick our butts right now, but we want you to make some money and we don't see the advantage in waiting to do it."

"I hear you," Chris said. "We're going to need a night to sleep on it."

"Fair enough," said Lynda.

SUMMARY OF CHAPTER 15
CONCEPTS

- Cell centers should be small to discourage loafing.
- Free money can be expensive.
- Do not let free money drive your decisions on capital investments and range improvement.
- Demand a 100% return on your capital.

Chapter 16
Nutrition, Reproduction, and the Calving Season

Once they were back in the truck, the teacher asked Wayne if he had any questions about anything they had talked about.

"I have some questions about stockpiling," Wayne said. "To stockpile feed, do you leave a pasture ungrazed during the growing season? And what about the quality? That stockpiled grass isn't going to be very palatable or nutritious. How do you manage that?"

"Dan, you want to tackle this?" the teacher asked.

"Sure. There's some people who leave pastures for winter grazing and don't touch them in the spring, but that's not the way we usually do it," Dan said. "We figure you got to graze it up before you can graze it down."

There was that phrase again. "Graze it up?" Wayne asked.

"Yeah. By graze it up I mean you don't come in and hammer it during the growing season. You leave lots of leaves. You take a little." Dan lowered his outstretched hand to about a foot above the bed of the truck. "Grazing lightly can delay the grass from heading out and can stimulate tillering. I think it improves the quality of the grass you have in your stockpile. Then, in the dormant season, you graze it down." Dan lowered his hand to about six inches from the bed. "You don't need to leave as many leaves. We leave enough to cover the soil. That's one of our goals, not to have any bare soil."

"And the quality?" Wayne asked.

"Hopefully, you've timed the production schedule so that you're using your stockpiled feed when the animals' nutritional requirements are low," Dan said. "You also have to know if you're feeding the cows or feeding the bugs."

"You mean the rumen microbes?" Wayne asked.

"Yep. That older grass, it's still got plenty of energy. Just put a match to it and it'll burn. There's energy in there, it's just hard for the bugs to get at it once its lignified," Dan said.

175

Dan explained that lignin is a substance that thickens the cell wall as the plants mature. "When the lignin content goes up, digestibility and the protein go down. The limiting factor is protein. The bugs need more protein to get the energy in that lignified grass."

Dan explained that there are two types of dietary protein, degradable protein and bypass protein. Degradable protein is broken down by rumen microbes. Bypass protein is not degraded by rumen microbes and is broken down farther down the digestive tract.

"Think of it this way," Dan said, "degradable protein feeds the bugs. Bypass protein bypasses the bugs and feeds the cow. If you have a cow standing belly deep in lignified grass, starving to death, what do you need to do?"

"I need to feed the bugs protein," Wayne said. "I need to feed them degradable protein."

"Right! That usually means using a supplement that is high in NPN, non-protein nitrogen," Dan explained. "But whether it's NPN or something else, they need degradable protein.

"And there's times when nature puts out a protein tub herself," Dan said. "When you have green grass under the stockpiled grass, that new growth might provide enough protein to help the bugs get the energy out of the stockpiled feed. Bottom line: to use old lignified grass the bugs might need a little degradable protein ... something high in NPN, probably. Spending a few pennies per head per day on the right supplement can add a lot of dollars to your gross margin."

"We provide some mineral and a protein tub in the fall, but I guess I don't really know what's in it," Wayne said. "It's not like we have a lot of stockpiled feed to go to. Then in the winter we supplement with hay."

"That's not supplementation. That's substitution," Joe said.

"Feeding hay isn't supplementation?" Wayne asked.

"No, it's not," the teacher said. "Supplementation makes up for deficiencies in *quality*. Substitution makes up for a lack of *quantity*. What Dan was talking about was feeding the microbes protein when forage quality is low. That's supplementation. People feed hay when there's no grass left or it's unavailable. That's substitution."

"I like the way you put it at the school," Dan said. "You told us that supplementation improves gross margin and substitution makes it real hard to make a profit."

Wayne had never distinguished between supplementation and substitution, but he thought it made sense.

"I've heard people say that this kind of grazing might increase production per acre, but it'll hurt individual animal performance. Is there anything to that?" Wayne asked. "Do most of the performance issues go back to problems with nutrition?"

"Most of the people who say that aren't talking about this kind of grazing. They're talking about rotational grazing and they don't have enough paddocks to keep the graze periods short and give plants the rest they need," Dan said. "If you have your act together with the grazing principles and provide a little degradable protein when the cows are grazing lignified grass, you really shouldn't have performance problems. If there are still performance issues in a cow herd, it either boils down to some kind of stress or one of the Wiltbank principles."

"The Wiltbank principles, what are those?" Wayne asked.

The teacher explained that Jim Wiltbank was an animal science professor who identified six keys to good reproductive performance in a cow herd. "They've survived the test of time. At Ranching For Profit we call them the Wiltbank principles. Dan, you've implemented these haven't you?"

"Sure have. They've been huge for us."

"How about explaining them?" the teacher asked.

"Sure thing. The first principle is to use a 60-day breeding season," Dan said. "Most people figure that's mostly to get a uniform calf crop, but the bigger impact for us was to get all the cows in about the same physiological stage at the same time. Used to be we'd have cows that weren't going to calve for another two months, some that had just calved, and others that calved two months ago. We'd try to meet the nutritional needs of the animals with the highest requirement and wound up wasting a lot of supplement and money on animals that didn't need it. Shortening the breeding season helped us meet the herd's nutritional needs more efficiently."

"Wiltbank talked about shortening the breeding season. It actually might be more useful to think about shortening the calving season," the teacher said. "You could keep the bulls in as long as you want to get all the cows pregnant. Then sell any cows that got bred late. They'll fit someone's program somewhere, and it'd add some value to your culls."

"Either way, the idea is to tighten things up to make supplementation more efficient," Dan said. "The second principle is to have cows in body condition five at calving. Condition at calving is the single biggest factor affecting her ability to re-breed on schedule.

"The third principle is to have cows gaining weight two weeks prior to breeding. If she's gaining weight, she's getting enough energy to be able to cycle and breed.

"Next is 48-hour temporary calf removal. Almost couldn't remember it because we don't do it anymore. There was a time when we had a lot of late-calving cows. By removing the calves when we turned in the bulls and keeping them from suckling for 48 hours, we got the cows to cycle a couple of weeks before they would have if we'd left the calves with them. Of course, if a cow has just had her calf and is deep in her post-partum anestrous period, this won't help. But for animals that are about to cycle, it's gold — provided you have the facilities and you're a decent stockman."

"I'd think that'd be awfully stressful. What kind of hit did you take on calf performance?" Wayne asked.

"Forty-eight hours after pulling the calves, we'd put 'em back in," Dan said. "They'd mother up immediately. We don't think there was any loss in performance. If there was, it was too small to measure. What we could measure was the number of late-calving cows that we used to have. That cost us big time until we started doing this. I'm confident that 48-hour temporary calf removal was a very useful tool, given the problem we had.

"Wiltbank's fifth principle is a no-brainer. It's fertility testing bulls. It doesn't take but one dominant bull throwing blanks to cost you a ton of money.

"The sixth principle is to use well grown replacements. You breed a heifer and she probably gets pregnant. But then she's an H2. She's trying to nurse a calf, she's still growing, and you want her to breed. That's a lot to ask of her. If she wasn't mature enough when she was first bred as an H1, odds are she won't breed back, or she'll breed back late, so even if she does get pregnant and have a calf this year, she's likely to miss next year.

"This doesn't mean growing heifers in a feed lot. We treat our H1s the same way we treat our stockers. In fact, if she's open she just becomes part of our stocker program. But from the point she's an H2, she does get a little extra TLC."

Wayne had been listening intently. "Let me see if I've got them," he said. "The six Wiltbank principles are:

1. 60-day breeding season
2. Cows in body condition five at calving
3. Cows gaining weight two weeks before breeding
4. 48-hour temporary calf removal
5. Fertility test the bulls
6. Use well grown replacements

"You've got a good memory," the teacher said.

"Thanks. It may be good, but it's real short," Wayne laughed.

A moment later Wayne asked, "These are mostly about nutrition, aren't they? I mean, the primary goal of shortening the breeding season to 60 days is to make the herd's nutritional requirement more uniform. Having cows in body condition five at calving is dependent on nutrition. So is making sure they are gaining weight prior to breeding and using well grown replacements. Even a breeding soundness exam on the bulls takes their body condition into account. Five out of six of these have at least something to do with nutrition."

"That's a good observation," said the teacher. "That's why syncing an animal's nutritional needs with the forage cycle is so important. Nature will provide nearly all of what an animal needs if you let her."

"I can't help but shake my head when I see what most people do," Dan said. "They are completely out of sync with nature. They time the animal's highest need to when the grass is at its absolute worst. That's crazy, but that's what we used to do too." Dan shook his head, adding, "Truth be known, when Roger and Jack told me that we were going to change the calving season I thought they'd lost their minds. Now I think it's everyone else who's crazy."

Wayne hoped no one would ask him when he was calving.

"They aren't crazy, at least not most of them, and they aren't stupid either," said the teacher. "They've just never looked at it ecologically or economically."

Wayne was puzzled. "If they aren't looking at the ecology or money, then what are they looking at?" he asked.

Joe, Lynda, Dan, Steve, Becky, and Roger simultaneously answered, "Production."

Dan continued, "Most people only focus on production. It's what the magazines and salesmen try to sell us. It's what the universities promote."

"And it's a big problem!" Roger said. "I was as bad as the next guy. We focused on getting high conception rates, high weaning rates, weaning big calves, and we were losing our shirts." Looking at Wayne he pointed at the teacher and said, "I remember when I took the school, over 25 years ago now, and he said something about hitting the bull's-eye but aiming at the wrong target. Man, that sure described us. We had the most productive cows and biggest calves around and were making huge losses. We were hitting the productivity bull's-eye, but we should have been aiming at profit, not production."

"But you have to be productive to be profitable," Wayne protested.

"Wayne," the teacher said, "in all my years of looking at ranches, I have yet to see the ranch with the most productive cows be the most profitable. And sometimes they are among the least profitable."

"That sure described us," Roger confessed.

Dan added, "The question isn't how high can you get your conception rates or how big a calf can you wean. The question is, what conception rate or what weaning rate and weight will result in the biggest profit? Once we started asking the right question, everything started falling into place. Everything."

"I guess one of the questions for us is, 'When should we be calving?'" Wayne said.

"Maybe, but that's *not* the first question," the teacher said. "Before you start thinking about when your cows ought to calve you really ought to ask if you should have cows in the first place, and if you should have cows, should they be *your* cows. It doesn't much matter when you calve if you shouldn't have cows. You need to look at what enterprises best fit your environment before you start thinking about the best production schedule for those enterprises. You need to consider markets and weather risk. You need something that gives you flexibility to destock quickly if you get into a drought. Maybe it ought to be completely seasonal with stockers or custom cattle. There are a lot of things to consider in determining the best enterprises and the best production schedule for those enterprises.

"The numbers will tell you what will work and what won't. Calculating enterprise gross margins and determining the impact on overheads, that's how you find what will work for your operation," he said.

"But a lot of people who come through your program wind up changing the calving season, don't they?" Wayne asked.

"Some do. If you want to get the hay out of the operation it's something folks probably ought to consider — that or getting rid of the cows altogether and going to seasonal enterprises. But other folks don't need to change when they calve. It's either a twig relative to other issues or its fine where it is. If you shifted to later calving and would still have to feed a lot of hay, it probably won't be a profitable strategy. The numbers will tell you if it's a smart move."

"I know that Chris and Kate are changing their calving season," Wayne said. "What's the best way to do that? Is it best to move it a couple of weeks each year until you get where you want to go or transition your cows all at once?"

"Nearly everyone who has changed to calving with nature will tell you they are glad they did it," the teacher said, "but most of them aren't happy with the *way* they did it. Roger, you want to tell them about your experience with this?"

"No!" Roger laughed. "It was too painful! We're like all the folks he just described," Roger said nodding to the teacher. "We'd never go back to calving when we used to, but we made the transition about as poorly as anyone could make it. We went two weeks later the first year, another two the next year, then another two."

"What was wrong with that?" Wayne asked.

"By shifting by just two weeks each year we still had all the costs of the old way and none of the advantages of the new way. It was an expensive lesson — a lesson that took us three years to learn."

"The other thing we did wrong was make the transition with our own cows," Dan said. "We figured we had good cows, and we did, for calving when we did. That's what they'd been selected for. But they weren't good cows for calving later. They were too big and milked too heavy. Breed up was bad. A lot of them volunteered to get on the truck and leave our herd!"

"Dan's right," Roger said. "And a late-calving cow is worth several hundred dollars less than an early-calving cow. Depreciation killed us. We took a half million dollar hit on depreciation alone!"

"How would you do it if you had it to do over?" Wayne asked, hoping he wasn't rubbing salt in the wound.

"All at once. I'd have a dispersal sale. I'd advertise our good set of early-calving cows and get top dollar for them," Roger said, looking directly at Wayne. "Then I'd either buy the kind of heifers I thought would work in our new program or buy everyone else's late-calving cows and let them shake out."

"That's pretty much the story you'll hear from a lot of folks who've made the transition," the teacher said. "Figure out where you need to get and then get there!" He shook his head, "Most people want to implement change slowly. It's like you're drowning in the middle of the ocean and a boat comes by. Would you say, 'Take your time with that life preserver'? I don't think so. You need it now! Most folks, most of the time, would be better off figuring out where they need to be and then getting there as soon as they can."

"And how," Roger agreed.

SUMMARY OF CHAPTER 16
CONCEPTS

- If you intend to graze livestock year-round, you may need to graze pastures up before you graze them down.

- Replacing hay by grazing stockpiled forage works best when animal nutritional requirements are low.

- As grass matures and lignifies, the energy in the grass becomes less available.

- There are two types of dietary protein, degradable and bypass.

- Degradable protein feeds the microbes. Bypass protein feeds the cow.

- Supplementation with degradable protein helps the microbes digest more of the energy in lignified feed.

- Supplementation makes up for deficiencies in quality. Substitution makes up for deficiencies in quantity. (Feeding hay is substitute feeding.)

- Proper supplementation improves gross margin per unit.

- Substitute feeding decreases profit.

- The six Wiltbank principles are:
  - 60-day breeding season
  - Cows in body condition five at calving
  - Cows gaining weight two weeks prior to breeding
  - 48-hour temporary calf removal
  - Use fertility-tested bulls
  - Use well grown replacements

- Calving with nature is a profitable strategy for many producers, but it is NOT the right strategy for every ranch.

- One consideration in creating the ideal enterprise mix for your ranch is your drought destocking policy.

- The ideal production schedule isn't just a biological question, it's an economic question.

- The transition to a new production schedule should not be phased in. It should usually be done as quickly as possible.

Chapter 17
Last Stop: The Transect

Wayne stood in the bed of the truck looking around as the others started climbing down. He wondered what was so special about this site. *Why did we stop here?*

"The teacher helped us set up our first transect yesterday evening. We thought we'd put a second one here," Kate told the group.

"Why here?" Wayne asked.

"Good question," Kate said. "The transect we put in yesterday is in a place with lots of weeds and bare, capped soil. We want to see what effect the changes we are making has on some of our worst ground. But we also want to monitor a site that's more representative of the whole ranch. We're putting one here because this is pretty typical of about half the ranch." She looked at the teacher and asked, "You want to show us how it's done?"

"Glad to. People who start cell grazing often tell me that they're seeing fantastic results. They say they're seeing grasses they never saw before. The problem is they may never have looked before. To know if things are really changing, we need to create a baseline from which we can measure that change."

Roger said, "I remember at the school you described the differences between a grassman and a cattleman. One that stuck with me is that cattlemen look *across* the land — they have to, to see their cattle. Grassmen look down into the land. Once I started looking down, I began to see things I never noticed before."

"And did you set up some photo points?" Chris asked.

"You bet. We've got at least two transects in each cell."

"You didn't happen to bring any pictures with you, did you?" Chris asked.

"No, I sure didn't," Roger admitted, shaking his head. "Should have. They show some dramatic changes. The key to documenting changes is to put the transect in a place that you can find each year. You want to take those pictures in the same place each year."

"That's right," the teacher agreed. "You've got to look down at *exactly* the same spot each year."

He pulled a long measuring tape and some fiberglass posts out of the back of the truck and demonstrated how to install a transect. In less than 15 minutes the 200-foot-long transect with four plots was installed.[1]

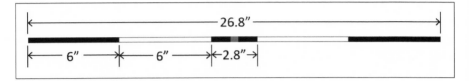

"Reading a transect is simple," the teacher said. "It starts with having a frame of reference. Literally!" The teacher held up a short 3/8-inch-diameter fiberglass rod. "I cut this 27-inch piece off a post Chris and Kate use with their temporary electric fence. Actually, it's precisely 26.8 inches. I wrapped black electrician's tape around the first 6 inches of either end. I left the next six inches bare and then I wrapped another piece of electrician's tape in the center. I like to put a piece of red tape in the middle of the rod, just so it's easy to know where dead center is. I use four of these sticks to make a plot frame. That's my frame of reference.

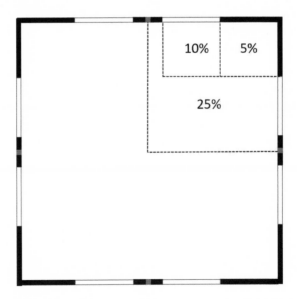

---

1 The procedure for installing a transect is provided in Appendix 1.

"When I walk around looking at ground like this, it's hard to say with any precision what's really going on. In some areas there's 10% bare soil. In others it's more like 80% bare." He laid the four sticks down on the ground, forming a square.

He pointed to one of the corners of the frame wrapped with black tape and explained that the six-inch square was 5% of the area in the whole frame.

"As I look at this, I ask myself, would all the bare soil in this frame fit into this corner? If not, what about twice this area?" He moved his hand down to the end of the first untaped six inches of the rod. "This is six inches by 12 inches. That's 10% of the whole frame. I think there's too much bare soil here to fit in that area. What about 25% of the frame?" He pointed from the red band at the center on one side to the center of an adjacent side. "I think that's pretty close. I'd call this 25% bare soil. Using the rods this way makes it much easier to come up with accurate estimates.

"When I'm out on ground like this, I like to take these rods and make some random plots." He tossed a rod, walked to it, and positioned the other three rods to make a square. "I'll toss a rod, make a frame and take a look. Then I'll toss it again, make another frame and take a look at that. I might not look at it for more than 10 seconds. By then I'll see what I need to see. I'll do this three or four, maybe even five or six times in an area to get a sense of what's happening."

The teacher then showed the group how to place the frames on the transect line so they could take pictures of exactly the same spot every year.[1] "Six inches this way or that way won't do," he said. "It's got to be exactly the same spot." He used his cell phone to take two pictures of the plot frame, one looking across the frame and the other looking straight down over the top of it.

"You can't evaluate range health through a windshield. Looking across the land gives us a distorted picture of what's really going on. We need to get out of the truck and look down *into* the range. Remember, boots on the ground, eyes looking down!"

Kneeling at the plot frame where he had taken the pictures, the teacher explained that a transect can help in the evaluation of several important indicators. He encouraged the group to pay particular

---

1 The procedure for taking transect pictures is provided in Appendix 2.

attention to the percent bare soil and the percent basal cover of perennial grass plants.

"Cover!" he stressed. "We want 100% cover. It doesn't matter if you have six inches of rain or 60. The goal is 100% cover. No bare soil."

"What about environments where it isn't possible to have 100% cover?" Steve asked.

"That's still the goal," the teacher said. "I'm not sure very many of us know what's possible. Most of our pastures and rangelands have been overgrazed for more than a hundred years. Most ranchers have never seen their land in really healthy condition. They've never seen what really good management can achieve. There may be places where 100% cover isn't possible, but I hope none of you will assume it's not possible on your place.

"It's not enough to look at canopy cover. Canopy cover is important. That's what captures sunlight energy. But when we talk about soil cover, we are talking about cover that is in direct contact with the soil.

"The flip side of soil cover is bare soil. That's what we're going to measure. We need to look past the canopy and estimate the amount of bare soil," he said, parting the leaves of grass plants in the plot frame. "Estimate the area that isn't covered by something in direct contact with the soil, living or dead, upright or laid over, pre-grazed," he pointed to some grass, "or post-grazed," he pointed to a cow pie. "What percentage of bare soil do you think we have here? Don't say anything — write it down."

Two or three at a time they knelt at the plot frame. No one took more than 10 seconds. As they made their estimates, the teacher explained that bare soil is the enemy. Bare soil leads to capping, runoff, compaction, lower productivity, and weeds.

Wayne reasoned that if he put all the bare soil in the frame in one corner it would fill up more than a quarter but less than half of the area. He wrote 35 on the palm of his hand.

"Let's see what you came up with. Show me your estimates," the teacher said. A few people guessed 30%. A few had guessed 40%, but most guessed 35%.

"We are pretty close to one another. Nice job. Do you see why it's helpful to have this frame of reference?"

They went through the same process to estimate the basal cover of perennial grass plants. As they each made their estimates, the teacher explained that there is a direct correlation between basal cover of perennial grasses and the health and productivity of the range.

"This is a very stable and meaningful indicator. If the basal cover of perennial grass plants is increasing, you can be pretty sure things are improving. If it's going down, it's a red flag."

The teacher explained that taking the photo points and estimating the percent bare soil and basal cover of perennial grasses at all four plots on the transect takes less than 30 minutes once a year.

"It usually takes more time to get to the transect than it does to read it. Once you're there, if you can spare a few more minutes, there are some other things you might want to look at."

He listed four things:
1. Soil health and the water cycle
2. Soil health and the mineral cycle
3. Energy flow
4. Community and biodiversity

He asked the group to form into four teams. He handed a laminated card to each team. "This is your score card.[1] It has guidelines for evaluating each ecological process. I'd like each team to go to one of the plot frames on the transect and evaluate either the water cycle,

---

1 The ecosystem health scoring criteria are provided in Appendix 3.

mineral cycle, energy flow or biodiversity at the site. Give it a score from one to 10 using the criteria on the card. That should take about five minutes. We'll discuss it when you're done."

Each team picked a process to evaluate and went to one of the plots on the transect. When they finished their evaluations, they gathered around the teacher to share their conclusions.

"Let's start with soil health and the water cycle."

"That's us," Becky said. "It doesn't matter how much rain falls. What matters is what actually soaks in and is available to the plant. That's called *effective precipitation*. We think the effective precipitation here is pretty low. We're guessing that it's less than half of the total precipitation."

"Why's that?" the teacher asked.

"There's a lot of bare soil and in some places the soil is capped," Becky said.

"Sorry to interrupt, but what is capping?" Wayne asked.

"No problem," said Becky. She knelt and dug with her hand, dislodging a portion of the soil surface. Holding the soil with one hand she pointed to the soil surface with the other. It had a crust that was at least an eighth of an inch thick.

"Do you see this crust?" she asked. "This crust is what we call a cap. It makes it really hard for water to soak in. It's caused by raindrops hitting bare soil. After the rain, when the soil dries, fine particles that were loosened by the raindrops seal the surface. Over time, unless it gets disturbed, that cap becomes thicker and thicker and eventually becomes nearly impenetrable so water can't soak in."

"The herd effect we talked about a little earlier ... That's one way to break a capped soil." Dan said.

"It'd be even better to keep it from capping in the first place," Becky said. "To do that we need a lot more cover than we've got here. We also saw signs of erosion. Our overall score for the water cycle here is four out of 10. There's a lot of room for improvement."

While the teams had been evaluating the health of the site, the teacher had grabbed a shovel from the back of a truck. Once Becky reported her team's water cycle score, the teacher walked a few feet behind the plot and slammed his foot down on the back of the shovel blade, driving it into the soil. It only went three inches before hitting a compacted layer. He chipped the dry soil with the shovel until he had dug a little over a foot. He knelt to get a closer look at the soil exposed in the hole.

"A shovel is about as good a monitoring tool as there is. I like to dig a hole or two near a transect and check for roots, organic matter, earthworms, and other organisms. I want to see how hard it is to dig, how compacted things are. I want to see what kind of moisture we've got." Looking up at Chris, he asked, "When was your last good rain?"

"We had a pretty good thunderstorm a couple of nights ago," Chris said.

"Do you think much of it soaked in?" the teacher asked.

"Doesn't look like it," Chris said with disappointment.

"Don't be discouraged. This is exciting stuff." Looking at Chris, he asked, "What's the average rainfall here? 14, 15 inches? Right now the plants here are getting about half of that. Just think about what's going to happen when you capture one or two more inches. That alone will increase your carrying capacity by 30% or 40%!

"Okay, who had soil health and the mineral cycle?"

"We did," Vince said. "As you can see from the hole the teacher dug, things are pretty compacted. Roots have a hard time penetrating that compaction layer. It doesn't look like litter is breaking down very well. We see a lot of dung pats from last year. Like Becky said, there's a lot of bare soil. Considering all those things and the other criteria on the card, we scored the soil health and the mineral cycle four too."

"More exciting stuff," Chris said sarcastically.

The teacher put his hand on Chris's shoulder and said, "It will be, when you start to see improvement. You've got a lot of potential here."

Turning to the group, he asked, "Who had energy flow?"

Pat stepped up. "Energy flow starts with plants capturing energy through photosynthesis. To maximize that, we want 100% green cover for as long as possible. We feel that this site has a long way to go to reach its potential. First, as everyone else has pointed out, there's too much bare soil. The plants here are mostly short-lived annuals. There are some perennial grasses, but they have narrow, pointy leaves. We want more perennials because they stay green and capture energy longer than annuals do, but we'd rather have perennials with broad flat leaves because they photosynthesize more efficiently than the ones with narrow leaves. We scored this site a four."

"We had community and diversity," Steve said. "One of the criteria is species richness. That's a count of how many different organisms are here. We looked within a yard of the plot frame. We saw six different forbs and four different grasses. There were five different bugs. Joe murdered a mosquito. We debated whether we should knock the count down by one, but we included the murdered mosquito and stuck with five. There were some deer pellets and a cow pie, and we heard a meadow lark. That makes the species richness count 18. We thought that was okay. But the plant species weren't particularly desirable, and we didn't see many young perennial grasses coming in. Overall, we gave it a score of four. We think there's a lot of room to improve."

"Thank you for sharing your observations," the teacher said. "This has been an interesting discussion. It becomes an important discussion when we shift the focus from how things are to what we're going to do about it." Turning to Chris and Kate, he asked, "So, given what we've seen, do you think there's potential to improve the health and productivity of this community?"

"Sure," Kate answered.

"Okay. How much?" he asked, turning to the group. "What if they captured another inch or two of rain, and increased the basal cover of perennial grasses from 10% to 15% or even 20%? What if they gave paddocks time to recover after grazing? What if that shifted this community from annuals and narrow-leaved perennials to more broad-leaf perennial grasses? If there was more litter and less capping, how much could they increase the capacity?"

"It could easily double," Jack said confidently. "We started with nearly identical conditions and that's what we've been able to do."

"That seems reasonable," the teacher agreed.

"How quickly could you see results like that?" Wayne asked.

"It's one of those 'it depends' things," the teacher said. "Will there be a drought? Will you be set back by a wildfire? Will you leave enough residue? Will you have a cold, late spring or will the next growing season start early? There are too many variables to know. Jack, how long did it take on Daisy Creek?"

"We doubled within five years," Jack said, "but we had a couple of really good years in that span and we'd been understocked. That made it easy to leave leaves. The carrying capacity is still increasing. Progress is slower now, but we still don't really know just how productive it will eventually become."

"What would y'all do here to produce those results?" the teacher asked.

"You'd need to get the rest right," Joe answered.

"You'd need to be able to change the recovery period as the growth rate changed," Becky added.

"I'd want to get the density up, but I wouldn't want to leave animals in too long," Mike said.

"Assuming they've already combined herds, they'll need to make more paddocks. That'd get the graze period shorter and ensure they didn't overgraze by staying in any paddock too long," Patty said.

"They need to make sure they get the stocking rate right," Vince added. "They need to look at matching the cows' requirements with the forage cycle and have a way to match the stocking rate to the carrying capacity year to year."

"Those are all things we are starting to do," Kate said.

"That's why this is so exciting," the teacher concluded.

"And why we need to create a baseline with the transects," Chris said. "We need to document the change. It's not enough to think things are getting better. We need to know."

"There's nothing more motivating than producing positive results," the teacher said. "And if the results aren't positive, you need to know about it so you can get back on track.

"Jack, you've been monitoring range condition at Daisy Creek for years, haven't you? Any advice for those who are just starting?" the teacher asked.

"We just take pictures mostly. I'm seeing that we probably ought to be measuring bare soil and basal cover too, at the very least." He paused. "My advice? Take pictures right now *before* you make changes. We didn't take enough pictures and we regret it. Also, when we started taking pictures, we didn't do it in a way that made it easy to take them in exactly the same way at exactly the same spot every year. We do now, but we didn't when we started. I think that's really important."

"We have done it well enough to be able to document improvements," Roger said. "We can stand at a microphone and tell the world what a great job we do, but a picture's worth a thousand words. It's not enough to talk the talk, we have to show we can walk the walk, and these transects and photo points are a great way to do that."

"Teach, you might be interested in this," Joe offered. "We have a neighbor, you know him, Bobby Heart?" The teacher nodded. "Well, Bobby uses his pictures documenting the improvement on his ranch to negotiate with landowners for leases. I don't know if he's been able to pay less because of it, but he says he's gotten leases because of it. And once he gets a lease, he sets up a transect so he can document the results he's getting for the owner."

"That's a great idea," the teacher agreed. "Look, this isn't an abstract academic exercise. This is a practical tool to give you actionable management information. If you think it's important to know if you're heading in the right direction or to have an early warning system to tell you when you may be off track, you need to do this. This isn't about collecting data. Data is useless unless you take the time to analyze and act on it. Some of your most important WOTB may be done sitting on a rock, under a tree, thinking about what the data is telling you and what you're going to do about it."

"Speaking of sitting under a tree," Kate said, "it's getting hot out here. If no one has anything else, let's head back for the turn-around session and lunch."

SUMMARY OF CHAPTER 17
CONCEPTS

- To determine the trend in range health you must monitor range condition.

- You cannot evaluate range condition by looking across the land. You must look down into it — boots on the ground, eyes looking down.

- Establishing transects with photo points can help you create a baseline and monitor the trends of several key indicators.

- Pictures showing the condition and trend of the range should be taken in exactly the same place every year.

- Whether you are in a high or low rainfall zone, one goal of management should be to maintain 100% soil cover. No bare soil!

- Basal cover of perennial grass plants is an excellent indicator of range condition and trend. If the basal cover of perennial grass plants is increasing, conditions are improving.

- Effective precipitation is the moisture that soaks into the soil and is available for plant growth. Effective precipitation is more important than total precipitation.

- In an effective mineral cycle, dung pats and litter on the soil surface break down rapidly.

- 100% canopy cover of wide-leaved, green perennial grasses is a good indicator of abundant energy flow.

- Biodiversity is an important indicator of range health. In most cases, the more diversity, the healthier the community.

- Species richness is a good measure of biodiversity,

- Soil capping occurs when raindrops hit bare soil.

Chapter 18
The Turnaround

It took Wayne a second to realize that he had climbed into a different truck. Jack scooted over to make room behind the cab and cheerfully said, "Welcome aboard."

"Thanks. I guess I was so distracted thinking about how all this applies to our place that I jumped in the wrong rig," Wayne admitted.

"No worries. We're all going to the same place," Jack said.

"You going to be here tonight for the barbeque?" Wayne asked.

"Gotta go up to Little Bear Butte this afternoon, but I'll be back. Wouldn't miss it. Free food and good people. How you going to top that? What are your plans? You want to come up there with me? We've got a contractor working on a water project. I told him I'd swing by and check in. If you want to come, I'll show you our cell up there. We should be back in plenty of time for the barbeque."

Wayne was surprised by Jack's invitation. "I need to check with Lori. She was going to come straight here from work. I was going to go back and bring Buddy and the kids. I'll call Lori as soon as we get back to the house." After a pause he added, "I didn't realize before today y'all were cell grazing."

"We don't talk about it much," Jack explained. "We used to. Part of the Daisy Creek mission is about community involvement and being good neighbors, so it seemed natural to try to share what we learned with folks, to help people learn from our mistakes. Believe me, we made plenty of 'em. But I think people thought we were showing off or trying to show them up. That wasn't our intention. We were just excited about the results we were getting and wanted to share."

"What results did you get?" Wayne asked. "You talked about the increase in carrying capacity."

"Ultimately that's the big one," said Jack. "That's the money maker. But that happened because a lot of other things happened. There's a lot more cover and a lot less bare soil. We went from over 60% bare soil to, well, my guess is that if we throw a couple of plot frames down, we won't see any bare soil. We've almost tripled the carrying capacity of the Little Bear Butte unit. The biodiversity is amazing. We've seen natives come in. In fact, Meryl, at NRCS, told us she didn't even know that some of the desirables we have now grew in this area."

Jack smiled and asked, "So you're interested in cell grazing?"

Wayne nodded.

"You ought to come up. I think we made every mistake known to man. We made the cell centers too big. We had too many paddocks coming into centers. We cheated on the rest period, tried to get away with using only eight or 10 paddocks per herd and treated the whole thing like a rotation. We started splitting up the pastures we already had ..."

"What's wrong with that?" Wayne asked. "Wouldn't that be the cheapest way to go?"

"It may be cheap in the short run, but it can be more costly in the long run," Jack said. "Doubling the carrying capacity is like getting another ranch for free. You can afford to spend a little on getting the infrastructure right to make that happen.

"The problem is that the infrastructure you have now wasn't built for this kind of management. You should start from scratch. You need a clean map so you can design the cell as though there was no existing infrastructure. Then, overlay the existing fences. Use them when they match up, which they usually will, but sometimes they don't. It's funny, if you start from scratch, nearly all the existing infrastructure will wind up being usable. But if you start by splitting the pastures you already have, you'll wind up with a terrible design — at least that's what we learned, the hard way. Trying to be cheap usually turns out to be really expensive"

"And it's not like we don't still screw up. No sense in repeating our mistakes and reinventing the wheel. You should come up," Jack reiterated.

"I'd like to," Wayne said. "I'll check with Lori."

It was a little past noon when they pulled into the yard. "Turnaround in 10 minutes," Kate shouted. As people made a beeline for the bathroom, Wayne stepped aside to call Lori.

He told her that Jack had invited him to come up to Little Bear Butte.

"That's great! Go! I can swing by home to pick up Buddy and the kids. No problem."

"I'm not sure Buddy wants to go," Wayne cautioned.

"Will Roger and Danny be there?" she asked.

When Wayne said they would, she said, "He'll go."

A few minutes later, Kate hollered from the porch, "Turnaround time!"

Everyone took a seat on the porch as Kate said, "Okay, we'd like y'all to summarize your thoughts from this morning. What are we doing that you think we ought to stop doing? And what aren't we doing that you think we should be doing? We'll do our best to keep up with you." With that, Kate and Chris turned their chairs and sat with their backs facing the group. They each had a notepad and were prepared to write. Kate turned and asked, "Can someone time this?"

"I'll do it," Becky volunteered. "Ten minutes starts … now."

"I'll start," Joe said. He turned so that he was talking to the group, not Chris and Kate. "One thing they're going to do that I don't think they should do is put up hay themselves. I think they ought to contract with someone else to put it up this summer. I would figure out the best time of year to sell their equipment, polish it up nice and pretty, and then SELL IT! Chris can take some of the time he would have had his butt in a tractor seat to build the cell now. I'd probably use the money from selling the machinery to finance the cell development. That's what I'd do that they weren't planning on doing. That free money seems awfully expensive."

"I think they ought to take some of that time and take the kids camping," Dan said. "All work and no play …"

"I don't think they ought to put up hay at all," Vince said. "Forget finding a custom guy. They ought to just buy what they need. Now that they have good gross margins, they need to increase turnover. Those hay fields — excuse me, *former* hay fields — could sure help with that. Given how dry they've told us it's been around here, I'll bet they could come up with some custom cattle right now to use it."

"It's pretty short notice," Pat said.

"It's pretty dry around here too," Vince noted. "I'll bet that it would take them less than five minutes to make a list of a dozen or more people in this area who need grass right now and would be willing to pay for it. Worst case, they make a few calls and can't find someone. In that case maybe they stockpile that extra grass for this winter."

"I'm a little nervous about grazing those fields with all the alfalfa in there. I'd think bloat could be a worry," Becky said.

"That won't be a problem," Jack said. "There's plenty of grass in there. They just need to let it get a little more mature than they would if they were haying it. They shouldn't graze it too severely and should leave plenty of residue. And they shouldn't move animals to fresh paddocks first thing in the morning. They ought to move them later in the day. "

"I like the idea of getting on with developing the cell right now," Kevin said. "They have enough work to do without stringing polywire all over the place and then building the cell. Build it and be done with it. And I'd take a serious look at hiring a crew to build it."

"I'd be looking at 25 paddocks, not 16," Mike said.

"I hope they'll take us up on our offer to visit with them about their cell design," Jack added.

And so it went for another seven minutes. Idea after idea on the design and management of the cell, the calving season, evaluating range health, and what to do about the hay enterprise. The board wasn't talking to Chris and Kate, they were talking to one another *about* them. No, not about them, about their business. Chris filled up three full pages of his notepad. Kate filled up five and was working on a sixth. The only words from Chris or Kate through the whole discussion were, "Can you speak louder?" and "Please say that again."

When the buzzer sounded at 10 minutes, the teacher asked, "Any more thoughts?" There were none. "I'll add this," the teacher said. "I am impressed. Congratulations are in order for the progress they've made. They have done a lot of work creating an exciting vision and crunching the numbers on various scenarios to figure out how to achieve it. They are laying the foundation for something special here. Impressive. And I know getting ready to host a summer EL meeting is stressful. I am grateful for the work they've done in making this so easy and valuable for all of us."

"Here, here," Joe said. Everyone nodded in agreement.

The teacher turned to Chris and Kate and asked, "Now, what did you hear?"

As Chris and Kate turned their chairs back around facing the group, the teacher said, "Board, listen closely. When they are done, tell them if they missed something and, if they have, ask them to write it down. If you think they might have misunderstood something, have them explain it so that you know they understood. If they didn't understand it, take the time to set them straight. Okay?" When everyone nodded, the teacher turned back to Chris and Kate and said, "Please read what you wrote."

Kate looked at Chris and said, "You first."

Chris read his notes. At one point, he looked up from his notes to explain why something might not be possible.

"Just read what you wrote," said the teacher.

When Kate finished reading her notes, the teacher asked the group if she or Chris had missed or misconstrued anything. The consensus was that they got it all.

"Great job," he said. "That was a lot to process."

Kate released a deep breath and said, "Thank you all. This has given us a lot to think about." Standing up she said, "And Jack, Danny — we will definitely be calling."

Wayne sat at a picnic table eating lunch with Joe, Mike, Patty, Becky, Steve, and Roger. He had conflicting thoughts about the morning. On one hand he was impressed by the frankness and the ideas people shared. On the other, he was a little disturbed at how blunt and critical everyone was.

"What'd you think of the morning?" Mike asked.

"You guys don't pull any punches," Wayne said.

"I hope not. I want these guys to tell me exactly what they think," Mike said. "I'm not here to hear how well we're doing. I come here to learn how we can do better."

"It's tough love," Joe said. "These guys care about my success almost as much as I do. And I care about theirs. If we didn't care, why would any of us work as hard as we do to help one another? It'd be a lot easier to pat one another on the back and tell each other how great we are, but what would we learn?"

"Think about the discussion on free money this morning," Steve continued. "I don't know if Kate and Chris ought to take it. Our job isn't to tell them what to do. Our job is to question their plans and challenge their assumptions. They have to make their own decisions. Hopefully, these discussions will lead to better decisions."

"It is sooo much easier to be objective about other people's places — to see how someone else ought to do things," Becky added.

"Don't you worry about revealing too much?" Wayne asked. He was thinking about when Chris told everyone what their gross margin was.

"No. We've all agreed to hold everything any of us see or hear in our board meetings in confidence. We renew that commitment at each meeting. My books are wide open to these guys. If they have a question about anything, I'll answer it the best I can," Joe said.

"The key is trust," said Roger. "In EL there is a strict code of confidentiality. If you tried to do something like this, especially the turnaround, with people you didn't trust, it would be a disaster. The only reason this works is because Chris and Kate trust that everyone here has their best interests at heart."

"I doubt that anyone here has had a selfish thought in their head this morning," Joe said. "Everyone was completely focused on helping

Chris and Kate. It'll be the same thing in our board meetings. During each business's meeting we'll all be focused on helping that business. That's a pretty special thing."

"Roger," Wayne asked, "Y'all got out of EL. Why'd you leave?"

"We got our stuff done," he said. "We were in for five years. That might have been a year longer than we really needed. We pretty much accomplished our restructuring after the fourth year. Restructuring a ranch doesn't happen overnight. But we got it done. And that's what EL is for."

"But you said you're thinking of coming back?" Joe asked.

"Yeah. It's hard to find a place in this industry where people are positive about the future and challenging conventional wisdom. It's easy to become complacent. And at what point do you stop needing people to challenge your thinking? EL was a lot of work, but I miss it."

Jack walked over and asked Wayne if he was ready to go. Turning to Roger he said, "Wayne and I are going to Little Bear Butte. I need to check with the contractor, and I thought it'd be good to show Wayne some of our dirty laundry."

"That's terrific. We've made just about every mistake you can," Roger said proudly. "In spite of that, it's pretty impressive. We'll see you tonight."

SUMMARY OF CHAPTER 18
CONCEPTS

- When planning a grazing cell, ignore existing fences and facilities.
- It is easier to be objective about someone else's situation than your own.
- Executive Link is a place where people are positive about the future and challenge conventional wisdom.

Chapter 19
An Unexpected Lesson

Wayne was excited to go to Little Bear Butte with Jack. He expected to learn a lot. He wasn't sure how much more he could absorb, but spending time with Jack was too good an opportunity to pass up.

"I sure appreciate your taking the time to show me what y'all are doing," he said as they pulled out of the yard.

"No sweat. Glad to do it," Jack said. "You see something that you have questions about, just ask. You see something that you think we ought to do differently, just say so."

"I don't know that I'll have much to offer. We've been doing what I thought was rotational grazing for years. I learned today it's actually been 'rotational overgrazing,'" Wayne said with an embarrassed smile. "We typically have five or six pastures per herd. How many do y'all use out here?"

"It depends," Jack said. "There's 25 permanent paddocks in the cell, but sometimes we split paddocks with polywire."

"Sometimes?" Wayne asked.

"Sure, like just before breeding. We like to make sure the cows are gaining weight a couple of weeks before we turn the bulls in. So, instead of staying in a large paddock for three or four days, we will cut paddocks in half or in thirds and move the herd every day or two."

"What's the biggest problem you've had with your cells?"

"Water," Jack said immediately. "At first, we didn't have water where we needed it, and where we had it our recharge rate was too low. Within a year we had another problem. We'd improved the water cycle so much that most of the rainfall soaked in. That was good, but there wasn't any runoff to fill our dugouts. In some pastures the dugouts were the only water source. As aquifers recharged, springs that had been dry for years started to flow again, but they didn't produce enough to water a big herd. At least they didn't back then. Then, within five years the demand for water doubled."

"That's right," Wayne said, "You doubled the carrying capacity. What'd you do then?"

"We dug a couple of wells and put in pipelines," Jack said. "Tell you what, if I was to do this all over again, I'd start by figuring out the water first. I wouldn't plan on relying on any runoff. I'd plan it so I could water the biggest herd I could conceivably run and then double it. I'd make sure the delivery rate could keep up with peak demand and I'd have enough storage to water that herd for at least a week."

"That's a lot of water!"

"It is. The challenge is to be able to imagine how you'd want to use a cell if it had two or three times the carrying capacity it has now. We went from watering 400 cows for six months to watering 600 cows for eight months. But as forage quality improved we found that seasonal stockers gave us a better return. So, for the last couple of years we've been running 1,500 stockers for four months. And now we want to take that to 2,000 stockers. When you're watering 300 to 400 animals, it's hard to imagine that a decade later you'd need water for 2,000 animals on a hot summer day."

"I see what you mean."

"That's why I wanted to get up here today," Jack said. "We're laying in larger pipe and increasing our storage capacity so we can water a bigger herd. The contractor called Dan to say he has concerns about where we want to put the tank. Dan asked me if I would talk to him. I'm supposed to meet the contractor up there this afternoon. I don't think it'll take long."

"Sounds like you all had a pretty steep learning curve."

"You can say that again," Jack nodded. "But it's so much better than what we'd been doing. I can't imagine managing grass and cows any other way now. You try something new, you're going to make mistakes. If you're afraid of making mistakes, you'll never change. You'll never grow."

"You and Dan probably have more experience with intensive grazing than anyone around. What's the key to making it *all* work?"

"Part of it is recognizing that it isn't intensive grazing. It's intensive management," Jack said. "But what's the key to making it all work?" After a long pause he said, "Listening."

"No, I meant about the grazing."

"I know," Jack nodded. "It's not like the grazing principles are separate things. Rest periods influence graze periods and carrying capacity. Carrying capacity dictates stocking rate and that affects herd size which influences herd effect and stock density. It's not like you can pick one thing and run with that." He paused for a moment and said, "I'm sticking with listening."

"Why listening?"

Because that is the key to making it *ALL* work. And I think listening is the hardest skill for most people to learn. It was for me.

"Roger and I got to the point where we were butting heads on just about everything. I knew he was the boss, but I felt like I knew better. I kept trying to convince him I was right. When he didn't seem to get it, I responded by explaining my point louder, and louder."

Loudest voice wins, Wayne mused. It was a communication style with which he was all too familiar.

"One day Roger gave me a copy of *The 7 Habits of Highly Effective People*, by Stephen Covey," Jack said. "He'd stuck a note in it that said something like, 'I'd like you to read pages something to something else and we'll talk tomorrow.' I read it. It was about working to understand someone else's point of view before expressing your own.

"I realized that I'd been so busy trying to make my point, I really didn't understand why he wanted to do things the way he wanted to do them. And it went farther than that. Whether it was Roger, Dan, my folks, my wife, my kids, I wasn't really listening to any of them. I was waiting. I was waiting for my chance to tell people what I thought. If I was listening, I was listening to correct them or judge them. I was listening to respond. Listening to understand was something I'd never done. But it made sense. In *7 Habits*, Covey wrote something like, before a doctor can prescribe a treatment, he has to diagnose the problem. Listening to understand is the first step in diagnosing the problem."

"Makes sense," Wayne said. He realized that this was the same thing Kate had said about their policy at the hospital — diagnose before you prescribe.

"It may make sense, but it's hard. It's not something I'd ever done, and it took a while to learn."

Changing the subject, Jack asked, "If you don't mind my asking, I got the feeling that you and your dad aren't always on the same page. Is that right?"

"That's an understatement," Wayne laughed. "I think we're working from two completely different books! And no, I don't mind."

"What's his book?" Jack asked. "What does he want?"

"His book is 100% old school. He doesn't want anything to change."

"He likes things the way they are," Jack paraphrased.

"Well, no. He's constantly complaining about the way things are too."

"He doesn't like the way things are, but he doesn't want to change anything," Jack summarized.

"That's right," Wayne confirmed. "He's as stubborn as they come. Old school all the way. He thinks things are tougher today than they used to be, but people aren't as tough as they used to be. I think he sees stuff like Ranching For Profit as snake oil or some gimmick."

"He realizes that things are more challenging than when he was your age and he's skeptical of people who claim to have answers," Jack said. "It sounds like he's uncomfortable with your going to the school."

"I haven't even told him I want to go," Wayne admitted.

"So, it's not a conversation you want to have."

"It's going to be ugly," Wayne sighed, looking out the window.

"Can I make an observation?" Jack asked.

"Sure."

"I think you're telling yourself a story about your Dad."

"A story?"

"Uh-huh, a story," Jack confirmed. "Look, your Dad says something like, 'That's a bad idea,' or 'That won't work here,' and when you hear it, you tell yourself a story about why he said it."

"I know why he said it," Wayne insisted.

"Why's that?"

"Because he doesn't want to change anything," Wayne said with a little annoyance.

"Okay," Jack conceded, "but a moment ago you said he complains about the way things are too."

"Yeah, well, he's a tough old bird," Wayne said as if that resolved the contradiction.

"Why do you think he's that way?" Jack asked. He wondered if he was getting too personal.

"I don't know," Wayne said. "He's ... well ..." Wayne searched for an answer but didn't find one. Eventually he said, "Don't get me wrong. I respect my Dad. No one has worked harder. No one's had it tougher. No one handed him anything. He earned it all himself."

"Sounds like you have a lot of respect for him," Jack observed.

"Well sure I do. It's just that he's always so negative. He always complains about the way things are. The weather. The government. The markets. He complains about how hard he works ... about how the deck is stacked against agriculture, and especially against him. He complains about how little money he has ... and me." With a laugh Wayne added, "Complaining about me might be his favorite topic."

"Your Dad is always complaining," Jack said.

"He's not *always* complaining."

"But that's what you said. You said 'always'. You're telling yourself stories. I do it too." He looked over at Wayne and explained, "Anytime you use words like 'anything,' 'everything,' 'always,' 'never,' you're probably telling yourself a story."

Jack turned onto a washboard county road. They had to shout at one another to be heard over the road noise.

Jack continued, "So last year Roger comes down to a project we're working on with this kid I hired to help for the week. It's 7 a.m. and the kid hasn't shown up. I'd confirmed with him the night before that he needed to be there by 7. So, when Roger comes down and asks where he is, I tell him that the kid's late. But I don't stop there. I tell him that this kid is always late. So, Roger asks how many times he's been late this week? I tell him twice. He'd been working with us four days. Since when is two out of four always? I was telling myself a story about the kid, and it was the worst possible story I could tell. It was also a lie. He wasn't always late. In fact, he turned out to be pretty reliable and a hard worker. I've hired him for other projects.

"So, Roger says, 'I wonder *why* he's late. I wonder if he's okay. I wonder if he's broke down?' Five minutes later the kid comes driving up. He'd blown a tire. A road like this will take its toll. He couldn't call because he couldn't get cell reception. Funny thing is, he'd actually left early to make sure he'd be there on time. He could have climbed up the hill where there'd probably have been cell reception and called to let me know what happened, but that would have made him even later. He made a judgment call. I probably would have made the same call. Oh, and the other time he was late? He got lost. He was too embarrassed to say anything, and I was too annoyed and self-righteous to ask.

"So, there's two things here. First, recognize when you're telling yourself a story. Second, when you recognize it, tell yourself a different story. Start the alternative story by answering this: What's a positive explanation as to why a good person would have done this bad thing? That doesn't mean you stick with that story forever. You just stick with it until you find out the truth. We poison relationships with the awful stories we tell ourselves. There's a great book about this, *Leadership and Self-Deception*. I'll loan it to you if you want. It says, 'When we hold on to resentment, it's like taking poison and expecting someone else to die.' Man, ain't that the truth? These stories we tell ourselves fuel resentments.

"It's none of my business, but it sounds like you might be telling yourself some stories and holding on to some resentments about your dad," Jack noted.

"I'm sure I am." Wayne felt like Jack was seeing right through him. "This hits pretty close to home. So, listening to understand ... is that some sort of process?"

"Kind of," Jack confirmed. "I was doing it with you a minute ago when you were talking about your dad."

"Really?" Wayne was genuinely surprised. "What were you doing?"

"I was listening to understand. You probably didn't notice, but I didn't give you my opinion about you or your Dad, and I didn't ask any questions, at least not at first. I simply reflected what I heard you say. There were a couple of times when my understanding wasn't quite right, and you corrected me. Can I ask you something a little personal?"

"Sure."

"Do you usually open up about your dad?"

"Actually, no, I don't." Wayne usually held his cards close to the vest when it came to talking about his family. He realized that he'd said more about his dad to Jack than he'd told anyone, except maybe Chris, and he had known Chris for more than a decade.

"That's the power of listening to understand," Jack explained. "We all want to be understood. When someone seems to understand, we feel a great sense of relief and it makes us feel safe to go deeper. I don't care if it's a family member, an employee, the boss, a lease negotiation, a bull buyer, business, or family ... if you want to get to the bottom of something, if you want to solve a problem instead of making it worse, listening to understand is the key. You've got to diagnose before you prescribe."

"Makes sense. Seems simple," Wayne concluded.

"It is simple," Jack said, "but it's not easy. It takes discipline and concentration. Most people want to jump in to ask questions or judge the situation or solve the problem. But if you want to let someone know that you understand, you should start by reflecting back what they tell you. Let them confirm that you got it right and give them a chance to set you straight if you got it wrong. Let them go deeper if they're willing *before* you ask questions."

Wayne wondered if he had the patience to try this with Buddy.

"'That's right,' are *the* magic words," Jack said. "When someone responds to you with, 'That's right,' you know they feel understood."

They pulled off the county road onto a dirt track. Stopping at the barbed wire gate, Jack asked, "How about getting that? You'll need to close it. We won't be coming back this way."

As Jack met with the contractor, Wayne wandered around. Jack told him that the herd had grazed the pasture four weeks ago. They were scheduled to graze it again in two weeks. Wayne didn't see any evidence that the pasture had been grazed. There weren't any cow pies and the grass was at least 18 inches tall. *So, this is grazing it up,* he told himself.

He got on his knees and pulled back the leaves to look at the soil. There wasn't any bare soil. He pulled out his buck knife and pushed the blade into the soil. It went in easily. He used the blade to scrape back the litter to see what the soil surface looked like, but the litter blended into soil and he couldn't really tell where the litter layer ended and the mineral soil started.

Wayne walked back to the truck and grabbed a shovel. The shovel sliced into the soil easily. Having dug about 18 inches down, Wayne put down the shovel and got on his knees to have a look. The first thing he saw was roots. Lots of roots. An earthworm quickly disappeared, slinking into the side of the hole. He touched the soil on the side of the hole. Cool and damp. He inhaled deeply and smelled the sweet smell of fermentation. *This soil is alive,* he thought.

A few minutes later Jack walked over. "What do you think?"

"This is impressive."

"It is, isn't it," Jack smiled. "This is one of our best pastures. We have others where the results haven't been this dramatic, but all our land has improved. Used to be if we got 15 inches of rain in a year, I'll bet only seven or eight inches would actually soak in. Now if we get 15 inches of rain, all 15 inches soaks in."

They stopped at a couple of other sites, including a spring they had fenced. "Last time we measured, this was producing a couple of gallons a minute. It'd been dry for all the years I'd been here, then four or five years after we started cell grazing, it starts flowing. Hasn't stopped since, not even in drought years."

They stopped by a hay field where they had been using compost tea to stimulate microbial activity in the soil and build back the fertility. Walking out in the field Jack said, "This soil was dead. We'd cropped all the fertility out of it and turned it into nothing but dirt. A healthy soil is a lot like the rumen of a cow, with billions of microbes breaking down organic matter and making nutrients available to the plants. We've used compost tea and the other things that we talked about at Chris and Kate's to bring the life and fertility back. Now the yields and quality are better than ever."

Checking the time Jack said, "Roger texted and asked if we could pick up him and Dan at headquarters and drive to Chris and Kate's together. We'd better get going if we don't want to be late."

Back in the truck, Wayne asked, "How long you been at Daisy Creek? It seems like you've been here forever."

"This October it'll be 25 years. The job title was manager, but I didn't know a lick about management."

"When did you become the general manager?"

"When I started here Roger was the GM," Jack said. "You know, there's something like 25 family members who have shares in this ranch. Grown-up kids. Aunts. Uncles. Second cousins. Heck, I have a hard time figuring out who is connected to whom and how! I think most of the family assumed Roger's oldest son, Kyle, would fill his shoes. Not sure exactly how they came to the decision, but they promoted me to general manager 15 years ago. Kyle is on the board. He's a great asset, but they made me the GM. By then I'd become a pretty decent manager. That was a very difficult decision for them."

"You said you didn't know a lick about management when you started here?"

"I thought I did, but I didn't have a clue. I was actually more like a foreman back then. Most of the people we call managers in this industry don't know a lick about management. They don't project stock flows or cash flows or profit or loss. They don't create plans or delegate authority or hold people accountable. They *react* to problems like drought and regulatory changes. A manager's job is to proactively *anticipate* these things and build contingencies. Most people come up with ideas. Managers turn those ideas into proposals. There are very few real managers in this industry.

"When I was working for my dad, I use to complain that he'd shoot down all my ideas. It never occurred to me to turn the ideas into proposals. Heck, if it had occurred to me, I wouldn't have known how."

"I don't think that I know how," Wayne said a little sheepishly.

"If you go to Ranching For Profit they'll show you. Of course, they can't make you do it, but they'll give you the tools," Jack said.

"Is that where you learned management?" asked Wayne.

"That was the start. It set me on a different trajectory. Since then I've taken all sorts of classes and read a lot of books. A while back, this kid just out of college, with an animal science degree, asked me for recommendations of books to read that would help him become a professional ranch manager. I think he may have wanted my job," Jack laughed. "I don't blame him. It's a great job. Anyway, I gave him a list of five or six books. *The 7 habits of Highly Effective People, Getting to Yes, Built to Last, Good to Great, The E-Myth, Leadership and Self Deception, Crucial Conversations.* It wasn't what he was expecting. He wanted books about *ranch* management. He didn't understand that management is management. Sure, you have to have production knowledge, but to be a good manager, you have to understand management.

"Back when I started, I thought management was about cattle and grass and money. But management is mostly about people. Far and away, the people part is the biggest, most important, and hardest part. It's the most rewarding part when you get it right. Get it wrong and it's the most frustrating part. At the end of the day, everything is a people problem. Everything. You can almost always figure out an economic or financial solution to something. You can solve production problems. But if you can't get people to buy in and step up, you will fail."

Jack glanced at Wayne, "And you've got a bigger challenge than I do when it comes to people. It's much harder to manage relationships with family members who are working together than non-family. Just imagine how much more complicated it would be if I were Roger's kid or Dan and I were related.

"When we have a WOTB meeting, there's no question that the people who are supposed to be there will be there. I'm held accountable and I hold people accountable." He shook his head, "But in a family business, it's much easier to make excuses, procrastinate, not respect one another's time, and no one holds anyone accountable. Building and maintaining effective working relationships is challenging. Family relationships can be challenging too. Put the two together and holy mackerel! How does anyone do it?"

Wayne shook his head. "I know what you mean. How does anyone do it?"

"It ain't easy," Jack said. "It's the reason I left home. I couldn't imagine working with my dad. Knowing what I know now, I probably could have made it work, but not then. It's also why Daisy Creek decided to hire a non-family general manager."

Jack turned into the driveway of the Daisy Creek headquarters as he said, "Roger told me something years ago that I think may be the key to the whole thing. He said, 'Family is too important *not to* separate business and family in your family business.'"

"To treat it like a business?" Wayne asked.

"No. Not *like* a business," Jack corrected. "To accept that it is a business and behave appropriately." He paused to let that sink in. "And I'll tell you what, if people are going to run a family business successfully, they'll be listening to understand before they start yapping about their own problems or opinions. It's the single most important tool I have in my management toolbox."

Jack parked in front of the office but didn't get out. Looking straight ahead he said, "I don't mean to poke my nose where it don't belong, but there's something else you might want to consider ..."

"No. Please." Wayne sincerely wanted Jack to continue. He'd never had anyone talk with him like this, not even Chris or Lori.

"Well, just keep in mind, your dad is doing the best he can." Jack paused to let that sink in. "Given the experiences he's had, the stresses he carries, the tools he's got, he's doing the best he can. I don't say that to excuse him. It's just something that might help you be a little more patient with him."

Jack gazed out the windshield as he spoke. "I've come to believe that we are all doing the best we can. In this moment, given what we know and what's going on in our lives ...

"I remember chewing out an employee. This was maybe 20 years ago. I still feel bad about it. The guy hadn't closed a gate after moving some stock. It was a mess. Cattle out on the highway. No accidents, thank God, but it could have been a train wreck. I jumped down his throat." Jack shook his head. "That night I come to find out that, the day before, his daughter had been diagnosed with leukemia. No, you never know what kind of pain people are dealing with. We are all doing the best we can."

They sat there another moment, then Jack said, "Let's see what's taking Roger and Dan."

SUMMARY OF CHAPTER 19
CONCEPTS

- *Everything* is a people problem.

- Listening to understand is a skill that can improve personal and business relationships.

- Listening to understand involves restating your understanding of what you've heard in your own words.

- We often tell ourselves unhelpful stories about other people's behavior and motivation.

- When we hold on to resentment it's like taking poison but expecting someone else to die.

- Family is too important *not to* separate business and family in your family business.

- Given the stresses they face, the experiences they've had, and the skills they possess, people are doing the best they can.

Chapter 20
The End Is the Beginning

Roger and Dan carried the lion's share of the conversation on the drive back to Chris and Kate's. It was almost 6 p.m. when they pulled into the yard. Wayne saw that Lori was already there. He wondered how Buddy was going to react to being around all these forward-thinking ranchers. Buddy was as good as anyone when it came to resisting new ideas. Would he think this was some kind of cult?

As they walked over to the porch, Wayne saw Matt, Justin, Sally, Robyn, and Patty and Mike's kids all hanging upside down from a tree branch. Allison was close by. It looked like the kids were having a blast and like Allison, though only 16, might need a stiff drink.

There were three picnic tables on the lawn. Lori was sitting at one of them, laughing with Pat and Becky. Wayne walked over with Jack, Roger, and Dan.

"Hi, Roger," Lori said, starting to rise.

"Don't get up for us," Roger insisted.

Looking at Wayne, Lori asked, "You have a good day?"

"It's been a great day. Very intense, but great," Wayne said. "Where's Buddy?"

Wayne's gaze followed Lori's nod toward the porch. There was Buddy with Joe, Steve, Mike, Vince, and the teacher. Buddy was sitting on the edge of his chair, obviously having an intense conversation. Wayne's first reaction was, *Oh no*, but then they all erupted laughing, Buddy loudest of all. Buddy looked up and, seeing Wayne, waved at him to come over.

Wayne opened the cooler, grabbed a beer, and holding it up, asked, "Jack? Dan? Roger?"

They all nodded. Wayne fished three more bottles from the bottom of the cooler. They all walked over to join the group.

"Good to see you, Buddy," Roger said as he reached to shake Buddy's hand.

"It's been too long," Buddy replied smiling. "How are you Dan? Jack, it's good to see you." Buddy shook their hands. Still gripping Jack's hand, Buddy said, "I guess you and Wayne have been seeing the sights this afternoon."

"Saw some really interesting things today, Dad," Wayne said.

"I'll bet. Don't get any crazy notion about dividing our place up into a hundred little pastures." Buddy leaned back on the back two legs of his chair and laughed.

Wayne refrained from rolling his eyes. He smiled and said, "No way. I only need 25."

Buddy lost his balance and leaned forward to avoid falling over. Laughing, some beer sprayed from his lips. Everyone laughed, Buddy included.

Wayne sat next to his dad.

Buddy raised his beer, put his other hand on Wayne's shoulder and toasted, "Here's to a new generation."

They all raised their drinks.

Mike toasted back, "Here's to the generations that came before, who gave us opportunities." They all took another sip.

Wayne felt a weight lift from his shoulders. *Dad's having a good time. He actually likes these guys.*

The discussion was light. It ranged from worst jobs to best trips to most embarrassing mistakes. It wasn't long before Kate rang the bell on the porch signaling that the food was ready.

Wayne and Lori sat with Vince and across from Buddy, Pat, and Mike. "So, what'd you see when you were out with Jack?" Mike asked.

"It wasn't so much what I saw, it was more what we talked about," Wayne said. "We talked about management — professional management."

"Well, Daisy Creek is big enough to have professional management," said Buddy.

"I wonder if they're big *because* they have professional management," Vince said.

Buddy looked at Vince and nodded. "Could be. They've been big all along, but once Jack got there, things changed."

"Like what? What changed?" Wayne asked.

"Well, Roger for one," Buddy said. "Used to be he didn't have time for anyone or anything. He was always going 100 miles per hour. I remember he'd say, 'You can have a ranch or you can have a life, but you can't have both.' After Jack came on, it seems like he got both. Can't think of a community thing he hasn't helped with or an industry event where he doesn't have some role. Didn't use to have time for any of that. Funny thing, they went from having something like six or seven hands to three, plus Jack."

"That's what capable management does for you," Mike said. "You can have a ranch and a life."

Buddy turned to Mike asking, "What's your story? How'd you get involved with this group?"

"Give him the short version," Patty said.

"I'll try," Mike said with a grin. "We first came to Ranching For Profit because we were going crazy. We have a complicated place. There were three, no, four generations on the place. We had shareholders who grew up on the ranch but that lived a thousand miles away and never saw the ranch. There were uncles, aunts, nieces and nephews, in-laws and out-laws, and I don't know what. The dynamics between parents and kids and siblings and … to make a long story short, we had people issues."

Patty shook her head. "You're such a politician. You should quit ranching and run for office. That's a kind way to put it," she said laughing. "We took the school for two reasons. First, we were working too hard and hemorrhaging money. We needed to stop the bleeding and change things so that nature did her share of the work. But the biggest reason was to figure out how to get everyone on the same page and working together without everyone wanting to kill one another."

"That's when we really started to turn things around," Mike said. "I mean, yeah, we changed enterprises and adjusted production schedules." Putting his hand on Buddy's shoulder he said, "And I'm afraid to tell you how many pastures we have, but the big breakthrough was getting everyone in the family to agree. Too many people saw the ranch as a lifestyle, not a business."

"I suppose everyone sings Kumbaya now?" Buddy asked sarcastically.

"Well, yeah. We kind of do," Mike said. "Oh, you'll always have people issues, but we have a corporate structure and policies, and we use procedures that help us consider all points of view in order to reach agreements everyone will commit to. One of the most important things we did was to separate the operating business from the land investment. There are over 25 of us that have shares in the land. But it's just Dad, Mom, Pat, and me that own and run the operating business. We pay rent to the landowners. Making that split was huge."

Turning to Wayne, Mike said, "How do you hold your dad accountable in the business, and how does he hold you accountable without it getting personal? Maybe that's not a problem for you, but it sure was for us. And how are you supposed to know how to do it if no one ever shows you?" Mike turned to Buddy, "My dad showed me how to work cattle, but he never showed me how to run a business. Did your dad ever show you?"

"'Fraid not," Buddy said, shaking his head. "There was a time when you didn't need to know all that. Being a good cowman was enough."

"Those days are long gone," Mike said.

The conversation shifted to other things. Vince impressed everyone by reciting the license plate numbers of every vehicle in the yard.

"No point writing them down to check," Pat said. "He was a cop. It's second nature for him to notice things like that."

After dinner they returned to the porch and to swapping stories. It was starting to get dark when Wayne noticed that Buddy wasn't with them. He turned to see Buddy talking with Roger and Jack at one of the picnic tables.

Lori left for home with the kids a little after 9. It was past 10 when Kate said, "Stay out here as long as you like, but we've got a big day tomorrow. Chris and I are turning in. Thanks for a great day everyone. Breakfast at 7. Meeting at 8, right?"

"Right," several groaned.

"We'd better hit the road, Dad," Wayne said to Buddy. "Thanks Chris. This has been quite a day. I can't remember a day when I learned so much — except maybe that workshop."

"I'm glad you could make it," Chris said. "And Buddy, I'm so glad you were able to join us tonight. What'd you think?"

"Thank you for inviting an old codger like me. This is a very interesting group. That Joe is a hoot. And ..." Buddy pointed to Mike as he struggled to remember his name.

"Mike," Chris offered.

"Right, Mike. He's a terrific guy. What a storyteller. I mean they've had their share of challenges and they come out alright. Anyway, thanks Chris. Thank Kate for me too. I enjoyed meeting your friends."

As soon as they were in the truck, Buddy said, "Mike's quite the guy, isn't he? Apparently they've had quite the turnaround."

"That's what it sounds like."

"You know," Buddy looked at Wayne, "I was joking about this Ranching For Profit being an oxymoron, but these guys are getting it done, aren't they?"

"It sure looks that way," Wayne nodded.

"That school's pretty pricey and cash flow is tight. We don't have a big margin for error," Buddy said.

"Margin for error?" Wayne laughed. "Lori and I can only stay here because of her job. We've been subsidizing the place with her paycheck since we came back. Margin for error? We are in constant error." Wayne regretted saying it as soon as the words left his lips.

"If you don't want to stay here you don't have to," Buddy snapped back angrily. "There's no one holding a gun to your head making you stay. You don't understand ..."

There's that word, understand, Wayne thought. The realization was like a slap in the face. *He doesn't think I understand.*

"I'm sorry, Dad. I know things are tight."

They rode a mile before Wayne said, "Dad, I think you're a great man. I really do. You've worked your butt off. But I'm worried. Lori's blowing and going nonstop. I wake up at 2 in the morning wondering how …" Wayne realized his venting wasn't going to do anything but pick an argument or make Buddy feel guilty. Suddenly he remembered what Jack had said about listening and he decided to restart the conversation.

"Why'd you bring up the Ranching For Profit stuff?"

"I don't know," Buddy said. "You get to my age and you start wondering what it's all been for. All along I treated life as though it was something that was going to happen later …"

Wayne remembered that a couple of months ago Lori had said the same thing.

"Dad, what's going to happen to the ranch when you die?" Wayne asked carefully. "Is there a plan?"

"I figured half and half," Buddy said looking straight ahead. "I got to be fair to Sam."

Wayne wanted to ask, is that fair to me? But instead said, "You want to be fair."

"Well, sure I do," Buddy said. "One reason I've put off doing anything is because somehow equal don't seem real fair. You came back to help when I needed you. Gave up college." Buddy looked out the side window. "I've always felt guilty about that."

They drove another half mile before Wayne said, "You feel like I made some sacrifices, and that ought to be factored in somehow."

"Well sure," Buddy said. "If I split the place, instead of having a place that will barely support one family, there'll be two that won't be able to support anyone."

"So, you don't really want to split the land. You want the place to stay intact." Wayne realized he was listening to understand.

"I've always said the only way I want to leave is in a pine box," Buddy said.

"Even then, you said you want that box brought back and buried on the place," Wayne reminded him.

Buddy laughed, "That's right." A moment later he said, "I suppose it's too much to hope for, but I'd sure like it if one day, Justin or Matt would be running things," Buddy said. "I guess if I had a dream, that'd be it. Somehow that'd mean that what I did here mattered."

"So, you want to be fair and you want to keep it in one piece. You see part of your legacy as keeping this in our family, but you don't know how to make sure that happens," Wayne summarized.

"That's right. I don't. Maybe it's time to talk to someone who does this stuff," Buddy said.

There it was, *that's right*, the magic phrase Jack talked about. Wayne couldn't recall ever having this long a conversation about anything serious with his dad. It occurred to him that it was easier to talk like this seated side by side, looking through the windshield, down the road, rather than face to face.

"Did you hear what Mike said about separating the land from the operating business?" Wayne asked. "What if you left the land to Sam and me, 50/50 with some kind of buyout agreement."

Buddy nodded. "I was wondering if something like that might work."

They passed the mailbox on the road and pulled into their long driveway. Wayne wasn't ready for the drive and the conversation to end.

"Dad, think about the ranch 5 years from now. What would you like to see happening here?" Wayne asked.

"Oh, well, you know. I'd like to see you run the place," Buddy said.

"You want to see me be successful here and you don't ever want to leave," Wayne said.

"That's right. I want your kids to have a future here … and their kids."

"You want this to go on for generations."

"That's right. I don't want Lori to have to work so damn hard," he said. "I feel like she blames me for her stress. You know she brings a lot of that on herself."

"You want to have a better relationship with Lori," Wayne said.

"That's right. I want her to feel like she can talk to me without having to apologize for missing this or that," Buddy said.

"What else, Dad?"

"Well," Buddy thought for a moment, "I don't want to work so bloody hard. I don't want you to have to work so bloody hard. I don't want to fight with you every time we talk for more than two minutes. I don't want ... you know it's a lot easier to tell you what I don't want than what I do want."

"Yeah, I've noticed that too," Wayne said.

They pulled up in the yard. Wayne turned off the engine, but neither moved to get out of the truck. "If you weren't working so hard, what would you do with yourself?"

"I'd slow down. I wouldn't do things half-assed. I'd do things right. I might ... "

"You might what?" Wayne asked.

"It's stupid."

"You might what?" Wayne asked again.

"Well, I'm too old now, but I'd always dreamed of going to Australia. I always wanted to see ranches there," Buddy said.

"That's not stupid. That's not stupid at all," Wayne said. "I think that's awesome. I never heard you mention that before."

"I never mentioned it because it's not in the cards," Buddy said. "Never had the money. Never had the time. I'm too crippled up now."

"You feel like it can't happen now," Wayne said. "Chris and Kate say they're going to Australia. They're going with the kids. I can't remember when. A couple of years from now I think."

"Well, I'm too old," Buddy said.

"You know, I was talking with Roger and Jack tonight," he continued. "Real interesting guy that Jack. One heck of a manager. You know, he left his family's place because he couldn't get along with his dad."

Wayne wondered how to respond. He chose not to.

"It got me wondering, with the way we get along, or don't get along sometimes ... have you thought about leaving?" Buddy asked.

"I've worried about our future here," Wayne said carefully. "I worry about Lori subsidizing our family and how little family time we have. The kids are growing so fast. None of us will get these days back. Lori and I both worry about what'll happen when you're gone. Will we be able to stay or will we have to leave? But, no, I've never seriously thought about leaving. I love this place. Lori does too."

They sat in the truck in the dark a few moments longer. "Dad, what if I was to put together a proposal to lease the ranch from you? We'd figure out what market rate rent would be. I'd need your help, and I'd pay you a fair wage, but it'd be my business to run. I'd want to run things by you. You'd be my senior adviser, but I'd make the final call on production decisions. Would you be open to considering something like that?"

"That guy, Mike, got me thinking along those lines. That's what I wanted to talk to Roger about. I know the Daisy Creek Ranch and Daisy Creek Livestock are two completely separate deals. I wanted to know how that works," Buddy said. "Gotta tell you though, it scares me."

"Scares me too, but Lori said something the other day that scared me even more," Wayne said. "She said if we don't change, we're going to wind up where we're headed, and where we're headed —"

"Ain't pretty, is it? She said that did she? Well she's right. Where we're headed isn't working very well for any of us, is it?"

Buddy looked at Wayne and said, "I read or heard somewhere that there are two types of regret. There's regret for things you've done and regret for things you never did. I don't regret too many of the things I did. I made some bad calls now and then but, for the most part, I made a decision and then I made it work."

"You taught me that 20% of success is the decision and 80% is the implementation," Wayne said.

"That sounds like some crackpot thing I'd come up with to try to sound smart," Buddy said. "But I really don't regret the things I did. The only regrets I have are for things I didn't do. Things I wanted to do but, whether I was too busy, too broke, too scared, for whatever reason, I didn't."

They sat listening to the crickets. Finally, Buddy spoke, "I'll look at your proposal under one condition."

"What's that, Dad?"

"You go to that school."

"Really? Lori and I'd like to go. I've been wanting to talk with you about it."

"You have, have you?" Buddy glanced at his son. "I'm not the easiest guy to spring a new idea on, am I?"

"That's actually been a worry for me," Wayne confessed. "I'm concerned that Lori and I'll come back from the class with a head full of new ideas and then —"

"You'll run into Buddy, the brick wall?"

"Something like that. What changed your mind?" Wayne asked.

"A few things. I guess it was mostly Mike," Buddy said. "His comment that it isn't enough anymore to be a good stockman, and that just because you know how to raise livestock doesn't mean you know how to run a business that raises livestock."

"That's something I've been thinking about too," Wayne said.

"I got myself believing that focusing on business would take the fun out of ranching, but I think I've had that backwards," Buddy said. "Getting the business side of things right might just be what it takes to make this fun again."

Wayne nodded. "Maybe we can have a ranch *and* a life."

SUMMARY OF CHAPTER 20
CONCEPTS

- Knowing how to grow crops and raise livestock is not the same thing as knowing how to run a business that grows crops and raises livestock.
- Transforming a ranch into a successful business can make ranching and life more fun.

Part III

Suggested Tasks, Appendices & Glossary

SUGGESTED TASK CONTENTS

Suggested Tasks

The tasks offered in this section are intended to help you apply Ranching For Profit concepts to your ranch. The task number refers to the chapter where the concept is introduced. Tasks 1.1 - 8.1 are recommended prework for the Ranching for Profit School. Additional tasks are provided to help you apply the whole RFP economic planning process to your ranch. It may be helpful to review the chapter before completing some tasks.

Rather than write on the sample forms that follow, you may want to make copies, preserving the forms here as templates.

NOTES

1.1 Efficient vs. Effective

Doing things right (efficiency) is a waste of time if you aren't doing the right things (effectiveness). Identify at least one thing that you suspect may be efficient but not effective on your ranch. Explain why each practice you identify may be efficient but not effective.

2.1 Fixed Assets & Working Capital

There are three types of assets in most businesses: fixed assets, working capital, and reserves. Simply put, fixed assets are things you intend to keep (e.g. land, breeding stock, infrastructure, vehicles, and machinery). Working capital are the things you intend to sell (e.g. growing stock and inputs).

A disproportionate share of the money in most ranches is invested in fixed assets. This is a problem because when most of the money is tied up in things you intend to keep there is very little to sell. Compounding the problem, a lot of the income from sales is often spent maintaining the fixed assets. The result is that most conventional ranchers are wealthy on the balance sheet and broke at the bank.

Estimate the value of fixed assets and working capital in your business.

FIXED ASSET	VALUE	WORKING CAPITAL	VALUE
Land		Growing Stock	
Infrastructure (buildings, fences, pipelines, etc.)		Other Working Capital	
Vehicles, equipment & machinery		Cash	
Breeding Stock		**Total Working Capital**	
Other Fixed Assets		**Reserves**	
Total Fixed Assets		**Total Assets** [1]	
% Fixed Assets [2]		**% Working Capital** [3]	

1 Total Assets = (Fixed Assets + Working Capital + Reserves)
2 % Fixed Assets = [(Working Capital / Total Assets) x 100]
3 % Working Capital = [(Fixed Assets / Total Assets) x 100][(Fixed Assets / Total Assets) x 100]

2.1 Fixed Assets & Working Capital (cont.)

Many Ranching For Profit School grads have increased profit by liberating money locked in fixed assets and reallocating it to working capital.

Points to ponder:

• What are the implications of having this percentage of your money invested in fixed assets?

_____

_____

_____

• What could you do to create income directly from fixed assets?

_____

_____

_____

• How can you increase the proportion of your money in working capital?

_____

_____

_____

3.1 The Breakthrough Question

Each day at the Ranching For Profit School we challenge participants with the following question: *What is impossible to do but, if it could be done, would be a huge improvement for you and your ranch?* We call this the *breakthrough question* because answering it requires that you challenge your paradigms about what is and isn't possible, and the answer frequently leads to a breakthrough.

At the Ranching For Profit School we suggest you answer the question looking at what is impossible for four areas in your business: 1. People, 2. Money, 3. Production and 4. Land.

What is impossible to do, but if it could be done, would be a huge improvement for you and your ranch?

1.   People

_____

_____

_____

2.   Money

_____

_____

_____

3.   Production

_____

_____

_____

4.   Land

_____

_____

_____

3.2 "I Want" List

Describe what you want your business to be 5 years from now. For the moment ignore any constraints that may make progress difficult. Imagine everything has gone perfectly and you can create whatever you want.

- What does your perfect ranch look like?
- What enterprises do you see?
- What products would it produce and what customer(s) would it serve?
- How profitable would it be?
- How would capital be deployed?
- What would it look like ecologically?
- What infrastructure would there be?
- How many people would be employed (family and non-family)?
- How would they interact with one another and ownership?
- How would the ranch be managed?

Each stakeholder in your business should make their own *I Want* list independently on a separate paper. Use short phrases of 3-5 words to answer each of the questions listed above. You may have several answers to each of the questions. The more the better.

Suggestions:

- Focus on what *you* want, not what you think others might want.
- Describe what you want, not what you don't want.
- Think about why you want these things. Identify the *why* behind the what.
- It may be helpful to discuss the things on each stakeholders list. However, if you share the lists with one another, it should be to understand, not to criticize what others want.

3.3 Profit Target

Before you can know how much profit you need, you need to determine what your profit is for. Profit can be used for a lot of things including:

- Building reserves for the business
- Reducing debt
- Paying dividends to the owners
- Paying a profit share to the employees
- Retirement savings
- Research and development of new enterprises
- Business expansion
- Off-farm investments
- Donations

Some businesses have a tiered strategy for profit, where the first $50,000 may be used to build reserves or pay down debt, the next $25,000 pays dividends or bonuses and the next tier is donated to causes important to the owners. Whatever your profit policy, it should be decided *before* you make the profit. Over time, as targets are achieved and your situation changes, profit targets may also change.

What is your profit for?

USE OF OUR PROFIT	AMOUNT NEEDED
Profit Target:	

4.1 Overhead Costs & Gross Margin Target

Overhead costs include land, labor and administrative costs. Estimate your overhead costs for the coming year. Don't worry about precision. Depending on your scale, if your estimates are within $10,000-$100,000, they will be close enough.

Labor Related Overheads		$
Employee Costs (salaries, deferred wages, benefits, payroll taxes, insurance, housing, etc.)	+	
Vehicles, Machinery, Equipment Costs (licensing, interest, repairs, depreciation, insurance, etc.)	+	
Other Labor Related Costs (cost of keeping working animals, contract labor, etc.)	+	
Total Labor Overhead Costs:	=	
Land Related Overheads		
Actual Rent (actual rents paid to others)	+	
Opportunity Rent[1] (the rent you could get if you rented your own property to someone else)	+	
Infrastructure Repair & Maintenance (buildings, roads, fences, corrals, pipelines, ponds, tanks, etc.)	+	
Other Land Related Overheads (weed control, fertilizer, etc.)	+	
Total Land Overhead Costs:	=	
Administrative Overheads (office supplies, professional fees, etc.)	=	
Total Overhead Costs: (Add total Labor, Land & Administrative Overheads)	=	
Profit Target: (from task 3.3)	+	
Gross Margin Target: (Add The Profit Target to Your Total Overheads)	=	

1 When including opportunity rent do NOT include property tax and other land ownership costs as overheads. You don't pay ownership costs on land you rent.

5.1 Enterprise List

After-hours coaching is available each night after class at the Ranching For Profit School. Among other things, the instructor helps students apply the RFP economic planning processes to their own businesses. The tasks 5.1 - 8.1 are intended to help you collect information and calculate statistics that will be useful in these coaching sessions.

List Your Enterprises

An enterprise is a portion of your business that could be run as a separate entity. Please identify the enterprises in your business:

1. _____

2. _____

3. _____

4. _____

5. _____

6. _____

7. _____

8. _____

5.2 Livestock Enterprise Inventory

The next several tasks will guide you through steps 1 - 6 of the of the Ranching For Profit 7-step profit planning process. (The 7th step involves completing tasks 8.2 - 10.1 but is not part of the recommended Ranching For Profit School prework.) We recommend you complete tasks 5.2 - 8.1 for one livestock enterprise as prework for the school. You will find it more valuable to project what you plan to do next year, rather than trying to reconstruct what you did last year. If you do not currently have an enterprise, it may be useful to use the exercises to determine the profitability of a potential enterprise.

Record the beginning inventory for one livestock enterprise.

Suggestions:

1. The production year does not need to match the fiscal year. The process will be MUCH simpler if you start the production year for breeding enterprises sometime after weaning and before calving or lambing.

2. Different enterprises in the same business can have different production years.

3. Project forward. Do not try to reconstruct last year.

4. List the inventory on hand at the *beginning* of the production year.

5. A Cow calf enterprise in which you raise your own replacements typically has six livestock classes: Cows, H2, H1, Heifer Calves, Bull Calves and Bulls.

Enterprise: _____

CLASS OF STOCK	BEGINNING INVENTORY AS OF _____

6.1 Stock Flow Mind Map

At the Ranching For Profit School you will learn a stock flow planning process for projecting livestock births, deaths, sales, purchases, and transfers. For now, use the mind-mapping technique Wayne used in chapter 6 to project from the opening inventory to your closing inventory for the enterprise selected in task 5.2.

Suggestions:

1. Rather than look up what happened last year, think through what will happen next year.

2. Accept that all of your numbers will be wrong. Close is good enough. In this task, the thought that goes into arriving at a number is more important than the number itself.

3. Complete a mind map for H1s and H2s before completing the mind map for cows.

4. After entering the beginning inventory for H1s, estimate and deduct anticipated deaths, culls, and opens. The remainder will be your closing inventory of H2s.

5. After entering the beginning inventory for H2s, estimate and deduct anticipated deaths, drys, culls, and opens. Add the remainder to the closing inventory of cows.

6. After entering the beginning inventory for cows, estimate and deduct anticipated deaths, drys, culls, and opens. Add the H2s that became cows to determine your closing inventory of cows.

7. Rather than cram your mind maps in the space below, draw them on a separate paper.

6.2 Livestock Valuation

Estimate the value of each class of stock in the enterprise identified in task 5.2. Complete the livestock valuation using the closing inventory projections on the stock flow mind map for this enterprise (previous task).

Suggestions:

- For breeding stock use a conservative value for a typical animal in the herd at the beginning of the production year. Ask, "What do I know I could get for these animals if I had to sell them all in a hurry?"

- For growing stock use conservative market values.

Enterprise: _____

CLASS OF STOCK	A VALUE/ HEAD	B BEGIN NUMBER	A X B BEGIN VALUE	C CLOSING NUMBER	A X C CLOSING VALUE
TOTAL:					

6.3 Sales, Purchase & Transfer Projections

To project a trading account for the enterprise identified in task 5.2 you will need to estimate the prices you will pay and receive and the value of animals that will transfer from one enterprise to another.

Enterprise: _____

PROJECTED SALES					
Class of Stock					
Number Sold					
Average Weight					
Price ($/lb.)					
Income per Animal					
Total Income					
PROJECTED PURCHASES					
Class of Stock					
Number Purchased					
Average Weight					
Price ($/lb.)					
Price per Animal					
Total Expense					

6.3 Sales, Purchase & Transfer Proj. (cont.)

Suggestions for transfers:

- Only show transfers between enterprises. Transfers within an enterprise should *NOT* be recorded here.

- Use your best estimate of market prices to value the transfers.

- Whatever value is used when an animal transfers out of one enterprise is the value that must be used for the transfer into the other enterprise.

PROJECTED TRANSFERS				
Transferring Out Of (Enterprise Leaving)				
Class of Stock Transferring Out				
Number Transferring				
Transferring Into (Enterprise Entering)				
Class of Stock Transferring In				
Value per Unit ($/head)				
Total Value of Transfer				

6.4 Livestock Enterprise Trading Account

A trading account measures the total value an enterprise produces. Complete this trading account for the enterprise identified in task 5.2. Use the inventory values calculated in Task 6.2 and prices and transfer values you calculated in Task 6.3.

Enterprise: _____

Closing Inventory Value	
+ Sales	
+ Transfers Out [1]	
- Transfers In [1]	
- Purchases	
- Beginning Inventory Value	
GROSS PRODUCT =	

1 Include transfers BETWEEN enterprises (e.g. steer calves to stockers). *DO NOT* include transfers from class to class *WITHIN* an enterprise (e.g. heifer calves to H1, H1 to H2, and H2 to cows).

7.1 Livestock Enterprise Direct Costs

Direct costs are costs that increase or decrease directly as the units of production in an enterprise increase or decrease. Project the direct costs for the enterprise identified in task 5.2.

Enterprise: _____

DIRECT COSTS	COST PER UNIT	# OF UNITS	TOTAL COST
Opportunity Interest @10% of BIV*	■■■■■■■■■	■■■■■■■■■	
Feed			
Health			
Ear Tags & Other Supplies			
Breeding (AI, preg. check, fertility testing, etc.)			
Shearing			
Transportation			
Brand Inspection			
Marketing (Commissions, advertising, etc.)			
TOTAL DIRECT COSTS =	■■■■■■■■■	■■■■■■■■■	

*BIV = Beginning Inventory Value

NOTES

7.2 Livestock Enterprise Gross Margin

Calculate gross margin for the enterprise identified in task 5.2 by subtracting the direct costs (task 7.1) from the gross product (task 6.4).

Enterprise: _____

	$
Gross Product	
-Direct Costs	
= Gross Margin	

7.3 Livestock Ent. Gross Margin per Unit

RFP Animal Units (AU) measure the relative demand of grazing animals. By using AU to calculate gross margin per unit you'll be able to compare the economic efficiency of grazing enterprises.

An animal unit (AU) is a 1,000-pound grazing animal. Add 0.1 animal units for each 100 pounds of additional weight. (A 1,400-pound cow is 1.4 Animal Units). If an animal is lactating, add 0.1 for each 100 pounds of calf nursing. (A 1,400-pound cow nursing a 300-pound calf is 1.7 AU). Assuming a cow is lactating for half the year and dry for half the year, use the average of the dry and wet AU values to show her annualized animal unit value:

$$\frac{(1.4 \text{ AU} + 1.7 \text{ AU})}{2} = 1.55 \text{ AU}$$

**The animal unit total for a herd of 400 cows,
80 H2s, 100 H1s and 24 bulls is 798 AU:**

CLASS	AVG WT. (LB.)	AU/HEAD			NUMBER	TOTAL AU
		DRY	WET	AVERAGE		
Cows	1,300	1.3	1.6	1.45	400	580
H2	1,100	1.1	1.4	1.25	80	100
H1	750	na	na	0.75	100	75
Bulls	1,800	na	na	1.8	24	43
					TOTAL HERD:	**798 AU**

A 600-pound steer is 0.6 AU. To calculate the annualized animal unit value for the steer, multiply the steer's AU value by the portion of the year it is in the enterprise. A steer starting at 500 pounds and leaving at 800 pounds (avg. weight 650 lb.) after 5 months is 0.27 AU:

$$0.65 \text{ AU} \times 5/12 \text{ Years} = 0.27 \text{ AU}$$

Multiply the annualized AU value by the number animals in the enterprise to determine the total AU in this enterprise. Use this value to calculate the gross margin per unit for the enterprise.

This scale (100 pounds of animal weight = 0.1 AU) applies whether working with cattle, sheep or bison. (A 170-pound ewe is 0.17 AU.)

7.3 Livestock Ent. Gross Margin per Unit
(cont.)

Calculate the total animal units in your enterprise:

CLASS	AVG WT. (LB.)	AU/ HEAD DRY	AU/ HEAD WET	AVG. AU/ HEAD	NUMBER	TOTAL AU
				TOTAL HERD:		

Divide the total gross margin task 7.2 by the number of animal units in the enterprise to calculate gross margin per unit:

_____ ÷ _____ = _____
Total Gross Margin   Animal Units   Gross Margin / Unit

8.1 Business Structure Diagram

A division is a part of your business with unique overheads. Please draw a diagram showing your business's divisions and the enterprises they include. (Examples are provided in Chapter 8)

8.2 Farming Enterprise Trading Account

Like the trading account for livestock enterprises, trading accounts for farming enterprises show the value produced. Please complete a trading account for a farming enterprise to project enterprise gross product.

Enterprise Name: _____

Closing Inventory Value	
+ Crop Sales	
+ Crop Transfers Out [1]	
+ Value of Grazing provided to Livestock Enterprises [2]	
- Crop Purchases	
- Opening Inventory Value	
Gross Product =	

1   Market value of crop fed to livestock enterprises (this must be charged as a direct cost to those livestock enterprises).

2   The value of grazing provided to your livestock enterprises should be recorded as a divisional overhead to your livestock division.

8.3 Farming Enterprise Direct Costs

The unit of production in farming enterprises is an acre, therefore land costs that increase or decrease as the number of acres increase or decrease are direct costs. (Rent is an important exception. Even in farming enterprises, rent is an overhead cost.) Project direct costs for the farming enterprise identified in task 8.2.

Enterprise: _____

DIRECT COSTS	COST PER ACRE	# OF ACRES	TOTAL COST
Seed			
Fertilizer			
Herbicide			
Irrigation Water			
Pumping Costs			
Custom Work			
Transportation			
Marketing Commissions			
		Total Direct Costs	

8.4 Farming Enterprise Gross Margin & Gross Margin per Unit

Calculate gross margin for the enterprise used in task 8.2.

Enterprise: _____

	$
Gross Product	
- Direct Costs	
= Gross Margin	

Divide the gross margin by the number of acres used in this enterprise to calculate gross margin per unit.

_____ ÷ _____ = _____
Total Gross Margin   Acres   Gross Margin / Acre

9.1 Division & Business Overheads

You made a crude estimate of overhead costs in task 4.1. Now it's time to refine your estimate. Complete the following tables listing division and business overhead costs.

Remember:

- Overhead costs should only be assigned to a division if the cost would be completely eliminated if the division were discontinued.

- DO NOT assign overheads shared with other divisions to any division. They are business overheads.

Division: _____(complete a separate form for each division)

DIVISION OVERHEADS	CASH	NON-CASH
Total Cash & Non-Cash Business Overheads		
Total Division Overheads:		

9.1 Division & Business Overheads (cont.)

Complete this table showing your business overheads.

BUSINESS OVERHEADS	CASH	NON-CASH
Total Cash & Non-Cash Business Overheads		
Total Business Overheads		

9.2 Division Profit or Loss

Calculate division profit or loss for each division in your business.

Division: _____

Division Gross Margin _____

                                (the total gross margin of all enterprises in this division)

– Division Overheads _____

                                (overhead costs that are unique to this division)

= Division Profit or Loss = _____

                                (Division Gross Margin – Division Overhead Costs)

9.3 Business Profit or Loss

Calculate business profit or loss by totaling the profit or loss for all your divisions and subtracting your business overhead costs:

Division Profit or Loss Total: _____

(total profit or loss of all divisions)

- Business Overheads_____

(these include any overheads shared by divisions)

= Business Profit or Loss = _____

(Total Division Profit or Loss – Business Overheads)

NOTES

10.1 Key Performance Indicators & the RFP Benchmarks

Calculate the gross margin and feed ratios for the livestock enterprises identified in task 5.2. Then calculate the overhead ratio for your business. Compare the indicators for your business to the Ranching For Profit benchmarks to identify potential profit drivers and deadwood.

a. Calculate the gross margin ratio for at least one livestock enterprise:

Enterprise: _____

$$\left(\frac{\quad\quad\quad}{\text{Enterprise Gross Margin}} \div \frac{\quad\quad\quad}{\text{Gross Product}} \right) \times 100 = \frac{\quad\quad\quad}{\text{Gross Margin Ratio}}$$

How healthy is the enterprise gross margin? (The benchmark for the gross margin ratio is $\geq 70\%$.)

_____

_____

b. Calculate feed costs as a percentage of gross product for the enterprise:

$$\left(\frac{\quad\quad\quad}{\text{Feed Costs}^1} \div \frac{\quad\quad\quad}{\text{Gross Product}} \right) \times 100 = \frac{\quad\quad\quad}{\text{Feed Ratio}}$$

1 Feed costs include hay, silage, supplement and mineral. DO NOT include rent for pasture or grazing fees.

How dependent is this enterprise on supplement and substitute feeding? (The benchmark for the feed ratio is $\leq 16\%$.)

_____

_____

10.1 Key Performance Indicators & the RFP Benchmarks (cont.)

c. Calculate the gross margin ratio for your business:

Before you can calculate this ratio you will need to project the gross margin for every enterprise in your business.

$$(\underline{\hspace{3cm}} \div \underline{\hspace{3cm}}) \times 100 = \underline{\hspace{3cm}}$$

| Total Gross Margin (Sum of all enterprise Gross Margins) | Total Gross Product (Total Gross Product of all enterprises) | Gross Margin Ratio for the Business |

How healthy is the overall gross margin in your business? (The benchmark for the gross margin ratio is $\geq 70\%$.)

_____

_____

d. Calculate the overhead ratio for your business:

$$(\underline{\hspace{2.5cm}} \div \underline{\hspace{2.5cm}}) \times 100 = \underline{\hspace{2.5cm}}$$

| Overhead Costs[1] | Gross Product | Overhead Ratio |

1 Include all division and business overheads. Include cash and non-cash overheads including opportunity rent and deferred wages.

The overhead ratio benchmark $\leq 40\%$. How does your business stack up?

_____

_____

10.1 Key Performance Indicators & the RFP Benchmarks (cont.)

e. Calculate the turnover required to hit your profit target:

Divide the Gross Margin Target (total overhead costs plus profit target) by the gross margin per unit of the livestock enterprise calculated in task 7.3.

(_____ ÷ _____) x 100 = _____

| Gross Margin Target | Gross Margin/ Unit | Number of Units Needed to Achieve Gross Margin Target |

f. Profit Drivers and Deadwood

What are your profit drivers? How can you take advantage of them?

_____

_____

_____

Where is your deadwood? What can you do to eliminate it?

_____

_____

_____

11.1 WOTB Meeting Policy

The only thing harder than running a business may be running a family business. It isn't easy for husbands and wives, parents and children, brothers, brothers-in-law, sisters, or sisters-in-law to be in business together. Too often disagreements over strategy and tactics discussed (or not discussed) during the day get brought to the dinner table or bedroom at night.

We need boundaries between our family and our family business. It may be unrealistic to think that we can suspend all of the complex dynamics involved in our family and just focus on business, but we need to try. WOTB (Working On The Business) meetings are key to doing that.

Traditional staff meetings focus on problems and lining out tasks over the next few days or weeks. In contrast, WOTB meetings focus on strategic and tactical issues. Think of strategic issues as the big-ticket items (e.g. your mission, vision, organization chart, enterprise mix and operating plans and policies). Tactical issues describe how you plan to implement the strategy.

A WOTB meeting is typically 2-3 hours and focuses on one topic. I recommend a regular schedule for WOTB meetings (e.g. every second Tuesday) and that everyone involved in making important decisions participate. Every meeting should end with an action plan showing who will do what and when it will be completed.

List the issues you might want to address in your WOTB meetings:

11.1 WOTB Meeting Policy (cont.)

Issues (continued)

_____

_____

_____

_____

_____

_____

List the people who should be involved in your WOTB meetings:

_____

_____

_____

_____

_____

_____

_____

_____

_____

When will you hold your meetings? _____

Where will you hold your meetings?
(If you are dealing with emotional
issues a neutral location may be advisable.) _____

Appendices

Appendix 1: Establishing Transects

Why bother installing and reading transects?

Our eyes and memories can't be trusted! Too often we see things we expect to see, or think we are seeing things that are new but are actually just newly noticed. To assess the impact of your management, we need to know what's really going on. Transects help us do that.

Having transect data will also help document your track record as a manager. Showing this track record to prospective lessors has helped several RFP alumni secure highly competitive leases, sometimes for lower rates than others were offering. This track record may also be helpful in protecting yourself from claims of overstocking, overgrazing, or other environmental degradation.

What are you trying to document and measure?

- Condition and trend of typical range sites

  If a community type represents more than 20% of the ranch by capacity, we strongly recommend installing at least one transect in that community. If a large area with low capacity (less than 20% of the total) has the potential to improve dramatically, it would also be a good idea to install at least one transect there.

- Condition and trend of special interest sites

  You may want to document changes on special sites (e.g. blow-outs, weed infestations, sites that have been disturbed with fire or tilling).

Where should you install transects?

Pick a site that is representative of the area you want to evaluate. It should also be easy to locate.

The start-point of a transect should be a place that is easy to find. On rangelands, keep the start point at least several hundred yards away from gates and water points (unless you want to document the condition and changes that may occur around these areas). Make sure you stay at least 100 feet away from fences and roads.

Installing a Transect

Materials for Installing a Transect:

- Two 48″ long, 3/8″diameter fiberglass rods (electric fence posts). Calibrate the rods by wrapping the posts with electrician's tape to make bands of tape six inches wide at six-inch intervals. Leave the bottom 12 inches of the post untaped. The taped posts make it easier to objectively assess the height of surrounding forage.

- One fence post clip mounted at the top of each fiberglass rod

- Black paint pen

- 200′ measuring tape

- Compass

- Hammer

- Two 5-gallon bucket lids with a 3/8″ hole drilled in the center of the lids

- Four 10″ spikes with cattle ear tags. (You will need to widen the hole in the ear tag using a drill to hammer in one of the 10″ spikes.)

- Two 12″ spikes with washers

48″
42″
36″
30″
24″
18″
12″
6″

You should run the transect in a west to east or east to west direction. You will always lay frames on the south side of the transect tape and read the frames from the north side. This will avoid casting shadows in the plot frame photos and ensure that you don't disturb the areas you are monitoring.

You will need at least one identifiable, relatively permanent feature within a couple hundred yards of the start point. Record the compass bearing and distance from the feature to the start point. It is also helpful to record the GPS coordinates of the start point.

Once you have selected the start point:

1. Lay down one of the bucket lids and drive a 12″ spike with a washer through the center hole in the lid. This is the start point

2. Write "S" (for "start") on the bucket lid with a paint pen.

3. Walk the tape out in a westerly or easterly direction. Make sure it is laid out in a straight line.

4. Tap in the end bucket lid as you did the bucket lid at the starting point.

5. Write "E" (for "end") on the lid.

6. Take a compass reading back to the start point. Write the compass direction on the bucket lid.

7. Go back to the start point and take a compass reading to the end point. Write the compass direction on the bucket lid with the paint pen.

8. If you can, it would be helpful to also record the GPS coordinates of the start point.

9. Tap in a 48″ calibrated rod 12″ into the ground at the 10′ mark on the transect.

10. Tap in 10″ spikes with ear tags at the 40′, 80′, 120′ and 160′ marks on the tape. These are the points at which you will lay plot frames.

11. Write the number of the frame on the ear tag

12. Tap in a 48″ fiberglass rod at the 190′ mark. (90′ mark on 100′ transects).

200′ Transect

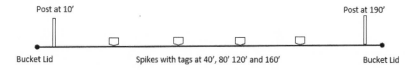

Post at 10′   Post at 190′

Bucket Lid   Spikes with tags at 40′, 80′ 120′ and 160′   Bucket Lid

Appendix 2:
Guide For Taking Transect Pictures

You will need:

- Two 48" x 3/8 inch fiberglass rods (temporary electric fence posts) wrapped with electrician's tape (see description in appendix 1)

- One fence post clip mounted for at the top of each fiberglass rod

- Four - plot frame sticks (These are made by cutting 3/8" fiberglass rods [temporary electric fence posts] to a length of 26.8" and calibrating them by wrapping them with electrician's tape as shown in the diagram.)

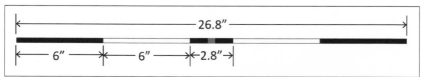

- 200' Measuring tape

- Clipboard with string so it can be hanged from the post clips

- Transect ID Form

Photographs documenting range condition should be taken in exactly the same location each year. The process for taking the pictures is:

1. Create a transect ID form showing the location of the transect, the position on the transect and the date pictures are taken. The position can be easily identified by including a large "S, 1, 2 ,3 ,4, E" on the transect form.

2. Tap in a 48" fiberglass rod about 12" to the side of the post at the 10' mark from the start of the transect. Hang the clipboard from the rod clips so that it faces the start bucket lid. If it's windy, use a small bungee cord to hold the clipboard steady

3. Circle the letter S on the transect ID form and hang the form on the clipboard from the two posts, facing the start point

4. Stand on the bucket lid and take a picture toward the end of the transect.

5. Remove the temporary post and put an X through the S on the transect ID form to indicate the picture at the starting point has been taken.

6. Lay out the plot frame sticks making a square on the south side of the transect tape. One stick should be centered on the spike with the ear tag.

7. Circle the frame number on the transect ID form.

8. Lay the clipboard with the transect ID form to the right of the plot frame.

9. Take a picture looking straight down so that the tape and ear tag marker, the entire plot frame, and the clipboard are in the photo.

10. Tap in the two fiberglass rods about 10 feet behind the plot frame (do not walk through the plot). Hang the clipboard from the clips on the rods so that you can clearly see the Transect ID form from the north side of the plot frame.

11. Take three steps back from the plot frame on the north side of the tape and take a picture so that the plot frame and the clipboard are both in the photo. The tape and front edge of the plot frame should be at the bottom of the picture.

If you prefer and the vegetation is short enough, you can prop the clipboard up with a rock or against a plant so that you can see it in the picture and you may not need to hang the clipboard on the fiberglass rods. It may still be useful to tap in a fiberglass rod to provide a scale against which the height of vegetation can be measured.

12. Once you've taken the pictures pull out the two fiberglass rods and cross out the frame number on the transect ID form.

You should repeat this process for each plot along the tape, however, before moving to the next frame to take pictures, you may want to record your estimate of percent bare soil and percent basal cover of perennial grass plants in the plot frame.

13. Once pictures have been taken at all of the frames and the other data associated with the frames has been collected take a photo standing on the bucket lid at the end of the transect looking back down the line (to the start of the transect) following the steps 1-5 of this procedure.

Appendix 3:
Range Site Evaluation Criteria

Soil Health & Water Cycle

	SCORE = 0-3	SCORE = 4-7	SCORE = 8-10
Soil Capping	Soil is severely capped.	Soil moderately is capped.	There is little or no soil capping.
Active Erosion	Clear signs of severe, active erosion (rills, pedestals, soil deposition, etc.).	Signs of moderate active erosion are noticeable	Soil surface completely intact. No signs of active erosion.
Litter Distribution	Little, if any, litter. Litter is only around obstructions.	Litter distribution tends to be patchy.	Litter is well distributed (not concentrated around obstructions).
Infiltration	Severe compaction. Major restrictions to water movement.	Moderate compaction. Some restrictions to water movement.	Little if any detectable compaction. No restrictions to water movement.
Moisture Retention	No obvious organic matter.	Some organic matter, but less than is desirable for this site.	Organic matter meets expectation for this site's distribution.

Soil Health & Mineral Cycle

	SCORE = 0-3	SCORE = 4-7	SCORE = 8-10
Grazing Severity	Obvious signs that most plants have been severely overgrazed or severely over-rested. Most plants are in phase I or III.	Signs that some plants have been overgrazed or over-rested. Some plants in phase I or III.	There a no signs that plants have been overgrazed or over-rested. Plants are in phase II.
Compaction	Severe compaction. Major restrictions to root growth.	Moderate Compaction. Some restrictions to root growth.	Little if any compaction. Roots are distributed throughout the soil profile.
Litter Decomposition	Litter is absent. If present, litter particle size tends to be uniform. Litter is not decomposing.	Litter distribution is patchy. Some differences in litter particle size. Litter is breaking down slowly.	Litter is well distributed. Wide variation in litter particle size. Litter is decomposing and becoming soil.
Dung	Year-old dung pats have not broken down.	Year-old dung pats are only partially decomposed.	Dung breaks down rapidly. There are no old dung pats.

Energy Flow

	SCORE = 0-3	SCORE = 4-7	SCORE = 8-10
Canopy Cover	Canopy cover during the peak of the growing season < 60%.	Canopy cover during the peak of the growing season 60-90%.	Canopy cover during the peak of the growing season > 90%.
Plant Type	Weedy annuals dominate. Perennial grasses are scarce. There are either C3 or C4 grasses, not both[1].	Broad leaved annuals may dominate. Perennial grasses are noticeable. There are some C3 and C4 grasses[1].	Perennial grasses with wide leaves dominate. There is a balanced mix of C3 and C4 grasses[1].
Growing Season	Photosynthesis restricted to < 50% of the potential growing season.	Photosynthesis restricted to 50 – 80% potential growing season.	Photosynthesis is not restricted during the potential growing season.

1   C3 and C4 Grasses: C3 grasses (cool season grasses) tend to grow rapidly in spring. C4 grasses (warm season grasses) grow rapidly in summer heat when moisture is available. The balance between C3 and C4 grasses is only important in environments that can support both types of plants.

Community & Biodiversity

	SCORE = 0-3	SCORE = 4-7	SCORE = 8-10
Biodiversity	There are only one or two plant types[1].	There are three or four plant types[1].	There are at least 5 different plant types[1].
Weeds v Desirables	Weeds dominate. Desirable perennial grasses are rare.	Desirable perennial grasses are present and easy to find but not dominant.	Desirable perennial species dominate. Weeds are inconspicuous.
Age Classes	All plants are about the same age class[2].	There is some variation in age classes[2].	All age classes[3] of desirable species present.
Other Life Forms	There are few, if any, signs of other life forms[3].	There are signs of several other life forms[3].	There are signs of many other life forms[3].

1 Plant Types include, annuals and perennials, cool season grasses (C3 grasses) and warm season grasses (C4 grasses), grasses and forbs, tap-rooted plants and plants with fibrous roots, woody plants and herbaceous plants, etc.

2 Age Class: check to see if there are diverse ages of each plant type. If only seedlings are present there is either a species change going on, or something prevents the plants from surviving past the seedling stage. If only mature plants exist (no seedlings) then the stand may be dying out.

3 Other Life Forms include any living things other than plants (dung beetles and other insects, earth worms and other invertebrates, reptiles, birds, mammals, fungi, bacteria, etc.)

Glossary
Economics & Finance Terms

Economics — The study of business profitability. Key question: Should I do this? (Is this profitable? How do I make it more profitable?)

Finance — The use and management of money to build and run a business. Key question: Can I do this? (Securing start-up capital, cash flow management, managing debt, etc.)

Good Debt — Debt on things that produce income.

Enterprise — A part of the business that could be run as a separate unit.

Division — One or more enterprises that share unique overhead costs.

Overhead Costs — Costs that tend not to change as the number of production units in enterprises change. In a livestock operation, nearly all land and labor costs are overheads.

Gross Product — The value an enterprise or business produces. It includes sales and the transfers out of an enterprise, the cost of replacements and the change in inventory value in the enterprise.

Direct Costs — Costs that increase or decrease directly as the number of units in the enterprise increase or decrease.

Gross Margin — Gross Product – Direct Costs = Gross Margin.

Gross Margin per Unit — Measures the economic efficiency of an enterprise.

Production Unit — The unit for calculating gross margin per unit. Livestock enterprises generally use an Animal Unit (AU). Farming enterprises tend to use acres as the primary unit. Other possible units are inches of rainfall, acre inches of irrigation water, dollars of capital invested, or full time equivalents (FTE).

Turnover — The total volume an enterprise or business produces for sale. In an enterprise turnover is synonymous with scale (eg. the number of units in the enterprise). In a business turnover is the scale of all of the enterprises.

Farming — Any activity that involves growing or harvesting a crop with something other than livestock.

The Three Secrets For Increasing Profit — There are only three things that any business anywhere can do to increase profit:
- Reduce overhead cost
- Improve the gross margin per unit
- Increase Turnover

Key Performance Indicators — Vital signs for a business.

Benchmarks — Profitability standards for key performance indicators achieved by highly profitable businesses.

Benchmarking — The process of evaluating business health using key performance indicators.

Gross Margin Ratio — [(Gross Product / Gross Margin) x 100] = Gross Margin Ratio. The benchmark is ≥70%. When the gross margin ratio is 70% it means that an enterprise earns a gross margin of 70 cents for each product produced.

Overhead Ratio — [(Overhead Costs / Gross Product x 100] = Overhead Ratio. The benchmark is ≤40%. When the overhead ratio is 40% it means that the business incurs 40 cents of overhead costs (including unpaid labor and opportunity rent) for each dollar of gross product produced.

Pre-Tax Profit — The sum of all enterprise gross margins minus overhead costs.

Business Profit — Pretax Profit minus opportunity costs.

Opportunity Rent — The rent you would receive if you rented your ranch to someone else. This is the rent your operating business must pay your land investment.

Deferred Wages / Sweat Equity — The value of unpaid labor. This is money the business owes to the laborer. It should be recorded with a reasonable interest rate so that it may one day be paid.

Cow Depreciation — The loss of value over time. Cow depreciation is often one of the biggest cost of keeping a cow.

Fixed Assets — Assets which are purchased for long-term use and are not likely to be converted quickly into cash, (eg. land, buildings, and equipment, and breeding stock).

Working Capital — The capital of a business which is used in its day-to-day operations.

Reserves — Money or easily liquidatable assets that can provide funding for periods of low income, emergencies and opportunities.

The 7 Step RMC Profit Planning Process
- Breeding Herd Statistics Chart (performance estimates).
- Stock Flow Plan (uses those estimates to project from opening inventory to closing inventory).
- Cash Flow Forecast (projects all cash income and expenses by month).
- Livestock valuation (uses inventory numbers from the stock flow).
- Trading Account (to calculate gross product).
- Gross Margin (= gross product – direct costs).
- Profit or Loss Statement (total gross margin – overhead costs = profit or loss).

Management Terms

Action Plan – A page showing a task, the person responsible for completing the task and the completion deadline.

Decision Grid – A structured process for evaluating the likely impact of various alternatives on important criteria.

Scenario Planning — Exploring alternative courses of action based on different financial, environmental and personal variables.

Effectiveness Areas — The area for which someone is responsible. Rather than describe the specific tasks associated with a position, effectiveness areas are used to describe the results the position is expected to produce.

Efficiency — Doing a good job quickly and with minimal resources.

Effectiveness — Doing the right job.

Working On The Business (WOTB) — Strategic and tactical planning, developing policies, documenting operating systems and doing other tasks required to develop a successful business. The phrase "Working On The Business was coined by Michael Gerber in The E-Myth Revisited.

Working In The Business (WITB) — Day-to-day operational activities.

Husbandry, Grazing & Ecology Terms

Cell Grazing — A management method relying on the flexible application of five principles:

- Give plants adequate time to recover after grazing before grazing again. The recovery required depends on the growth rate of plants.
- Use the shortest graze period consistent with the required recovery.
- Use the highest stock density practical.
- Use the largest herd possible consistent with good husbandry.
- Adjust the stocking rate to match the carrying capacity annually and seasonally.

Grazing Cell — An area managed for grazing usually consisting of several paddocks.

Cell Center — A place where several paddocks meet.

Paddock — A relatively small unit of pasture or range within a grazing cell.

Overgrazing — Repeatedly grazing a plant before it has recovered from a previous grazing. Overgrazing weakens roots, depletes soil organic matter, promotes compaction, run-off, erosion, less desirable plants and lower productivity. Overgrazing has nothing to do with the number of animals grazing. It is strictly a function of time. It occurs in two ways:

- Keeping animals in a pasture too long
- Bringing them back too soon, before a plants have recovered

Overstocking — The forage demand of the herd exceeds the forage supply. Overstocking results in severe grazing and lower animal performance. Repeated overstocking promotes less desirable species, compaction, runoff and erosion and results in lower range productivity.

Rest Period — The time given plants to recover following grazing.

Graze Period — The length of time animals are left in a paddock for grazing. Short graze periods generally result in better animal performance than longer graze periods because when animals are frequently moved to fresh feed their intake increases. Cell grazing practitioners use short graze periods while providing paddocks the recovery time they need. This usually requires at least 14-16 paddocks per herd.

283

Growth Phase — Three phases of grass growth have been described to provide a general description of the condition of grass plants. These phases are referred to in the Range Site Evaluation Criteria provided in Appendix 3. The three phases are:

Phase I: Plants have been grazed and most leaves have been removed. Regrowth may have started. The nutritive value of regrowth is excellent, but growth is relatively slow. Plants in phase I need time to recover and enter phase II.

Phase II: Plants are growing relatively rapidly. Forage quality is high. Grasses in phase II are ready to graze.

Phase III: Plants have been over-rested and growth is slow. There is a lot of biomass but leaves are highly lignified and forage quality is extremely low.

Stock Density — The number of animals per acre at a given moment of time. 500 cows grazing a 2,000-acre pasture is a stock density of 0.25 (500 cows/2,000 acres = 0.25 cows/acre). 500 cows grazing a 5-acre paddock is a stock density of 100 (500 cows/5 acres = 100 cows/acre). High stock density improves the uniformity of use and improves the quality of the pasture.

Animal Impact — The physical impact animals have on soil and vegetation.

Herd Effect — Concentrated animal impact resulting from the excited behavior of a large group of animals concentrated in a small area. High stock density will not necessarily result in herd effect.

Animal Unit (AU) — A measure of the relative dry matter intake of raising animals. One AU is a 1,000 lb. grazing animal. 0.1 is added for each additional 100 lbs. of animal weight. (A 1,250 lb. cow is 1.25 AU.)

Carrying Capacity — The supply of forage available for grazing. Carrying capacity is usually expressed as the number of acres required to support an animal for one year or the animal days of grazing per acre available.

Stocking Rate — The forage demand of a herd. The stocking rate measures the grazing pressure put on an area. It is usually measured in the number of acres it takes to support an animal for one year or the animal days grazed per acre.

Photo Points — A specific location at which photographs will be taken annually to document and track changes in range condition.

Transect — A line across an area of rangeland that can be reestablished annually to make observations and measurements to monitor range health. Photo points are taken at fixed points along a transect.

Bare Soil — Exposed soil without anything covering it. When measuring the percentage of bare soil do not include rocks, or area covered with manure or plant residues. The higher the proportion of bare soil, the less healthy the community.

Basal Cover of Perennial Grass Plants — The area occupied by perennial grass plant stems and tillers coming out of the soil. Basal cover of perennial grass plants is an important measure of range health. The higher the basal cover, the healthier the community.

Capping — A hard crust on the soil surface. Bare soil is susceptible to capping and over time, as the cap thickens, it will severely reduce effective precipitation.

Effective Precipitation — Moisture that soaks into the soil and is available for plant growth.

Water Cycle — The movement of water from the atmosphere to the soil and back to the atmosphere.

Energy Flow — The volume of sunlight energy captured by plants and harvested by animals in a community.

Mineral Cycle — The movement of minerals from soil to plants to animals and back to soil.

Biodiversity — The variety of living things including the variety of species and the variation within those species. When evaluating biodiversity it is important to consider species diversity, genetic diversity and habitat diversity. Generally speaking, the higher the biodiversity, the healthier and more stable the community.

Species Richness — The number of different species present in a community. Measuring species richness includes a count of all species present including animals, plants, insects, fungi and bacteria.

H1 — A weaned heifer calf. An H1 will be exposed to the bull. If she is confirmed pregnant she is reclassified as an H2.

H2 — A first calf heifer. Once a heifer is confirmed pregnant, she is an H2. She will have her first calf and go through her second breeding season as an H2. If she is confirmed pregnant for a second time she is reclassified as a cow.

Made in the USA
Monee, IL
04 October 2021

79368477R00173